Rethinking Reintegration and Veteran Identity

"Dr. Hunniecutt's personal accounts as a military service member, her transition into full-time civilian life, and her academic research combined with her own journey of reconciling how her Veteran status is part of who she is has led her to develop a compelling new framework for understanding Veteran identity. Hunniecutt's conceptualization of Veteran identity is based on the identity recruits bring to the military and a natural continuum of their experiences as a service member in relationship to the ultimate sacrifice. As a civilian trying to understand an important group of people in my country and as a researcher looking to do research with Veterans, I will be regularly using this book as a resource to do the best I can to learn about Veterans and be there for them."
  —Aaron T. Anderson, PhD, *University of Illinois Urbana-Champaign*

"For anyone who has ever used the term "veteran", I urge you to read Jeni's story. It is a raw, honest look at the struggles that come with trying to find one's identity before, after, and during military service. It's also a glimmer hope that through research, communication, and deconstructing our preconceived notions that maybe we can better understand what each warrior carries in their rucksack of life. In return we may just save more warriors from taking their lives."
  —Abbie Holland Schmit, Iraq War Veteran

"In this book, Dr. Hunniecutt considers a new way to conceptualize the archetype of a military "Veteran" as an identity, product, and process. She vulnerably walks the reader through her own journey before enlistment and then guides an investigation of her own destructive "non-deployment emotions" after her service. She then deftly identifies the invisible apex of "Veteran" identity and the resulting identity conflict and distress that occurs for all people who have made it out of the military alive."
  —Jacob N. Hyde, Psy.D., Iraq War Veteran, Clinical Psychologist

Jeni Ruth Hunniecutt

Rethinking Reintegration and Veteran Identity

A New Consciousness

Jeni Ruth Hunniecutt
Ronin Institute
Montclair, NJ, USA

ISBN 978-3-030-93753-9   ISBN 978-3-030-93754-6   (eBook)
https://doi.org/10.1007/978-3-030-93754-6

© The Editor(s) (if applicable) and The Author(s), under exclusive licence to Springer Nature Switzerland AG 2022
This work is subject to copyright. All rights are solely and exclusively licensed by the Publisher, whether the whole or part of the material is concerned, specifically the rights of translation, reprinting, reuse of illustrations, recitation, broadcasting, reproduction on microfilms or in any other physical way, and transmission or information storage and retrieval, electronic adaptation, computer software, or by similar or dissimilar methodology now known or hereafter developed.
The use of general descriptive names, registered names, trademarks, service marks, etc. in this publication does not imply, even in the absence of a specific statement, that such names are exempt from the relevant protective laws and regulations and therefore free for general use.
The publisher, the authors and the editors are safe to assume that the advice and information in this book are believed to be true and accurate at the date of publication. Neither the publisher nor the authors or the editors give a warranty, expressed or implied, with respect to the material contained herein or for any errors or omissions that may have been made. The publisher remains neutral with regard to jurisdictional claims in published maps and institutional affiliations.

This Palgrave Macmillan imprint is published by the registered company Springer Nature Switzerland AG.
The registered company address is: Gewerbestrasse 11, 6330 Cham, Switzerland

For all of you,
under the red, white, and blue,
who feel broken
and true
under the rule
of power, domination, and oppression.
I breathe you hope, light, and resistance.
Courage,
to adapt and overcome
the pain of a disparate self.
My wish for you,
is union
and
love.
This story is dedicated to SGT Baker, who was a soldier in my National Guard unit and died by suicide. I once heard that a person never truly dies until their name is spoken for the last time. I write your name here, Travis Baker, to be forever scribed into this world and into my path.

PREFACE

The timing of the completion of this book could not come at a better (and more painful) time. As our nation ends our longest war to date (the war in Afghanistan), military Service Members and Veterans across the country are facing difficult questions about the meaning and impact of their military service. *What did it all mean? Did I make a difference? Did any of it matter at all?* These are hard questions, and the realities and truths behind them are even harder.

At the end of the day, most of us didn't join and serve in the U.S. military to fight for some esoteric concept of "freedom." We joined for the benefits, for the escape, to continue the legacy of service in our family, to feel a sense of pride and accomplishment within our life, for citizenship, or maybe we just wanted a chance to travel the world. Regardless of our "why," we joined. We stayed and we fought (in many ways). We sacrificed all we were asked and more, not for the military institution, not for Uncle Sam—but for each other, for the women and the men to our right and our left. This book is my own journey of military service and though it tells *my* story, which is unique only to me, it's about all of you too—my brothers and sisters in arms. It's about the questions we have, the liminal space we exist in once we leave the military, and the challenges we face in trying to understand what it all meant and how it all changed us.

It's for the researchers, the policy makers, and the leaders too. Because the power for systemic and lasting change lies with you. It is up to you to head the responsibility to hold yourself accountable to Truth, to justice, and to progress. This book is a blueprint for change. This book is a story of my truth as I unmask "the truth" of military service and Veteran

vii

viii PREFACE

identity. This book is a plea, a request, a demand—to do better. With this book, I invite you to feel, to mourn, to laugh, to grieve, and to take up arms and *make a difference* in our lives.

Champaign, IL, USA   Jeni Hunniecutt

CONTENTS

1 (The) U.S. Military: (My) Service   1
Introduction   1
Joining   3
    Where I Come From   5
    From Pom-Poms to Combat Boots   10
Doing Time   12
    Initial Entry Training   14
    Time in Service   18
Freedom Rings   26
    Lower Your Head and Drive On   27
    Little Things   31
Works Cited   35

2 My Veteran Identity (Crisis): Suicides and Reintegration   37
Fall 2014: Feeling Loss   38
Winter 2015: Seeing What I Lost   46
Spring 2015: Finding Myself in the Loss   50
Searching for Answers: Veteran Suicides   54
Conceptualizing Veteran Reintegration   57
    Military Assimilation   61
    Military Culture   65
    Military-Civilian Divide   66
Works Cited   70

x CONTENTS

3 Writing Through Layers of Veteran Liminality   75
Theoretical Framework: Liminality   76
Sacred Liminality: "Communitas"   77
Institutionalized Liminality: Belonging to a Total Institution   82
My Research and Writing Process   86
Autoethnography   87
Works Cited   93

4 Loss of Community: Searching for and Finding Home   95
Spring 2015–Winter 2016: Building My Self Communally   96
Spring 2016: Facing my Community   103
Works Cited   114

5 Loss of Structure: Resisting and Finding (My) Voice   117
Fall 2016: Resolving Ambivalence   120
Winter 2017: A New Redemption   123
Spring 2017: Duality and Liminality   127
Works Cited   133

6 You Can't Go Back   137
Freedom: "Give me Liberty or Give me Death!"   138
Freedom Isn't Free   144
*Freedom?: Give me Liberty (of Self) or Give me (Psychological)
Death!*   149
Assimilating   150
Serving   155
Separating   158
I am No Hero, nor am I Wounded   165
Works Cited   166

7 Adapt and Overcome   169
Building Blocks   175
Model for Analyzing Human Adaptation to Transition   176
Theory of Differential Adaptation   179
Ecological Framework and Family Systems   182
Veteran Identity: A New Consciousness   186

CONTENTS xi

Model of Veteran Identity Hierarchy	189
Reconceptualizing Veteran as a Noun and a Verb	192
Unifying Ambivalence: Moving Toward Indigenous Perspectives	198
Critical Reflection	200
Suggestions for Future Research	203
Works Cited	206

Index 209

ABOUT THE AUTHOR

Jeni Hunniecutt grew up in a small community tucked away deep in the Appalachian Mountains. She joined the Virginia Army National Guard at the age of 19 and honorably served 6 years as an enlisted soldier. Through her time in the military, she earned her Bachelor of Arts in Technical and Professional Communication from King University and her Master of Arts in Professional Communication from East Tennessee State University. She separated from the U.S. Military in 2014 and then moved to Denver, Colorado, where she earned her PhD in Communication Studies from the University of Denver in 2018. She now lives in Champaign, Illinois, where she worked for over three years facilitating "research with, not on" Veterans within a Veteran center at the University of Illinois Urbana-Champaign. She is still affiliated as an Adjunct Research Assistant Professor at UIUC. She is also a Research Scholar at the Ronin Institute. Continuing her work bridging academic and military/Veteran spaces, in 2021 she established Veteran Research Consulting LLC in Illinois. As a globe trotter, yoga instructor, gardener, entrepreneur, and scholar, she believes in unlimited potential in the continual creation of self and life. She happily resides with her partner, Ryan, and their cat, Moon, in Illinois and frequently travels back to Appalachia to ground in her roots and receive inspiration from the majesty of the mountains.

ABBREVIATIONS

ACU   Army Combat Uniform
AIT   Advanced Individual Training
BCT   Basic Combat Training
CAM   Complementary and Alternative Medicine
DoD   Department of Defense
DU   University of Denver
ETS   End of Time in Service
ETSU East Tennessee State University
HHD   Headquarters and Headquarters Detachment
IET   Initial Entry Training
MEPS Military Entrance Processing Station
MOS   Military Occupational Specialty
MRE   Meal Ready to Eat
MST   Military Sexual Trauma
NCO   Non-Commissioned Officer
NG   National Guard
PFC   Private First Class
PhD   Doctor of Philosophy
POW   Prisoner of War
PTSD Post-Traumatic Stress Disorder
RSP   Recruit Sustainment Program
SGT   Sergeant
SM   Service Member
SPC   Specialist
SSMP Sturm Specialty in Military Psychology
SVA   Student Veterans of America
TBI   Traumatic Brain Injury

xvi ABBREVIATIONS

TIS	Time in Service
U.S.	United States
VA	Department of Veterans Affairs
VSO	Veteran Service Organization
YMCA	Young Men's Christian Association

LIST OF FIGURES

Fig. 4.1   Home
Photo of a metal bunk bed with a green blanket neatly made
on the bed. A piece of tape with my name on it is on the top
of the bed   109

Fig. 6.1   Body
Two photos side by side; photo on the left is of me saluting
while in the Army Combat Uniform and photo on the right is
of me in civilian clothing and pulling up my t-shirt to reveal a
fresh tattoo of a flower on my hip   160

Fig. 6.2   Visual Narrative of Redemption
Picture of tan stock paper with white lines on it resembling sun
rays. A military crest cutout is on the left side of the paper and
shows a red background with a spear breaking through a chain.
The crest has handwriting over it. Two cut out drawings of
people are on the right; one is of me in military uniform and
the other of me in cheerleading uniform   162

Fig. 7.1   Model of veteran identity hierarchy
The figure shows a triangle and has word descriptions at the
peak of the triangle as well as on both sides   190

CHAPTER 1

(The) U.S. Military: (My) Service

Introduction

The purpose of this book is to create a new way to think about and understand the U.S. Military Veteran identity. If we can understand Veteran identity in a more comprehensive, holistic, nuanced way, then we can better understand experiences related to the Veteran identity, such as transitioning (reintegration), Veteran suicides, resiliency, and the meaning of military service. If we have a better understanding, we may come up with better solutions—better policies, programs, services, and treatments. My whole purpose here is to help—help myself through this writing and research process, help researchers understand these topics in new ways so we can produce better outcomes with our work, and, most importantly, help my brothers and sisters in arms, because we have suffered enough and because we deserve better. We *earned* better. We do not have to be pawns in the system; we have agency, we have choice. I hope this book shows you that.

Throughout this book, I share my own story. I lay my own self bare between the pages. I do so with complete purpose and intention because I adamantly believe that if I can get you to *feel something* about my story, it might stick with you. It might even motivate you. I use a research method called "autoethnography" throughout this book, which is a form of research designed to be solely subjective, affective, emotive, and disruptive. Autoethnography is about writing out one's own lived experiences in

© The Author(s), under exclusive license to Springer Nature
Switzerland AG 2022
J. R. Hunniecutt, *Rethinking Reintegration and Veteran Identity*,
https://doi.org/10.1007/978-3-030-93754-6_1

1

relation to larger, systemic, cultural narratives. Telling my own story about Veteran identity will help you to understand larger narratives and systemic complexities about Veteran identity. Telling my own story about joining, serving in, and separating from the U.S. Military will help you to understand and contextualize nuances of these experiences in a way reading statistics and facts cannot.

Statistics and facts about things like Veteran suicides, Veteran reintegration, and Veteran identity are all included throughout the chapters, but they are not the focus. Rather, they weave between and among my stories in a way that purposefully prompts you to see, interpret, and question [my] lived experiences in relation to the objective knowing that quantitative research facilitates on very *real* topics like Veteran suicides and reintegration. I vulnerably tell you my own stories related to Veteran suicides, reintegration, and identity so that you may feel something related to these facts and statistics. Feeling something facilitates another form of knowing, one that is not privileged or often seen as legitimate not only in the Ivory Tower but in our Western world as we know it. Thus, I also write this book to *disrupt*. Perhaps if we *feel something*, we can understand something in a new way, a better way, and just maybe, that will foster change. By moving you to feel, I aim to disrupt and shatter current conceptualizations of Veteran identity because quite frankly, they are not working. Too many U.S. Military Veterans die by suicide each day; too many lose themselves in a pit of psychological darkness during times of military transitions, such as coming home from war or separating from the military completely. More Veterans have died by suicide than by fighting in our nation's longest war to date; this is simply unacceptable. My aim here then, with this book and with showing and telling my own story, is to change this. Thus, with this book, I offer up a new way to name, define, and conceptualize Veteran experiences of transitions and identity. I hope that it makes a difference.

I start with a condensed overview of my own military story. Chapter 1 is almost exclusively a story and covers my own lived experiences of joining, serving in, and then separating from the Virginia Army National Guard. Chapter 2 continues with my story and illustrates the psychosocial challenges I faced when I separated from military service. It also introduces literature on the topics of Veteran suicides and reintegration. In the discussion of Veteran reintegration, I include background information on military assimilation, military culture, and the military-civilian divide in U.S. culture to give readers a foundation to best understand the military institution. Chapter 3 takes a break from my linear story to introduce a theory that frames the entire second half of the book. Chapter 3 also includes two guiding research questions that frame Chaps. 4, 5, and 6. In Chap. 3, I overview autoethnography as a research method and explain why this form of research is needed in the field of Veteran Studies, including why it is the most effective way to answer the research questions I propose.

Following this, Chaps. 4 and 5 pick the story back up and show [my] Veteran identity tensions (i.e., psychosocial difficulties) that exist during separation from the military institution. I shift a bit in Chap. 6 and focus more on how the conditioning and assimilating that takes place during the initiatory training processes in the military create a space of "liminality" or "betweenness" for Veterans once they separate from the military. And finally, Chap. 7 brings us full circle. In Chap. 7, I first overview a few additional theories that are useful in understanding the complex topics of Veteran identity and reintegration. Following this, I propose a "new consciousness" for Veteran identity—I share a new Model of Veteran Identity Hierarchy and then I propose an entire reconceptualization of Veteran identity. I conclude the book with a critical reflection of this work and suggestions for how the research can and should continue. First, we start with my story.

Joining

It was a sweltering June day when I attended my first drill with my new unit in Gate City, Virginia, as a fresh-out-of-basic, *trained and proficient* soldier of the United States Army. I was assigned to 1030th Headquarters and Headquarters Detachment (HHD), a small battalion headquarters unit in the Virginia Army National Guard (NG) that had just about 40 soldiers or so in it. The armory that my unit drilled at was only a 45-minute drive from my hometown of Bristol, Virginia, so I could drive there in the morning for drill and then sleep in my own bed in my hometown that same night. It was the best of both worlds. I graduated Army Basic Combat Training (BCT) in Fort Jackson, South Carolina, that spring of 2009 and then completed my job training for 92Y, unit supply specialist, in Fort Lee, Virginia, later that summer. Within my unit, I was part of S4, unit supply. There's a saying in the Army that goes, "Make the cook your #1 best friend and the supply person your #2." In supply, we made sure everyone had all their equipment, gear, and necessities to do the work. My job (and that of S4) was to make sure everyone always had what they needed to do their job and accomplish the mission.

There were only four of us in S4, all working under our senior noncommissioned officer (NCO). It was me—one of the lowest ranking as only an e4 Specialist (SPC), Sergeant (SGT) Wilde (the only other female in the section and one of the only few in our entire unit), SPC Dillan, and SGT Baker. Dillan and Baker were close friends, having both grown up in the same region of Appalachia and having been part of the same unit for several years. Wilde, Baker, and Dillan had all been part of 1030th when the unit was deployed to Iraq in the initial invasion and start of the "War on Terrorism" during the early 2000s. That was before I was in, but I could tell there was a strong bond between them and a handful of other people still in the unit through how they interacted and joked around with each other.

Upon meeting everyone in S4, I liked Wilde immediately, but to me (originally being from and spending my early days in Florida), Dillan and Baker were mostly stereotypical Southern, redneck guys with their diesel trucks, heavy drawn-out accents, and constant banter about things like hunting, fishing, and whisky. Wilde had a much different background though, one I related to more. She grew up in a dysfunctional family system and joined the military at 17 years old. When she joined, Wilde was just looking for a way to put a roof over her head—a way to gain a sense of security and even belonging. She once told me that she'd once or twice spent a night in her car in the armory parking lot when she had no other place to go. Like many others, she joined the military as an escape and as a way to gain security. From what I could tell, it seemed to have really worked out well for her; she had a steady civilian career in healthcare now and seemed to be good at the whole Army thing.

Wilde quickly became my mentor and friend. In addition to being in the same section, she was friendly and outgoing, assertive when she needed to be, and had one of the highest physical training (PT) scores in the entire unit. Wilde was the highest ranking of us four in S4, and after our senior NCO noticed how much we were clicking, he officially assigned Wilde to be my "battle buddy" on that day of my first drill. As my assigned battle buddy, she was responsible for showing me the ropes during my first several months with my new unit and making sure I was trained and up to speed on all the things required of us as soldiers in 1030th. One of the first things she instructed me to do was to train for my Humvee license. She assigned SGT Baker to teach me.

I was nervous as hell as I climbed into the passenger side of that boxy, black and green, camo-painted hunk of steel on that warm summer afternoon. I imagine SGT Baker could feel my anxiety because shortly after he settled into the driver's seat next to me and started the loud humming engine, he looked over at me with a big grin and deviant eyes and said, "You wanna go off roadin'?" He made a right turn out of our armory motor pool and drove us just out of town back into what us folk in central Appalachia would call a "holler." When we finally got deep enough into the woods, at the base of a mountain next to a small creek, he had me switch seats with him and take the wheel. My anxieties about belonging in my new unit, being a recruit fresh out of boot camp, and absorbing the stark reality that I was now a soldier in the United States Army faded into the background as I drove that giant Humvee through the creek, over tree stumps, under wide oak leaves, and up our green mountain side.

Where I Come From

I don't come from a family legacy of military service. My grandfather on my dad's side served one enlistment in the U.S. Air Force, but I was raised in a different state than him so never really knew him that well, much less anything about his service. The military wasn't a direct part of my story as I grew up. However, like most households in Appalachia, I grew up in a low-income family with conservative values and strong allegiance to evangelical Christian doctrine. And if you know Christians, especially the Baptist part of the Bible Belt that encompassed my hometown, you know that general patriotism and pride for country just seem to be inherently part of it all. *God and country*, you know.

My dad never even considered joining the military—he was one of the rebel rock-and-roll types in the 1970s, and the discipline and control of the armed forces was just something he wasn't about back then. My mom didn't have any military service in her family at all, so it simply never entered her trajectory as she came of age. Neither of my parents graduated from high school, but instead each went on to earn their GEDs and learn a trade over time—my dad was a telephone technician and my mom a hairdresser. We were the kind of blue-collar family who earned barely too much to qualify for government assistance but entirely not enough to pay for three kids' college tuition.

6   J. R. HUNNICUTT

My dad came from a middle-class family that was overall healthy and connected. His parents—my paternal grandparents—were kind, loving, and warm. I didn't grow up around them in the same way I grew up around my mom's side of the family though—and her family background was very different from my dad's. I'm very close to my maternal grandmother and I've witnessed her endure much hardship throughout her life. She's one of the strongest women I know. My maternal grandfather (whom she was married to for 50+ years) was a kind man, but he came from extreme poverty and abuse and passed down cycles of intergenerational trauma through his line. My grandma once told me that his father, my great-grandpa, whom I never met, was kicked out of the Army for misconduct. He was a drunk, she said. I know my grandpa had a hard life, and because of it, my mom witnessed and experienced various forms of violence throughout much of her childhood too. And as trauma cycles tend to do, they impacted her into adulthood. They impacted her parenting, which meant they also impacted me (and my siblings). My parents did the best they could raising my sister, brother, and me along with some of my cousins here and there (my maternal aunt had five kids she struggled to raise alone between her five different marriages during my childhood). But between my parents' own unresolved trauma, the intergenerational trauma passed down through my relatives on my mom's side that I grew up around (including my aunt and the men she would bring around), I experienced my own fair share of compounded and prolonged trauma throughout my early childhood and teenage years.

As is the case for many trauma-infected family systems, on the outside looking in, things looked normal; they looked okay. *It's just the way things were.* Even though I can look back now as an adult and clearly see signs I exhibited as an adolescent and teenager needing help to cope with what was happening in my home, no one ever asked. I had three close girl friends as a child and teen though, and their mothers cared for and loved me, so I had chosen family I could lean on and escape to when the going got especially rough. Still, growing up in a low-income rural town in the Deep South in a home that was often unsafe, I wanted and needed another, more permanent escape. My light at the end of the tunnel was *finding a way to get out.*

But my hometown was tucked neatly in the middle of central Appalachia where drug abuse and mental health disorders are significantly higher than the national average ("ARC Study"). And, of course, my family was no exception. Several of my cousins grew up in and out of foster care (often living with us) and as we all came of age, drug addiction, sexual, psychological, and/or physical trauma, and even serving time incarcerated seemed to be more of the rule than the exception. The opioid epidemic was no stranger to southwest Appalachia or to my family. Several people I graduated high school with served prison time for cooking and selling meth or died by overdosing on prescription pills. A few of my cousins serve/d time for it too. In my teen years, my mom developed opioid dependence—she had surgery for chronic low back pain from her work (cutting hair), and nearly a decade later, the suffering caused by overprescribing and lack of viable, accessible alternatives for healing still plagues our entire family system through the reverberations of her ongoing opioid dependence. But it's not just the failing systems. Depression, anxiety, and intergenerational trauma are all consequences of the cycles passed down in my lines and, as a result, a deep part of my story and family history. But again, growing up, I couldn't have known that. *It's just the way things were.* With the decline of the coal industry in the early 2000s around the time I was coming of age, my hometown that borders the edge of the Cherokee National Forest surrounded by the Blue Ridge Mountains was riddled with endemic poverty, aging infrastructure, environmental issues and a deficient K-12 education system and was number one in the country for opioid and methamphetamine abuse (Rudd et al.).

There was a growing migration pattern of young people leaving the area. I, too, was eager to spread my wings and leave not only the suffering in my parent's home, but rural Appalachia altogether. But with poverty rates so high, drug addiction so prevalent, and hegemonic cultural discourses of "family is thicker than blood," leaving to go on some self-serving quest of upward mobility was frowned upon at best and downright sinful at worst. Being in the Bible Belt of the U.S. Deep South, there's a saying where I'm from that goes, "You can stand on any street corner and throw a rock and you'll hit a church." Culturally, my hometown epitomized stereotypes of "the South," with confederate flags waving in front yards, 9 mm pistols strapped casually through belt loops, secret KKK gatherings in the woods behind that barn in the pasture, and gossip that's whispered around salon chairs and into the ears of preachers' wives. Environmentally, it was a beautiful place to live and grow up, encompassed by the peace and tranquility of the ancient and expansive Appalachian mountainside. With the charm, however, comes a painful, discriminatory, and violent history carrying an unspeakable evil that deeply penetrates the culture of the U.S. Deep South. I was not immune to this evil. Under the shadows of patriarchy, white supremacy, and intergenerational trauma and abuse, I grew up wanting and *needing to get out.*

I started working toward independence at an early age. I was 15 years old when I started lifeguarding and teaching swim lessons at the Young Men's Christian Association (YMCA)—the perfect job to have as I finished my last two years of high school. My job at the YMCA helped me to make new friends and gave me a valid reason to not be home—both of which were things I was struggling with at the time. When I got kicked off the cheerleading team my junior year of high school for getting caught drinking at a party, being able to still go to work gave me a sense of purpose and belonging, an escape from my home life, and a way to earn money/gain some independence all while making new friends. Working at the YMCA during the summer months was especially awesome because it meant working at the outdoor aquatic center, so my days were full of sunshine, swimming, and friendly faces.

I was 16 and it was the summer before my junior year of high school when I met Shawn at the outdoor center. He was a newly hired lifeguard, just working there for the summer season. He was older than me—19 years old—and had just gotten home from a deployment to Iraq prior to starting at the YMCA. He was in the Army National Guard, belonged to a unit just up the highway from the outdoor pool we worked at. When we met, Shawn was a young soldier, high from the rush of just having returned home from the new war in the Middle East. It was 2005 and he had been part of a unit that deployed in 2003–2004, during the initial invasion of Iraq. He had joined when he was 17 years old, and he spent his 18th birthday at war in Iraq, he once told me with a sense of pride. Upon just meeting and getting acquainted, Shawn didn't share too many details about the military or his experiences of war, just that he was in the NG and had recently gotten back from a deployment. I felt a special connection between us back then, but at that time we couldn't have known it yet; we were mostly just work friends who occasionally partied together at our lifeguard after-hour pool parties. When summer ended, we parted ways and didn't really keep in touch.

A year passed and eventually I reached my final year of high school—a year that felt particularly lonely as I was no longer part of the cheerleading team and didn't have a clear path forward for what my future could look like. Since neither of my parents had gone to college, there wasn't a clear script for me moving forward or how to do it. My parents wanted my siblings and me to have a better life than them though, so they encouraged us to figure out the whole college thing. But again, given the cultural discourses of our region and the intergenerational trauma in my family, they wanted us to do better, sure, but they didn't want us to go *too* far. After much pressure from my family to stay nearby after graduating, I decided to follow in my older brothers' footsteps and attend a local private Presbyterian college in my hometown.

After being accepted for admission, I tried out for and made the cheerleading team at my new school. Then, as soon as I was legally and financially able, I moved out of my parents' house into a shared home across town with some of my new cheerleading teammates. My parents were not able to support me financially living on my own, but my dad had made a promise that he would do his best to pay for some of our first year of college. I got some scholarships and financial aid, but with it being a private school (the closest option to home), I still ended up taking out student loans to cover the remaining of what my parents couldn't. I was willing to do whatever it took to be out on my own, including accruing debt and working nearly full-time at multiple jobs while I was in school (and a student-athlete).

That first semester of college and living on my own went by fast and was a wild one full of experimenting, irresponsibility, and general debauchery. I was a full-time student and a member of the college cheerleading team. I also worked part-time waiting tables at a local chain restaurant while still lifeguarding and teaching swim lessons on the side. Likely because I was out from under my parents' roof for the first time, all the unprocessed, compounded trauma that I'd carried inside me for most of my childhood rapidly started rearing its ugly face at this time. The environment I was in, however, made it easy to find ways to numb and evade; I was a freshman college cheerleader living in the "cheerleader house" near campus. The partying was nonstop. I was drinking to excess several nights a week, experimenting with cannabis for the first time and occasionally smoking cigarettes, and I even tried prescription pills a few times. Somehow though, I made it through that semester, barely passing my classes. Eventually, my grind caught up to me.

I got caught drinking underage at an off-campus party during winter break that first year of college. It was my first real "run-in with the law." I got a misdemeanor citation, and thanks to the small-town nature of where I lived and went to school, my cheerleading coach and athletic director knew about the incident before the sun came up the next day. I was put on probation on the cheerleading team and sentenced by the university to attend a six-week-long substance misuse treatment group to maintain good standing as a student. Things only got worse from there. As the spring semester started, I continued to party, became less involved in cheerleading, and contemplated dropping out of school entirely to just work and make money. I was doing worse and worse in my studies and didn't know how to get ahead of it. Under no circumstances would I have been able to admit it at the time, but I was lacking direction, purpose, and a sense of belonging. All the intergenerational trauma, mental health instability within my family system, and lack of resources to pay for school and create a life of my own were catching up to me. I was alone and could barely keep my head above water.

From Pom-Poms to Combat Boots

Toward the end of that spring semester of my freshman year of college in 2008, I ran into my old friend Shawn from the YMCA at a party off-campus. That chance encounter changed everything. We hadn't seen each other in a few years, so it was a pleasant surprise for both of us to run into each other that night. We sat on a couch together, beers in hand, and spent a couple of hours just catching up on life. I explained my situation to him about being burnt out working so much trying to pay for school and living out of my parents' house, not doing well in classes, and getting in trouble with partying. Shawn had since taken a job working in recruiting for the Virginia Army National Guard, and after I vented all my problems to him, he was quick and eager to offer up a solution to all my woes. He pointed me straight toward enlisting. The NG was offering an abundance of benefits at that time; it was a no-brainer.

At first, the idea seemed absurd to me. *I was a college cheerleader. Shawn was really the only person I knew in the military. Me in Army boot camp?* But once I got in front of a recruiter and came to fully understand the benefits I could get from signing up, it didn't take long for me to make up my mind. They were offering a $20,000 sign-on bonus (just for signing up and completing boot camp!), federal and state college tuition assistance, a monthly living stipend I could earn while being in school, student loan repayment for the loans I already had, a "college-first" option that would contractually ensure I was "nondeployable" the first two years of my service, access to affordable and quality health insurance, and a good, reliable monthly paycheck for my regular training throughout my entire contract. Not only that, but it could also teach me discipline and purpose, and give me access to experiences I would never have otherwise. *It was the answer to all my problems at the time.* Plus, I trusted Shawn; I felt safe with him and like he was steering me in the right direction. I made my decision quickly and easily—I was going to join the Virginia Army National Guard.

The process of joining wasn't quite as quick or easy though; there were a few challenges to overcome. First was telling my parents. Once I had officially decided, I called my mom up on the phone to tell her I was coming over that evening to talk with her and dad about something important. She tried to pry around what this was about, but I wasn't budging. "I'll explain it all tonight when we talk," I told her. When I got there, the three of us sat down in the living room, and after a few moments of silent anticipation, I anxiously word vomited "I'm joining the Virginia Army National Guard!" Their initial reaction was to just look at me with confusion and bewilderment, mouths open and eyebrows raised. I stared back at them with a cold, expression-less face. Next, they both erupted into laughter, exchanging looks with each other and then back at me, assuming this was some kind of prank or joke. But when I didn't laugh too, the energy in the room shifted quickly as they started to realize I was serious. "What? Where is this coming from?" my mom spoke first with a cracked voice and sincere worry in her eyes. That was my cue! I sat up straight, cleared my throat, and then dove right into explaining all the benefits I would get, in particular the money to pay for school. The more I talked, the more my dad perked up as I explained all the resources and financial benefits, especially the part about money for school. My mom, on the other hand, wanted to know more about the dangers, the unknowns, what I would be doing, and what this meant for the safety of her girl.

I would be doing unit supply, I told them. I used the language my recruiter and Shawn had used, "If I did ever get deployed, and unlikely because I have the college first option and will be in a small unit here in the national guard, I have a safe job, I would never need to go outside the wire." After I completed boot camp and my job training, I would only have to attend drill (training) one weekend every month and two weeks every summer. The costs and personal sacrifice seemed minimal, but the benefits were something I couldn't fathom getting any other way. My dad was the first one to come around to the idea. My mom needed more time. I was happy to give her that, but the decision was already done; I had already made up my mind and had started the process. I was joining the United States Army. *I had found my way out.* They nor anyone else could stop me—or so I thought.

12   J. R. HUNNIECUTT

My unresolved compounded trauma had different plans for me. It continued to surface through my actions and behaviors at the time. I had another "run-in with the law" sometime between deciding I was going to join and waiting to go to the Military Entrance Processing Station (MEPS) in Knoxville to get my physical exam (including a drug test), sign the papers, and swear the oath. Prior to deciding, I was still partying a lot, mostly [underage] drinking. Once I had officially made the decision to join, my recruiter and I scheduled my date for going to MEPS a couple of months out to give me time to clean my system (of cannabis) so I could pass the mandatory drug test. By this time the spring semester of my first year in school had ended and summer break had officially begun.

With little to do other than work and wait for MEPS, I was still regularly going to parties and clubs. It didn't take long for me to get caught underage drinking again, this time at a bar with a fake ID. I was charged with my second misdemeanor of underage consumption and another for public intoxication. I spent that night behind bars for the first (and I fully intend for it to be the only) time in my life. I know now but didn't know then that my race and class privilege likely had a lot to do with consequences, or lack of, rather, that I faced after this incident. When my court date arrived, I was given the opportunity to present my case and explain my situation to the judge. I shared with him that I was scheduled to enlist in the military and that being charged with this offense would ruin my chances of it. After hearing this, the judge dismissed my charges and let me off rather than administering the typical punishment for this (second) offense of underage drinking, which should have been a probation sentence. I walked out of the courtroom that day with an overwhelming sensation that I had just made it *out of there*, barely, by the skin of my teeth and with the help and protection of Uncle Sam. By *there*, I didn't just mean the courtroom and the sentencing; *I had made it out* of the scripted path before me of drug abuse, co-dependency, poverty, and cycles of intergenerational trauma.

DOING TIME

On August 27, 2008, I went to MEPS, passed all my exams and physicals, signed my contract, raised my right hand in front of the U.S. flag, and officially swore the oath to join and serve in the United States Army. At MEPS, I was assigned a "ship date" for basic training, which was scheduled for January 2009. Until then, from that August until the following

January, I was enrolled in the Recruit Sustainment Program (RSP) that the Virginia Army National Guard had at the time. RSP was a retainment program that brought recruits together to essentially train and prepare for BCT. We drilled monthly and learned things like how to put on and wear the uniform, military rank structure, customs and culture, and basic skills in weapons identification, usage, and maintenance. It was incredibly useful to prepare me for what was to come, BCT—aka, "boot camp."

I will never forget the day I shipped to go to MEPS to leave for basic training (you go to MEPS then are "shipped" to basic from there either via getting on a plane or being driven in a bus or van to the military installation where you do basic at). That morning, my mom and dad drove me up to the local NG armory about 15 minutes from my house, and from there, Shawn would meet up with us and then drive me two hours up the road to MEPS again, where I would spend one night in a fancy hotel room and board a van for Fort Jackson, South Carolina, early the next morning. When my parents and I got to the armory to drop me off, my mom was so upset that she refused to get out of the car. Plenty of time had passed since that day in their living room when I told my parents I had made the decision to join, but my mom still didn't want me to and was terrified of what it would mean for me and my life. This was my first time leaving home—my family or the town I was raised in—for any extended period of time; it was new to all of us and we weren't sure what to expect. My mom was scared, and so was I. *What would happen to me? Who would I be when I came back home?* It broke my heart to leave her that way, but I was in the Army now, and that meant I no longer had a choice to do what I wanted; I had to move forward. We said our goodbyes and she stayed in the car, laying in the backseat sobbing while my dad grabbed my bag and walked with me into the armory to meet Shawn.

I felt prepared in many ways for basic because of RSP. I was grateful for the several months I spent training and learning customs and culture before shipping. I felt like I knew what to expect physically—I was already in good shape because of cheerleading, plus I knew they slowly built you up and shaped you to be fit like a soldier once you got there. I also had a good idea of what to expect psychologically—I knew I would be cut off from my life back home, no cell phone, very limited and monitored phone calls, and no access to media of any form. I knew I would have to deal with the yelling and degradation and humiliation from Drill Sergeants—it was just part of it all. Altogether, I would be in basic for 12 weeks and from there I would ship to Fort Lee, Virginia, and spend another two months or so training for my specific Military Occupational Specialty (MOS). In all, I would be gone in my Initial Entry Training (IET), which includes basic and job training, for around five to six months. I had taken the semester off school that spring and would pick up where I left off once I was back. I even left all my things in the house I shared with the other cheerleaders and would continue paying rent during the time I was gone. I wanted to be able to simply move right back in when I was back and pick my life up where I left it off, just with more resources and a little more discipline.

I made the decision before I shipped, however, to quit the cheerleading team. I wasn't in good standing anymore because of my run-ins with the police and my less than par grades and class attendance; I had been close to academically failing the prior semester. Beyond that though, I could feel something starting to shift in me. I was no longer a college cheerleader aimlessly partying, failing in school, and heading down a path that many others around me, both in my family and peer group from high school, were on. I was moving in another direction. I had joined the United States Army, and everything was about to change.

Initial Entry Training

Don't be first, don't be last. Stay in the middle. That was the advice Shawn left me with before driving away and leaving me alone at MEPS, where I would board a van to ship to Fort Jackson, SC, the next morning. It was good advice—advice that was quickly illuminated once I actually got to basic. One of the first things Drill Sergeants tell you when you get there is that the fastest way out of there is to graduate. None of us—the other recruits nor I—knew what they meant by that at first, but we quickly learned. If you refused to train, or you did something like fake sick or disclose a non-heterosexual orientation (it was still Don't Ask, Don't Tell then, which was an exclusionary policy that prohibited anyone from disclosing a non-heterosexual orientation while serving in the military—you would face dishonorable discharge if you "came out" in the military) as a way to try to get out, they would keep you there for processing way longer than you'd be there if you just did the training and graduated. One of the things many people who never served in the military often don't understand is how all-encompassing the military is. You can't just quit, or leave, or get out when you want to. When you sign the contract and swear the oath at MEPS, you are legally obligated to carry out your contract or face serious consequences like jail time. There are, of course, always outliers and loopholes, but in general, the military owns you once you join. That part was daunting.

BCT was generally what I expected it to be. There were scary Drill Sergeants who yelled a lot, sometimes hit or shoved recruits, and forced us to do exhausting, infuriating, and sometimes humiliating and degrading things. The whole purpose of it was to strip you of your individual identity and form you into a soldier. We were supposed to all be the same. Difference was punished. We were assigned "Battle Buddies" (affectionally known as "Battles") in basic. You can't go anywhere, at all, ever, in any way, without your Battle. Not even to the bathroom. You sleep next to each other, always stand next to each other, and the whole idea of it is to train us to keep each other accountable. My battle buddy was a black woman named Starla from Atlanta. In general, Starla and I strongly disliked each other (though we had a few moments of bonding near the beginning and end of basic). She was a black girl from the city, and I was a white girl from the Deep South—our differences were stark.

Apart from our cultural identities and my unpacked, conditioned feelings of white supremacy at the time that heavily influenced my perception of and interactions with her, Starla often was one of the *last* ones in training (last to wake up, last to show up for formation, last to be finished eating, etc.). I was doing all I could to head Shawn's advice and *stay in the middle*; I didn't want to stand out or be noticed by the Drill Sergeants. One day, Starla was running late for a formation. I was getting angry because I didn't want to be late, so I made the big mistake of leaving her and going to the formation by myself. I got in line and once she showed up a few minutes later, my Drill Sergeants called me up to post in front of the entire formation. Once I was standing stiff in the position of attention, the screaming and humiliation began.

"WHO DO YOU THINK YOU ARE, RECRUIT HUNNIECUTT? YOU THINK YOU'RE BETTER THAN YOUR BATTLE BUDDY? WHEN YOU GO TO WAR, ARE YOU GONNA LEAVE YOUR LOST AND INJURED COMRADES BEHIND? YOU THINK YOUR LIFE IS MORE IMPORTANT THAN HERS?! GET YOUR ARMS ABOVE YOUR HEAD AND EVERYONE ELSE DROP TO THE FRONT LEANING REST POSITION!"

I was being punished for leaving Starla alone. They were making an example out of me. I was made to hold my M16 (about 7 lbs.) over my head with my arms extended straight while I repeatedly chanted, "I AM A

BLUE FALCON," in full volume for all to hear. In the military, "Blue Falcon" is a code term for "buddy fucker" and is used to describe people who leave their battles behind. As I stood in front of the entire formation chanting this, the Drill Sergeants made the rest of the formation get in the "front leaning rest position," which is the plank position. I don't know how long this went on before they let us all stop. Probably around five minutes, but it's hard to say. As I stood up there, body frozen in a painful position, humiliating myself as I screamed a phrase degrading to both myself and everyone there, ashamed by the emotions leaking from my eyes, time seemed to stand still.

Many moments like this sprinkled through my experiences in basic. The training was vigorous and there was little down time, which helped somewhat in keeping home off my mind. In the tiny bit of down time we were allowed in the evenings before lights out, I wrote in a journal, where I unknowingly at the time documented my own transformation from civilian to soldier through writing about many of my experiences there. Mostly though, I wrote about missing home. I wondered and worried, *what was going on back home, without me?* Every evening in our final formation, the Drill Sergeants would issue out mail. We were allowed to send and receive letters. And the letters I got! Despite my mom being distraught when I left and generally disagreeing with my decision to join, she was my biggest fan my entire way through basic. Nearly every single day I received a letter from her. Mostly, the letters contained chitchat about the mundane happening of home, but for me, receiving a letter from home each night during that transition helped keep me anchored and grounded in who I was. It felt like having a warm hug from my mama every night.

I wrote to her too, about all the different experiences I was having—from the exciting things like passing fitness tests and qualifying with my weapon to the bad stuff like the Blue Falcon incident and other things that were new, unfamiliar, or different. I wrote to her and told her about an incident with a girl in my bay who, during the first few weeks of basic, would frequently come over to my bed after lights out and try to make unwanted advances on me. I didn't word it that way at the time because I didn't clearly see it that way then (I had never been advanced on by the same sex before, so I brushed it off as an overly friendly and affectionate female). As I continued to confront experiences of stark *difference* in basic, I also wrote her and told her about my Battle Buddy, Starla, and how I felt weird being around black people because I never really had been before. As a white girl who grew up in a white family in rural central Appalachia, a region that is 90% white ("ARC Study"); my exposure and relationship to diversity, of any form, was minimal.

The first time I remember ever thinking about race was in my early teenage years when my older cousin gave birth to a biracial baby boy with an African American man—my maternal grandfather was so infuriated that she conceived "out of yolk" (a term my family used to describe anyone of a different race or religion) that she and her child stopped attending family gatherings for years. The second time was when a biracial student enrolled in my entirely white high school—I remember feeling sorry for him and being complicity silent when I witnessed him experience overt racism in our hallways and classrooms, from both my peers and teachers. And now, the third time was there at basic training, when for the first time in my life, I was surrounded by people of racial, ethnic, religious, and sexual identities different from my own. Unlike at home where I was mostly surrounded by and interacted with people just like me, Army basic training was the first organized setting I was ever in where my success depended on my ability to communicate across differences.

Difference was incredibly heightened in basic. People from all over the country with immensely different backgrounds and identities were all brought together for a common purpose, mission, and experience. At the same time, however, difference was something we were being trained and conditioned to minimize, to make disappear. *We were all Army Green,* which meant we were all the same, had the same mission, the same purpose, and were made to behave and look the same as a way for us all to believe and embody it. For me, as a white, cisgender, heterosexual woman, the main difference between me and most others there (white, cis, hetero, men) was gender. I noticed and reacted to differences other than gender—things like race and sexual orientation, but I did not yet have the tools or consciousness to think critically about these issues. Although I did experience unwanted advances from a female that I trained, slept, and showered alongside in basic, and my experiences (and the consequential feelings from them) are not to be negated because of her gender and sexual orientation, it's also true that I was uncomfortable at the time by her sexual orientation. Again, this was still the time of Don't Ask, Don't Tell. More than that, I had been conditioned by ideologies of white supremacy and homophobia having grown up in the Deep South. The only gay person I had ever been around (to my knowledge) up to this point was a gay man in church who I witnessed "have the demons cast out of him" in one of our church revivals. Because of my background and upbringing, I wasn't very interested in or empathetic toward others who didn't look like or have similar experiences as me. In basic, I was noticing and bumping up against these differences, but I didn't yet pay them much mind. Rather, I was focused mostly on the transition I was experiencing and preoccupied with the transition I knew would be next. Front and center in my mind at that time was: *what was it going to be like once I got back home after basic?*

The NG is different from active duty, in that we don't get stationed to an active-duty base somewhere and, thus, don't have to relocate from where we were living when we joined the military. In the NG, when you join you choose a unit within the state you're joining in, which is where you will be assigned to and drill with once you finish basic and your Advanced Individual Training (AIT). Thus, after you complete this initial training, you simply transition back home, to where you came from before you shipped for basic. You resume your civilian life, drill with the NG one weekend a month and a couple of weeks a year, and just basically go about your normal life as a civilian-soldier. In basic, training progressed through phases, and as we got closer to graduation and entered our final phase of training, we were given more autonomy and more free time. Free time meant time to think. As the day I would return home got closer and closer, I felt nervous and anxious about what was next. I could feel that something inside me had changed. I knew I was different from the girl I was when I got there. I turned 20 in basic too; it was symbolic for me to transition out of my teenage years as I transitioned from civilian to soldier. By the time basic came around, I could no longer really imagine myself fitting right back into the same life I was living before. I had purpose now. I was part of something greater than myself. I had tools and resources now—I had *a way out.* What I didn't have, however, were tools to prepare me for integrating my new identity as a soldier into the life I lived before joining.

Time in Service

I spent the first few days and weeks home from basic and AIT celebrating and indulging in all the things I couldn't do or have while I was in my IET. I was living with my old cheerleading roomies again and we quickly resumed our *drink too much too often* ways. It was summer though, so I gave myself permission to take it easy for a while before classes started. After six months of mandatory physical training in IET, I was very opposed to any sort of organized exercise and ate whatever and however much I wanted to since I could again. I got my first tattoo (something my sister and I wanted to do together before I shipped, but it was against policy, so I had to wait until I was out of training and had the tattoo approved by my unit). I cashed in some of my bonus money and bought a new car. Generally, I just did a whole lot of nothing in the first few weeks after I was home from IET. As the weeks started to pile up though, I started to feel a kind of way about being back—a way I struggled to understand or name.

It was summer so fall classes in school hadn't started yet; I had quit the cheerleading team before I left so I didn't have any practices to attend, and I wasn't working because I had plenty of money from the Army that I'd just earned through joining and all my time in training. I went from having my entire day and routine planned out for me in every detail for about five to six months straight in BCT and AIT, to absolutely nothing to do and no one to tell me what to do that entire summer. My roommates were busy with practice and working; their lives had moved on while I was gone. Feeling alone, bored, and annoyed with the civilian culture that thanks to my new lenses of Army Green, I now saw as frivolous and self-centered, I spent weeks doing nothing but staying up too late, sleeping most of the day, eating, and smoking cigarettes (an addiction I had picked up in my job training during off time when I was at Fort Lee).

After attending my first drill with my new unit that summer, I realized that *that* was what I was missing more than anything. I wanted to be back within the structure and the community I felt at basic and AIT. I didn't want to have to live part-time in the civilian world—a world I now felt very disconnected to and aimless in. I knew I didn't want to go full-on active duty because I was happy to finally be out from under the intensity of basic training where I had no agency and autonomy. I feared being full-time military (active duty) for a full enlistment contract would be too much. I wanted a balance of something in between. In basic, I had heard a lot about how in the NG and reserves, you can volunteer to be placed with another unit who is on rotation to deploy to war next, if there was a slot open for your job. This seemed like it could be the middle ground I was looking for. I started to seriously consider volunteering for a deployment to war at that time. I knew the idea of volunteering to go fight in a war was absurd, but I missed the cohesion, challenges, and rush of BCT. I inquired with my unit leadership about this and was told my first step was to write a letter to leadership. I started writing it immediately.

Within the same week, Shawn reached out to me and introduced me to a friend, Berry, as a sort of blind date—something to distract me, I think.

Shawn didn't want me to volunteer for a deployment. Berry was in the NG too, served in a unit near mine, and had been in the military a few years longer than me and was higher ranking. He was handsome, was college-educated, served too, and seemed like he had a good head on his shoulders. Berry had a motorcycle, and for our very first date, he picked me up on his bike and took me to a Mexican restaurant right down the road. After our meal, he took me for a long, summer evening bike ride down 421 highway that goes by the NASCAR track and out past the Holston Dam in my hometown. After I got the hang of leaning into the turns and flowing with the back-and-forth grooves of the bike, I let myself relax for what felt like the first time since getting home from IET. I tightly wrapped my arms around him from behind and held on as I closed my eyes and lifted my face to the sky for the warm summer sun to kiss my cheeks while the wind whipped my hair wildly behind me. Berry and I clicked immediately. Our first date turned into two, then three, and before I knew it, Berry and I were a couple. Shawn's distraction worked because, with Berry's encouragement, I changed my mind about volunteering for a deployment. I even let Barry delete the letter I had written only a month before.

Time passed quickly for the rest of that summer and when classes began in the fall, I was ready to give it my all. I no longer had to have a job outside of the NG, so I had my time freed up to focus on school and generally had less stress as I had plenty of reliable resources now from the military. I focused on school and partied way less. As I became less interested in the clubs and drinking, my friendships with people I was close with before joining were diminishing. Most notably, I wasn't getting along with my roommates anymore. There seemed to be a disconnect. To them, I had left for one semester and was back and things were supposed to just go back to normal. To me, I was completely different and couldn't go back— I now saw their way of life as frivolous and unfocused and wanted nothing more than to create a new, different normal that was now congruent with my military service. I moved back into my parents' house for the rest of that semester, and not long after, Berry and I moved in together.

Months passed and I slowly worked to create that new normal. I was drilling regularly, enjoying my time in S4 with 1030th HHD, enjoying the resources from the military, and finding the military was giving me something else that I hadn't anticipated when I joined. It was trumping my family system obligations and giving me an "out" just when I needed one. It was paying for school, giving me health insurance, paying my rent, and helping me to feel like I belonged somewhere and was doing something that mattered. *I was serving in the United States Army.*

Uncle Sam became my surrogate parent—always showing up for me when I needed him most. And because of how much I felt like I owed him for all he was giving me, it was easy for me to overlook some of the not-so-great and hard-to-believe things about him. Something had happened to another woman in my unit, someone I had gone to high school with. SPC Chase was a year younger than me, and we never interacted much in high school because our social circles didn't cross. She was already part of 1030th HHD when I joined. But shortly after I became part of the unit, she transferred to another one. I didn't know much at all about it at the time, except that she had filed a report against someone in my unit for sexual harassment. I knew this because every time she walked into a room, males around me would say things like "don't look at her or get too close to her or she'll file a report again you." She was ostracized in our unit, and not only did she switch to another unit, but she ended up moving to an entirely different state in the months after. I never talked to SPC Chase about what happened to her or asked anyone any questions about it. But through witnessing the consequences she experienced because of filing a report against one of the males in our unit, I quickly learned it would serve me best to always keep my mouth shut if anything ever happened to me. I never wanted to experience what I witnessed her go through. And if I'm being completely honest about it, at the time, I'm not sure even I believed her. Believing her would have meant that Uncle Sam who had given me a way to *get out*, maybe couldn't always protect me.

I pushed any feelings about her and what happened away, and I kept on keeping on. My last two years of college flew by. I graduated with my bachelor's degree in 2011 and started a master's program at a university a town away, East Tennessee State University (ETSU), studying communication. My unresolved and unprocessed early childhood and adolescent trauma was still showing up in disruptive ways at that time—most notably in my romantic relationship with Berry. Our relationship ended that summer before I started grad school. After the breakup, I moved into an apartment about an hour away, living on my own for the first time ever (and I could afford it, thanks to the military!). I continued to drill every month and attended our two-week-long annual trainings each summer. The Army was paying my tuition at ETSU and providing me a modest living stipend while I was a student. To generate some extra income, I joined Honor Guard. Being part of Honor Guard meant attending funerals (in your military dress uniform) to conduct military honors at the ceremony, doing things like folding the flag or performing the 21-gun salute. I found it humbling to be part of the funeral ceremonies of so many people who had served our country. SPC Dillan, who was in S4 with me, did Honor Guard too, and so did another older man in our unit, SGT Kaye.

I enjoyed being part of Honor Guard. It felt patriotic to be performing these rituals at the funerals of men who had served our country. I did notice though, that it was always men. Not only were the funerals always for men (I can't remember a single service for a woman Veteran we did honors for), but I was also on a team full of men; I was the only woman in Honor Guard. I didn't necessarily mind this though because *it's just how things were* in the military. I was used to being one of the only females in this male-dominated world. I had learned how to hold my own—I ignored the looks and the off-handed comments about my appearance or body and was continuously figuring out how to dodge the unwanted flirting and advances in general. Besides, I felt safe in Honor Guard because of who was there with me—SPC Dillan felt like a protective brother and SGT Kaye like an uncle or even Army father figure of sorts. Nothing was amiss.

As the first couple of years in my unit passed, I didn't think much at all about gender. Then, in my first semester of grad school, which was my third year in the Army and second year with my unit, I took a class in my master's program called "Gender in the Media." In this class, I learned how gender and socially constructed roles of femininity and masculinity were produced and reproduced through media. For my final paper in that class, prompted by my wise professor, I chose to do a research project examining how women service members were represented in military media. To gather data for this paper, I spent hours combing through military magazines, analyzing photos of women serving, text written about them, and generally how they were being portrayed. The results both shocked and horrified me. Women were rarely portrayed at all, but when they were it was in a maternal light (accompanied by text describing them as mothers and wives), they were smiling, never near a weapon. Sometimes, they were even represented sexually (like their military top opened with cleavage showing or photos of them wearing red lipstick in uniform, which was highly against regulation).

After I parsed through all my resources and collected data for this class project, I finally sat down to write the paper and found myself overwhelmed with confusion, anger, and general perplexity. I related to what I was finding, and it didn't feel right. Because of this class, I had new language to name my feelings and experiences, which before I didn't know how to put words to. I often felt invisible in the military, sexually objectified, or like my place was not to be in the military at all. I had frequent experiences my first few years that reminded me I was a woman in a man's military, but more often than not, I didn't really *see* it. It was easier not to. *I chose not to.* I learned early on what survival in that space looked like. I remembered SPC Chase in my unit that I had gone to high school with who was ostracized and punished for *seeing* it and naming it. So instead, I laughed at the sexist jokes, I distrusted most other women I crossed paths with during my service and was happy to "sit there and look pretty" when my senior NCO (literally) instructed me to do so. The military—Uncle Sam—gave me so much, it felt uncomfortable to critique it in the way I was doing in this paper for grad school. It was much easier to push it to the back of my mind and do as they had taught me, *lower your head and drive on.* So that's what I did.

As the months went on, occasionally at drill I'd hear some gossip about how we were up next in a rotation for deployment to the Middle East. The thought that I could get called up to go was always in the back of my mind. It was a weird feeling; sometimes I wanted to go and hoped it happened because, well, that's what all this training was about and because as a country we were at war, and I wanted/felt conditioned to do my part. Usually though, I feared it and hoped it never happened. I also knew it was possible to get called up to go with other units too if your MOS was ever in high demand. I had seen it happen when SGT Baker, who was in S4 with me and taught me how to drive a Humvee in my very first drill, was pulled from our National Guard unit in early 2011 to deploy to war in the Middle East with another unit in Virginia who had a slot open for his MOS. There was a vacancy in the deploying unit, and as is common practice in the NG, SGT Baker was pulled for that deployment because his job filled the vacancy and met a quota.

After over a year away at war, we got used to operating in S4 with Baker's spot vacant; things moved on as normal. When he finally finished his tour, returned home, and started drilling with our unit again in 2012, he was isolative and mostly kept to himself. Sometimes, you could smell alcohol on him if you stood close enough. Smelling alcohol on him wasn't entirely out of the ordinary though, and as far as I knew, everything was normal, and he was just adjusting to being back. A few short months went by after his return and then one Sunday during our morning formation at drill, our unit commander stood in front of our formation and uncomfortably announced that SGT Baker had taken his own life the night before. They told us they would let us know about upcoming funeral arrangements and then said something about looking out for each other. "Keep an eye on your battle buddy," he said with a solemn face. We were all invited to a church service with the unit chaplain following formation. Then, they just continued with the other announcements. Formation was dismissed and as we were walking out of the room after, SPC Dillan walked up to me with blood-shot eyes and muttered under his breath, "he put a pistol in his mouth and ate a bullet." Travis Baker died by suicide on April 10, 2012, at age 43. He had a wife, a son, and a daughter. His obituary read, "He was an avid hunter and fisherman who loved being in the woods."

I never talked about it after that day, but Baker's suicide impacted me. After they announced it at drill that morning, things just went on as if it never happened. I know a handful of people from the unit who attended the funeral, but apart from that, that seemed to be it. No one ever talked to us about what happened and why. In the unit, we had regular annual trainings that covered things like sexual assault, drug use, and suicides, but it was all taken lightly and even turned into a running joke in the unit. It was never really taken seriously. Maybe it was just how we all coped with it.

But it happened. His life ended, by suicide, shortly after he returned home from war—war that the military sent him to. I remember wondering if it was because of that, because he had just gotten home *from war*. I assumed what happened was because something there, *at war*, must have happened. It frightened me. I could not visualize myself ever being in a war. I knew I was a soldier; I was *trained and proficient*—I was literally trained how to kill—but I still couldn't imagine it ever happening, ever really doing it. I wondered many times about Baker and about the truth of what happened. I thought many times about that day on the mountain side he taught me how to drive the Humvee—how he had helped make me feel comfortable and showed me kindness on my first drill with our unit. He "loved being in the woods" and I am so grateful he shared that with me. I didn't understand how someone so kind, laid back, and giving could do something like end his own life. It didn't make any sense to me. I never got any answers. No one ever told me, and I never asked.

Drive on, soldier, drive on. Time continued to pass and the more it did, the more jaded I became. I developed what I used to call a "love/hate relationship with the military." I loved how it felt like the military—Uncle Sam—was always there for me. I had the resources I needed to get through school mostly debt free, I had access to more ways to supplement income if I needed to (like in Honor Guard), I had good health insurance, I had consistency and discipline and order, and I had community—I had grown to feel a sense of kinship, family really, with my unit. The military came first in my life, it had to, because I was under contract. This helped to shift some of the relational dynamics in my nuclear family that were long overdue to be shifted. The military came first—before the family obligations and duties—and it was a tool for me as for the first time in my life, I learned how to establish and implement healthy family boundaries. Uncle Sam became my surrogate parent, caring and providing stability for me in a way I desperately needed at the time—a way my parents were never fully able to. It was hard not to love, or at least not feel a deep sense of loyalty, to the military. What I realized over time though is how clouded this loyalty caused my vision to be—how much it impacted what I chose to *see* and, subsequently, name and process around my own experiences in service. Again, it was easier, and I was conditioned, to just push it all away. *Lower your head and drive on.*

But the longer I was in, the harder and harder it was getting to do that. It was my second to last annual training with my unit when I had an experience that was incredibly difficult to just push away and pretend didn't happen. My unit had just arrived at Fort Pickett, a military installation a few hours' drive up the road from our armory in Gate City. We usually did our two-week-long annual trainings there. After just arriving, we were trying to figure out barracks and bunks. As per usual, our unit formation was in the male's barracks because there's way more of them and that's *just the way things were.* The female soldiers, including myself, didn't yet know what barracks we were assigned to. In a row, the handful of females in our unit filed into the male barracks and dropped our stuff at our feet. Among the rest of the males in our unit, SGT Kaye, my friend from Honor Guard, was sitting on a bed just a few feet away from where I stood. After everyone was accounted for, one of the males asked the females, "Where is yall's barracks at?" I responded, "We're not assigned one yet." Without missing a beat, SGT Kaye blurted out, "You can sleep right here with me, Hunniecutt," and looked at me with a wink while he seductively rubbed the spot on his mattress next to him where he sat. *What?!* Laugher erupted across the barracks. *Why did he say that? In front of everyone.* I looked around at the other females. A few rolled their eyes and shook their heads. *I can't believe he just said that. No one is standing up for me and saying that's not ok?* My leadership remained quiet. My body froze and I felt a rush of emotion overtake me. I felt a knot in my stomach form. *I trusted*

SGT Kaye. I thought he respected me. I felt violated. My eyes lowered to the floor, and I stepped back, moving out from the center of the group formation and backed up against a wall, where I stood silently for the rest of the time I had to be in that room.

Throughout my years in service up to that point, a lot of men I served with made sexual comments to me, about me, with me. I had learned how to go along—how to not *see it*. It was an act of self-survival. This felt different though. SGT Kaye was old enough to be my father, he was a senior enlisted soldier that I had grown to trust, respect, and look up to over time. *This one hurt.* It was humiliating, disgusting, and violating. I know that he saw in my nonverbal response how much the comment had impacted me, because later that evening after chow, he approached me when I was standing outside of the female barracks alone, smoking a cigarette.

"Hey, I just wanted to come over and apologize," he said.

I looked blankly at him, unable to find any words. I took a few steps back from him as he approached.

"I didn't mean anything by it. But I know I shouldn't have said it," he went on.

"It's fine," I quickly responded with a shrug.

He hesitated before nodding in agreement and then awkwardly walked away.

After that interaction, I never wanted to be around or interact with SGT Kaye again. I never reported this incident because any time I considered it, I remembered what happened to SPC Chase. I stopped showing up for my Honor Guard duties in the months after this incident. I would either show up late, show up in the wrong uniform or sometimes even not show up at all. Eventually, I was removed from my position.

Freedom Rings

By this time, I had served five years of my six-year contract, and I had been in grad school long enough to have some basic skills in critical thinking. It was getting much harder to ignore and dismiss all the gender inequities and misconduct I witnessed and experienced in service. I was beginning to feel angry, but I didn't feel like there was anything I could do about it, so the anger faded into a type of flat indifference. And the more indifferent and jaded I became, the more I saw the military as only a means to an end for accomplishing my goals in my civilian life—get school paid for and then get out. The hate part of my love/hate relationship with the Army kept growing, and the love part, dwindling.

Lower Your Head and Drive On

I finally graduated with my master's degree from ETSU in the spring of 2013 and had to decide what was next. I had fallen in love with research during my master's program and knew I wanted to continue in academia and make a career of it. My goal was to earn a PhD (Doctor of Philosophy) in Communication. I was incredibly intimidated to even apply to PhD programs, as it just seemed like something so far-fetched from what was possible for me. After all, neither of my parents had even graduated high school and there was not a single person, on either side of my family, who held a doctorate degree. This dream felt far, far away. *But I was a United States soldier.* Through all my experiences of adapting and overcoming in service, I had come to believe in myself in a way that helped me to keep pushing forward toward my dreams and goals. *Drive on, soldier, drive on.* Though I had decided I was going to apply to PhD programs decently late into the application process of that admissions cycle, I went for it anyway. I submitted applications to a handful of schools around the country that had doctorate programs in communication studies. Only a month or so passed before the admission letters started showing up: I didn't get accepted to a single one.

At first, I was devastated and crushed. Once I read the letter from the last school to respond and saw I had been rejected, I knew it meant any chance of starting a PhD program that next fall was gone. After I finished reading that last letter, I threw on my tennis shoes, put in my earbuds, turned on rock music at full blast, went outside, and then took off in a mad sprint toward the longest and steepest hill in my neighborhood. I ran that hill up and down, up and down, up and down, as fast as I could and as many times as I could, until I was ready to collapse. I wobbled home with my cheeks wet from tears and sweat and decided that very night that I would try again the next year. I was angry and felt like a failure, but I could see a silver lining. I only had one year left before my End of Time in Service (ETS) with the military. Waiting a year made more sense because then I wouldn't have to transfer to another unit in another state for the last year of my contract with the Army. I hadn't officially decided yet, but I was leaning toward getting out of the military once I finished my contract. This plan could work—I could reapply to PhD program the next year and this time get accepted and be able to move to a new place for school around the same time I finished out my time with the Virginia Army NG. I still had a year before I had to make that decision though. I busied myself in the meantime.

I took part-time jobs adjunct teaching at various colleges and universities in the area; I spent time helping my mom organize and market her new hair salon business, and I met someone online, Peter. He was in the Army, with only a few months left in his contract, and was stationed at Fort Knox, Kentucky, which was only a half day's drive away from where I lived in Bristol. After a few weeks of texting and video calls, he came to meet me for the first time when he got a weekend pass from the base. We hit it off and jumped into things together quickly. The last few months of his contract neared an end, and he made the decision to move to the town I lived in once he was released from duty at Fort Knox. His hometown was in northern Virginia, so moving to where I lived in southwest Virginia wasn't far-fetched for him. I didn't think much of it other than being excited he would be much closer to me. He had plans to enroll in school and I agreed to allow him to temporarily stay with me until he got settled and found his own place.

I didn't yet know what Post-Traumatic Stress Disorder (PTSD) looked like, what it felt like, or how to name it. Peter was a combat engineer and had served a tour in Afghanistan the year before he got out of service. Within the first couple of months of him leaving the military and temporarily moving into my small duplex, I started to notice some behaviors I wasn't very comfortable with. Most notably, he was smoking a lot of pot. Once the habit turned to smoking several times daily, I started expressing to him how much I didn't like it or understand why he was using so much.

"It helps me feel relaxed," he told me one afternoon we were arguing about it.

"I don't get it. Aren't you like, *high*? How can you function being so high all the time? Why don't you go for a run or something instead to destress?" I replied.

"No—I don't feel *high* like that. With weed, I feel normal, like leveled out," he told me.

I didn't understand, but I didn't push too much. Over time, his usage started to influence me, and when I could, I started to smoke weed with him. I was still in the NG, which meant still subject to random drug tests, but I had the system pretty figured out by then. I knew that after drill weekend each month, I had about a week window where I could smoke weed and still have enough time for it to clear out of my system before drill the next month. It also helped a lot that someone in my unit had insider status on when we were likely to have drug tests and regularly told me (and the other soldiers in our unit who he knew used cannabis) when to expect the next one. This person smoked too. There were even times when a group of us from the unit would smoke together. It was like this small group of us who all wanted to get out of the military used smoking weed together as a form of defiance against the system and I see now, even a way we attempted to reclaim our own agency. For me, the more I began to use cannabis, the more I started to understand what Peter had been telling me about feeling relaxed and leveled with weed. I was starting to feel it too—it felt good not to *feel* so much all the time. So, I began pushing the bounds of how much I was using it too. Even though I had a layer of protection by having insight into when we might get drug tested, I was still teetering a risky line using enough to risk "popping hot" on a surprise drug test at drill. If I were to be caught, I could have been dishonorably discharged from the military—something that I knew would carry serious consequences throughout the rest of my life if it happened.

But as dependence on cannabis began to form, care about potential consequences began to fade. Peter and I had a new routine on the weeks I was able to smoke. We would sprawl out on the couch in the living room, take turns hitting the bong we passed back and forth between us, and zone out watching something on TV, and then about an hour or so in when the munchies hit, we'd binge eat together. There was a bakery just up the street from my house that just happened to be open 24/7. There were so many nights we would drive the few blocks down the street to the bakery, stoned off our asses, to get boxes of baked goods to come home and chow down on. It didn't take long for this new habit to catch up to us—we both started gaining weight, arguing more, and generally just seemed to be unhappy with ourselves and each other. He seemed to be more impacted by it all than I was though as he was smoking (and binging) much more than me since I was limited to only about a week out of every month I could indulge. As things progressed, I eventually realized I wasn't happy in the relationship, and it wasn't working for me anymore. I told him I wanted it to end and that he needed to find another place to live as soon as possible. He wasn't happy with my decision, and he started acting out. Things escalated quickly.

Once he and his stuff were completely out of my house, I changed the locks. He was doing things by this point that were scaring me—sending text messages to my friends telling them inappropriate things about me and even tried to show up at my mom's work once to talk to her about me and my decision to not date him. One evening when I was at home alone, he showed up. He knew I was there because my car was in the driveway and the lights were on inside. But when I didn't answer the door and he realized I had changed the locks, he became angry and started pounding on it while yelling obscenities at me. I was terrified he was going to try to break in and hurt me. There were a lot of windows around my house he could see in, so I got on my hands and knees and crawled through the kitchen, past the front door, and into my bedroom where I kept my pistol. I got the gun, called 911, and crouched down waiting for the police to arrive, hoping he would leave. After a few seconds of silence, I heard a loud noise, like glass shattering, followed by his truck starting and tires burning on pavement as he sped off down the road. He had broken one of my windows. I called 911 and, eventually, he was caught and arrested. He spent a night or two in jail and, eventually, I dropped the charges.

Looking back, knowing what I know now, I realize he had PTSD and that specific incident was an episode. But I had no idea at the time. I knew he was a Veteran. I knew he had been to war. I knew he had cannabis dependence and anger problems, but somehow, I never attributed any of it to his service. Now I understand he used cannabis as a way to cope and self-medicate with his own military transition stress and trauma. But at the time, I only saw his cannabis (and my own) in a negative light and had no insight into how to support him through his military-connected stressors during his transition out of service. I just wanted away from him. So, once the experience had passed and I had enough distance from him and felt safe, I pushed it all down and away and *lowered my head to drive on.*

Despite the turbulence of that relationship, I had still managed to submit my PhD admission applications for the second time during those several months we spent together. Once early spring of 2014 rolled around, the admission letters started coming in. This time, I got offers from every single school I had applied to! I was thrilled. It felt surreal. I couldn't believe it was happening. I was bursting with pride at all the acceptances but simultaneously riddled with fear about actually being capable. *Me, get a PhD? How could I do something like that?* I kept reminding myself to look back to see just how far I had come. *Other people can do it, why can't I? I'm in the United States Army—I can do anything!* Of all the different admissions and financial aid offers, the University of Denver (DU) stuck out to me the most. I was impressed by their faculty; the award package they offered me was generous, and I thought it would be an incredible experience to live in Denver, Colorado. About a week later, I officially accepted the offer from DU and, with much anticipation, made the decision to move across the country to Denver that summer, shortly after my military service ended and I completed my very last drill with my unit. By that time, I knew what my decision about staying in or getting out of the Army was. I was getting out.

Little Things

When I was serving my time in the military, it was the little things—or rather, a reflective look at the collection of the seemingly mundane experiences of my service—that ultimately led to my decision to walk away. At that point, I didn't yet feel like any of my experiences in service or connected to my service were traumatic, but I did feel like all the "little things" added up to a big thing that was impacting my life in a big way—I didn't want to give any more of myself. By the time my six years in the military were almost up, I longed to be free of Uncle Sam; I no longer wanted to feel him breathing down my neck. I knew though that being free from him was a double-edged sword—it also meant I could no longer count on him. When I walked away from the Army, I had to walk away from everything the Army gave me. Ending my time in service didn't just mean gaining my individual freedom and autonomy back, it also meant losing the security, comfort, and structure the Army offered me.

I had to walk away from the financial security—from the money. I had to walk away from the psychological security—I knew it would always be there—THEY would always be there. I had to walk away from the experiences I had yet to have—I would now never deploy with the unit I had spent six years training with. I had to walk away from the soldiers—leaving behind the memories, the secrets, the kinship I'd grown to know and feel safe within over the past six years. But it came down to them or me. It was stay in and have those things or get out and have the freedom to be whoever I wanted to be. It became about the little things for me.

It was not having to wear my hair in a tight, rounded, perfectly tidy bun on the back of my head for hours upon hours at a time. It was being able to wear red nail polish or any nail polish for that matter. It was being able to walk into a room full of soldiers and not have everyone turn around and stare at you because of your gender. It was having the freedom to have my mom add an undertone of violet color to my hair to add some dimension. It was being listened to and heard. It was wanting to feel sexy but needing to silence that need. It was wearing clothes that actually fit my body—the body of a woman. It was not being sexually harassed. It was not having to pee in a cup every month while someone with a higher rank on their top watched. It was being able to wear the normal clothes that I wear the other 28 days of each month without being slut shamed. It was not worrying about if my hips moved when I walked. It was being able to put my hands in my pockets without fear of reprimand. It was being able to talk back and say no when I disagreed. It was being able to voice my opinion and be listened to. It was not being looked at like a giggly little girl. It was having privacy again. It was not being out in the middle of the woods when I'm exhausted and hungry and angry and having to "hurry up and wait" just one more time. It was not having to take a PT test every year and stress and stress for months prior about if I can pass the two-mile run or not. It was not having to have my pants tucked perfectly into my boots. It was not having to have yearly physical health assessments where I had to put my feet in stirrups in an RV in a parking lot where a strange doctor gave me an exam. It was not being ignored anymore because I'm a woman. It was being allowed to say no and walk away if I wanted to. It was not having to give respect to someone because of the rank on their uniform rather than because they earned it. It was not having to any longer give respect to those people who have so blatantly and intently violated mine. It was not having to be quiet and take it when that happened. It was to be seen for who I am—for the person that I choose to be.

By the time I had made my decision, I still had about five months or so left of drills before my contract officially ended on August 26, 2014. As I started being open with my decision about choosing not to "re-up" my contract at drill, the more the Army tried to offer me things to keep me in. It's cheaper to retain a soldier than is it to train a new one. I stood firm in my "no" and felt empowered by it. And the more empowered I felt in my decision to choose myself again and say no to Uncle Sam, the less I cared about the rules and regulations anymore. Leaving the military felt like making the decision to move out of my parent's house for the first time when I was 18 years old. As time got closer and closer to my ETS date, I was consumed with thoughts of "freedom." Just like when I was 18 years old, ready to bust out of my parent's house and experience the world on my own, I once again wanted nothing more than to make my own rules and my own decisions, unencumbered by anyone or anything else. I could see the light at the end of the tunnel, and it was permeated with thoughts of making my own path and being able to do whatever I wanted without the hovering presence of Uncle Sam. I just wanted freedom.

My very last drill with my unit, in June of 2014, was a strange day. My contract was through August, but my unit would be at their annual training then, so I made up my drill a few days early before they left and before my official ETS date. I felt like something should have happened to somehow mark that day of my last drill with my unit—my last ever drill with the Army—but everything just went on per usual. We did the same normal, routine training drills and missions we always did. A few people acknowledged it was my last day and said goodbyes to me, but mostly it just felt strange and surreal. Something was missing for me; I needed a way to ritualize that last day—the end of that chapter. So, immediately after that very last drill, I went and got my nose pierced. It seemed a little silly, but piercing my nose was something I had wanted to do for years and wasn't able to because of the Army. I tried it once though.

I knew I wasn't allowed to and that it was against regulation, but I had heard of other women doing it anyway and just using a nude-colored nose stud during drill weekends, so it didn't close up. Or some just stuck a small Band-Aid on it. I went for it. About a year before my ETS date, I got it pierced one week between drills. Before the next drill happened, I got the nude-colored nose stud and put it in (even though I was not supposed to change the ring that soon!). It looked utterly ridiculous like I had a very strange-looking, large zit on the side of my nose. When I attended that first drill with it pierced, I did my best to play it off as being a zit and acted really offended (because it was a "zit") when someone pointed it out. I preferred them thinking I had a gross zit on my nose over my new nose piercing closing because of having to be at drill (when it's a fresh piercing, it closes up very quickly—within hours—if you remove the ring). Somehow, I got away with it for a while. It went on for two or three months before someone higher ranking than me finally made me take it out. It closed up before we were dismissed from final formation that same afternoon.

On my last drill, I knew re-piercing my nose was the perfect way to celebrate and ritualize the ending of my chapter in the military. It would be my *freedom ring*. After I got home from the armory that day, I changed clothes before driving up to the tattoo parlor. I was slow and self-conscious when I changed clothes that day; I knew it would likely be the last time I ever wore that uniform. I grazed my fingers over the unit patch on my shoulder before pulling it off. I untied the shoelaces of the sandy brown boots I had worn for the past six years, the same boots issued to me in basic training. I let my hair down out of the tight bun on the back of my head. I walked into the bathroom and looked at myself up close in the mirror. I didn't feel any different. I got dressed and drove to the tattoo parlor.

There were still a couple of months before I would move to Denver. Sometime between ending the relationship with Peter late last winter and that summer, I had started another [unhealthy] relationship. It was with someone I had known for most of my childhood—we grew up in church together. Early that spring we had run into each other at a bar and had a drunken hook up that night. One hook-up turned into many hook-ups, and once again, I found myself deep in a cycle of unhealthy co-dependency and attachment, seeking love and acceptance in any place and in any form I could find it. I had still yet to face or resolve any of my childhood trauma (much less any I faced during my military service), and my behaviors around sex and relationships at this time were reflective of this hard truth. My new boyfriend, Josh, was also a heavy and regular cannabis user. He even dabbled some in dealing it. Even though I had ended my relationship with Peter, the weed habit I picked up when I was with him stuck with me after. Being with Josh only further enabled me. Our entire relationship revolved around getting high together. But since we knew each other for most of our lives and had grown up in a very close church community together, we had a strong bond through shared experiences and, with this, deep respect for each other too. I think Josh felt a deep sense of obligation to help care for and protect me. He knew about my plans to move to Colorado late that summer and he also knew I was absolutely terrified of going by myself. I had never even been there. My parents, especially my mom, were even more terrified. I was leaving; I was moving far away from her, my family, my hometown, and the only life I had ever known. She didn't want me to go alone. It didn't take much convincing for Josh to agree to move with me. He was excited to move to Colorado because weed was legal there (at that time, it was one of the only states with recreational legalization). We packed up my duplex that first week of August 2014 and when the morning for us to go finally arrived, my parents and his mom came over to help load up the U-Haul. As we drove away, Josh in the driver's seat and me in the passenger, tears streamed down both our cheeks as we watched our parents, our hometown, and our old lives fade in the rear-view mirror.

WORKS CITED

"ARC Study: Disproportionately High Rates of Substance Abuse in Appalachia." *Appalachian Regional Commission.* August 2008. www.arc.gov/news/article. asp?ARTICLE_ID=113

Rudd, Rose A., et al. "Increases in drug and opioid overdose deaths—United States, 2000–2014." *Morbidity and mortality weekly report* 64.50 & 51 (2016): 1378–1382.

CHAPTER 2

My Veteran Identity (Crisis): Suicides and Reintegration

In the previous chapter, I shared a condensed version of my story of joining, serving in, and choosing to separate from the Virginia Army National Guard. The purpose of Chap. 1 was to lay a foundation and provide background as a jumping off point for explicating psychosocial challenges that were consequential of my lived experiences of military service. In this chapter, I continue with my story. Becoming a researcher of Veteran studies blends with my story of separating from military service, as told throughout this chapter. Given this, I narratively weave literature on topics relevant to separation from military service into this chapter, including Veteran suicides, reintegration, and identity. Taking a linear approach, the first three sections of this chapter flow chronologically in time through Fall 2014 to Spring 2015 and include specific stories that illustrate feeling lost, seeing loss, and finding myself through loss. Woven throughout these stories, I include, overview, and analyze literature on Veteran suicides, Veteran reintegration, military assimilation, military culture, and the military-civilian divide. The purposes of this chapter are (1) to illustrate the crisis of identity I experienced when I separated from military service and (2) to provide a literature review while situating my own experiences within existing research relevant to Veteran identity.

© The Author(s), under exclusive license to Springer Nature
Switzerland AG 2022
J. R. Hunniecutt, *Rethinking Reintegration and Veteran Identity*,
https://doi.org/10.1007/978-3-030-93754-6_2

Fall 2014: Feeling Loss

It was late morning when Josh and I finally arrived in Denver. One of the first things that stood out to me was how many sunflowers there were! Growing up, my mom had always decorated my room with sunflowers and my sister's room with daisies. Sunflowers had become symbolic for me, eliciting a feeling of home. It was so sunny in Colorado, sunflowers lined the streets, and everything looked so clean and maintained. "It's all the tax money from the weed," Josh told me when I pointed out the lavish landscaping among the side streets in town we were driving past.

A woman who was in a cohort a couple years ahead of me in the PhD program had offered to let me and Josh stay in her apartment for a week or so until we figured out housing; she was out of town anyway, so it wasn't an inconvenience, she assured us. When we got there, found the right apartment, and made our way inside, I found a note she had left for us explaining the sleeping arrangements she had made. The note also mentioned there was beer in the fridge for us. I texted her to let her know we had arrived and thanked her again. "Oh yeah, thanks for the beer, but we don't really drink. Do you happen know of a good place we can go buy some legal weed?!" I asked. By this point, coping with harm emotions through self-medicating with cannabis had become the norm for me.

The first few weeks in Colorado were hazy and flew by. We smoked a lot of pot, searched for, found, and moved into a house, and Josh found a job working as a cashier in a department store near where we lived. As the beginning of September rolled around, it was time for classes to finally start! I had already met a few of my new peers from my PhD program, one of which was Josh's and my new roommate. But more than anything, I was eager to jump into the work—to learn more about research.

When I submitted my applications to different programs, I had to articulate what my research interests were, what I wanted to study, and with whom. I had written my master's thesis at East Tennessee State University (ETSU) about infidelity and trauma of betrayals in romantic relationships and how that impacted child development in family systems where it occurred (it was part of my own story). It was in my program at ETSU where I first learned about autoethnographic research—which is essentially research where the author writes about their own lived experiences as it relates to larger systems of power and culture. I fell in love with research learning how to do autoethnography because the process of examining my own personal struggles and experiences in relation to larger systems was both cathartic and healing. It was through doing this work in my master's program that I first started to gain a foundation of understanding that it's not always *just the way things are*. And so, when I decided to continue with the pursuit of my doctorate degree, I knew I wanted to continue in this line of work—doing research that was messy and vulnerable but second to none in its ability to touch and move those who engage with it. It was how I felt like I could use my own adversity and experiences to help others, while also healing myself.

My focus at this point was solely on family systems and romantic relationships. Those were my research topic interests when I was accepted into and started my PhD program; nothing to do with the military at all. At this point, the military was the furthest thing from my mind. During my six years in service, occasionally I would miss a drill, or one would be canceled on a certain month, which meant that it wasn't an uncommon experience for two or even three months to pass without me wearing the uniform or being in any military settings. This helped make my first couple months out and not attending drill seem easy and normal—I didn't really notice it because I had gone two to three months at a time without drilling before. Plus, I was too busy during those first few months in Denver scrambling to find housing, securing financing, adjusting to my new living situation, and situating myself as a new student and teaching instructor to even notice, much less process, how much separating from the military may have been impacting me.

The first time I gave the military much thought was during my first month in school as part of a class I was taking called *Visual Narratives of Women's Health*. We had been discussing the concept of redemption in class, particularly how it related to the health and wellbeing of women. To reflect on what we were learning, we were assigned a class project. When reading the prompt for the assignment, I immediately thought of the military: *we were to visually narrate a time in our lives we had experienced a form of redemption*. I knew exactly what I was going to do.

I looked up, printed, and cut out a picture of the crest of my old NG unit. I drew two small versions of myself—one in a cheerleading uniform and one in my Army Combat Uniform (ACU). I wrote my name with descriptions under each picture: under the cheerleader drawing of me I wrote: "Jeni Hunniecutt: college student, cheerleader, civilian," and under the Army drawing of myself I wrote: "SPC Hunniecutt: civilian soldier." I found a large piece of stock paper that looked like rays of light shooting up from the bottom of the page. I glued the unit crest and the two cut out drawings of myself to the paper and then I wrote the Soldier's Creed that

I had been made to memorize in basic training over the entire picture. On the day in class when we were to share our projects, I did so with pride and excitement for not only what I had created, but that I had served in the military. It was the first time since I had gotten out that I had talked about my military service. After class, I hung it up on the wall over my desk in my shared office I was assigned to as a graduate teaching instructor.

Life moved forward. I was having a hard time adjusting. I was doing great academically, but socially I was having a hard time connecting with my peers. Sometime around late October, I was in a biweekly meeting with all the other graduate teaching instructors in my program. The advisor of this group had assigned us an article to read before the meeting, and we were to come ready to discuss the article in our large group setting that day. The article was written by a black academic, and it was about his experiences trying to reconcile and construct meaning around how his life growing up in poverty as an African American child and teen was so drastically different from his life as an academic in the Ivory Tower now. To get the discussion going, the group advisor led with questions asking us to how experiences we may have had in our own lives could relate to what the author was speaking to. After a few moments of silence, a woman next to me shot up her hand. Her name was Sara, and like me, she was also from a part of the Deep South. "Well, like us for example," she gestured to me and to herself, "we're from the south and so sometimes we get judged a certain way for things like having an accent or even wearing certain kinds of clothes, like camo . . ." She wasn't even finished speaking when several people cut her off at once. "What! Wearing a camo shirt is NOTHING like having black skin," one person interjected. "Talk about privilege!" said another.

My body tensed up. I wasn't sure what was going on. I hadn't even spoken yet and suddenly half the people in the room seemed to be yelling at me. I looked over at Sara. She had sunken down in her seat and her eyes were looking down, arms tightly folded across her chest. I sat silent for what was only a few more moments, but felt like a lifetime, before I finally spoke up. I said something along the lines of how growing up in a white bubble in the South, in a place predominately white, we didn't have the tools to understand or think critically about race. I backed Sara up too as I explained that the Deep South indeed is a distinct culture of its own that comes with its own challenges and forms of oppression. Most of my peers balked in response to what I said and continued to verbally attack Sara and me. Finally, it became too much. I stood up abruptly and grabbed my things with force. "I've had enough. I don't have to sit here and listen to this," I said before storming out of the room.

In the hours following this experience, I felt very confused. I didn't understand what had happened and why the others were so angry with what Sara and then I said. The way they treated us made me feel like I had done something awful and offensive, but I didn't understand what. I wanted to find a way to show my classmates, my new peers, that I wasn't a racist bigot from the South. I thought of a song by one of my favorite musicians at the time. It was titled "I Love All People," by Corey Smith. I posted the song on my Facebook page. Early the next morning, I had an email from my graduate teaching advisor, the one who had led the meeting the day before. She wanted me to come in and meet with her as soon as possible. We set a meeting for later that day.

Upon walking into her office, the first thing I saw was a printed out copy of song lyrics on her desk. I looked a little closer and saw it was the lyrics from the Corey Smith song I had posted on Facebook the day before; parts of it were even highlighted. "Do you understand the implications of this song?" she asked once I was seated. "It's about loving everyone regardless of their race or any other identity," I responded with confusion. "No, it's about color blindness," she said.

"I don't understand this, and I don't understand what I did wrong," I told her.

She did her best to explain the concept of white privilege to me, but I was incredibly resistant. "You are telling me that just because so and so is African American or Latino, it means they've had a harder life than me?" I asked in bewilderment.

"Yes," she responded without hesitation.

"I just can't accept that. You don't know my life or what I've been through," I said back defiantly.

We went back and forth a bit more before finally she told me that I had to remove the song from my Facebook or risked facing serious consequences in the department. Then, she asked me about "something that looks like the rebel flag" hanging over my desk in my graduate teaching office.

"THAT'S MY UNIT CREST FROM THE MILITARY! I MADE THAT IN YOUR CLASS" I responded with loud anger.

"Oh," she said, "I didn't realize. Some other students think it resembles the rebel flag."

"I'll take the song off my Facebook, but I'm not taking that picture in my office down. It's about my military service."

She paused for a moment, obviously contemplating what I had just told her.

"Okay," she finally agreed as our meeting came to an end.

From there, things only continued to get worse. After I refused to take the picture in my office down, my office mate requested to be moved out of our shared office. Only a couple of peers out of my entire cohort would speak to me; everyone else actively avoided me or worse, blatantly ignored me and walked away if I tried to speak to them. I was angry, confused, isolated, and incredibly lonely. My roommate that Josh and I shared a house with was still willing to engage with me because we lived together but made it very clear where she stood on everything that was happening at school: she thought I was wrong and didn't want to be associated with me. I did my best to just *lower my head and drive on*. I used cannabis more and more, and I buried myself in my academic work.

It was toward the end of that first academic quarter in November of 2014 when I had my first panic attack, one that lasted around 12 hours in total. It was late, around 11 pm, and I was staying up to finish a research paper that was due the next day. It was my very first research paper that I would turn in as a PhD student. Josh had already gone to bed, and I was sitting in my recliner, laptop in my lap, and on the table next to me was a glass of water and a bowl of weed I was sporadically taking hits from. I tried to concentrate on writing, but my mind was just going full speed and wouldn't focus. By this point, I was a high-functioning cannabis user, so I believed my lack of focus wasn't about that. Something else was going on. The symptoms worsened. First the words on the screen in front of me began to blur. I felt my heartbeat speeding up and sweat starting to surface in my pores. It was getting harder to breathe. I put my laptop down and stood up, but it kept getting worse. I took another big hit of weed, but that only made it progress faster. It felt like I was dying. I was terrified and didn't know what to do. I just kept drinking water and hitting my bowl. I was sobbing and even tried praying. It wouldn't subside. Eventually I turned on the shower and curled up into the fetal position on the cold tile floor while the warm water encompassed me. The sensations of the warm water with the cold floor helped put me back in my body enough to calm me down to a state where I could begin to make sense of what was happening.

Once, years earlier, when I was still in the military and was dating Berry, something similar happened. I was outside jogging, trying to prepare for the two-mile run that was part of the upcoming physical training test I had to take at my next drill when suddenly, I felt like I couldn't breathe. I felt like there was an elephant sitting on my chest. It only lasted a few minutes, but it worried me so much that I scheduled a doctor's appointment for the next day to get checked out. I saw a local Physician's Assist who I babys at for. After doing several tests over the course of a week, he gave me his final diagnosis for what had happened, "anxiety," he said gently as he handed me a prescription. "Take one of these next times it happens."

That night in Colorado, I didn't have anything to take to help me, so I smoked more pot. Between smoking weed and taking the shower, I finally calmed myself down enough to be able to sleep a little bit. After only a few hours, I woke early the next morning to the same crippling anxiety. I franticly emailed my professor and asked for an extension on the paper and then had Josh drive me to the nearest dispensary to look for a strain of weed that would help more with the anxiety I was experiencing. After a short drive from our house, we arrived at our favorite dispensary. Josh parked the car and we both got out. As we walked toward the door, a wave of nausea overcame me. Without saying anything to Josh, I quickly turned around and started walking back toward the car. Standing there in the dispensary parking lot, Josh held my hair back and I braced myself against my jeep as I vomited and vomited and vomited until there was nothing left in my stomach. I knew what was happening: I was sick with anxiety—very sick. Finally, after there was nothing left to vomit, my stomach settled enough for me to get back into the car and wait for Josh to return from inside the dispensary. He had found a strain that would help with the anxiety and another they told him would help with the nausea. He drove me home, and I spent the rest of the day in bed smoking weed and crying in between small bouts of rest.

As days and weeks passed, the attacks became more and more common. The anxiety I developed then drastically impacted my gastrointestinal health and my relationship with food, causing me to lose a significant amount of weight in a short amount of time. What started as a loss of appetite when feeling nervous quickly turned into a battle with disordered eating as the anxiety (that manifested physically in my stomach) drastically changed my relationship to and with food. To cope with all this stress, I relied on substances: caffeine to wake me up, cannabis to treat my anxiety, stomach pain and stimulate appetite, and sleeping aids for rest. I was struggling to adjust to my new environment, struggling to financially sustain myself solely on my student stipend (I no longer had income from the military), and my relationship with Josh was going downhill quickly. I felt so incredibly alone. I was battling daily with severe anxiety—all while juggling teaching and taking classes in the first quarter of my PhD program.

November of 2014, within three months of ending my six-year enlistment with the Virginia Army National Guard, I found myself suffering with clinical anxiety, disordered eating, and substance dependency. The military, however, was still the furthest thing from my mind. There were a lot of other things happening too—being away from home and my family, what I was experiencing with my peers at school, and the decline of my relationship with Josh. I did think of the Army sometimes, most often when I was awake early, and the world felt still and quiet. It reminded of the times in basic training I was up with the sun, outside in formation with all of my battle buddies, ready to spend the day training and learning the cadences of soldiering. In these brief and fleeting moments that I did think of it, the military felt like another life I had just smoothly stepped out of and left frozen in another place and time. I felt a pang of loss when I did think about those I served with, particularly my brothers and sisters in 1030th. I felt fear sometimes when I thought about the loss of resources and the feeling of belonging to something greater than myself. I no longer had reliable income from the NG, and it was taking a toll. Still though, I didn't yet make any connections between what I was experiencing then in terms of my mental health and my separation from, or any experiences of, military service. During my time in, I did not deploy to war, experience trauma as I defined it (I never saw combat, and I wasn't raped or assaulted so I didn't believe I had any military-related sexual trauma) or sustain any type of physical injury. My experiences in the military did not align with the dominant narrative of military service. I was not wounded, and I was no hero (Purtle). Despite the real struggles around mental health I was battling at the time, I attributed none of it, in any way, to my military service.

Research tells us that Veterans experience above average rates of mental health challenges and disorders, such as anxiety, depression (Caan), drug and alcohol abuse (Golub and Bennett), disordered eating (Breland et al.), impaired functioning (Smith et al.), and suicide ideation and attempts ("Department of Veterans Affairs"). Within three months of ending my time in service with the military, I was experiencing anxiety, depression, substance misuse, disordered eating, and impaired relational and vocational functioning. However, *these are things a person who reintegrates home from war is likely to experience, not someone who reintegrates out of the*

National Guard with no deployment experience. Because of my experience of military service, or lack of experiences, rather, I do not qualify for healthcare benefits with the Department of Veterans Affairs. National Guard and Reservist Service Members must have been activated to federal duty apart from for training purposes (or have been injured during training) to be considered a "Veteran" by the Department of Veterans Affairs or to qualify for benefits. My unit never deployed to war (so we were never activated on federal duty orders) while I was in the military, and I was not physically injured during any of my training—so my experiences of service did not count and did not qualify. When I left the military and had my last drill with my unit, no one ever talked to me about qualifying for any benefits from the VA (disability, housing, or healthcare benefits) or any type of support I might be able to get once I separated. No one told me I might experience transition stress and mental health challenges after I got out, despite what my experiences were (or were not) while I was in. Because none of this ever happened and because I am not considered a Veteran by the nation's largest and most comprehensive Veteran organization (the VA), I did not consider myself one. I did not think I would be impacted at all, in any way once I separated. Yet, my lived experiences tell another story.

A handful of scholars claim that some Veterans experience crises of identity during periods of transition (Demers "When veterans return"; Demers "From death to life"; Mascarenhas; Smith and True). Tyson Smith and Gala True explain that upon ending military service, Veterans often confront identity questions such as: "How have I changed?" and "Who is my new self?" (149). Anne Demers finds, Veterans who have separated from the military often "used a variety of metaphors to describe the crisis of identity they experienced, each of which illustrated either psychological darkness or death" ("When veterans return" 171). The "psychological darkness" I experienced as I was transitioning out of service aligned with the dominant narrative—I was struggling in the ways articulated; I was clearly amidst an identity crisis. But *my* experience of military service did not align with *the* dominant narrative—I didn't have the military service experiences of war, Post-Traumatic Stress Disorder (PTSD), Traumatic Brain Injury (TBI), or what I considered to be Military Sexual Trauma (MST) at the time. I never thought my struggles were about transitioning out of military service, because I did not have the military experience that dominant narratives tell us makes one susceptible to these challenges. I believed my struggles were about everything *but* military service. So, I didn't identify. I never ever used the word "Veteran" to describe myself or my experiences. I didn't fit, so I didn't acknowledge it. Yet even though I couldn't yet see how intricately a part of me the military institution was, my behavior exhibited this truth. Amidst all the struggle, I was resilient, as most Veterans are (Green et al.). *I did not accept defeat.*

I kept going in school, doing what I could to keep my head above water. I pushed through and I chose to *drive on* as I worked to gather healthier tools to cope. I enrolled in therapy at the counseling center on campus and started spending time in the evenings practicing yoga watching YouTube videos on my computer. I made it through the end of that first quarter (passing all my classes) and then flew home to Virginia right before Thanksgiving to spend the holidays and winter break with my family. By that point, Josh and I could both sense that things were over between us. I suspected he was cheating on me with someone he worked with, but he denied it and gaslighted me any time I brought it up. I was eager to get out of that house and that city, away from him and my roommate and all my classmates (and professors) who I felt like didn't understand or *see* me. A month off from school and away from all of it was a welcomed and much-needed break. I had only one concern before leaving Denver. I called my mom up, and in between sobs, I asked, "Mama, can I smoke weed there in your house? It helps me with my stress and anxiety."

"Well, that's one I've never heard from you before," she said. "But yes, honey, you can. Just come home."

WINTER 2015: SEEING WHAT I LOST

One of the first places I went once I was back in my hometown was to visit my friends from 1030th. I went to see the friends who I used to smoke weed with when I was in, and we sat in their basement and passed a bong around in a circle and caught up on life in between taking hits. Being around them again felt like being home. They told me the unit Christmas dinner was coming up and that I should go—that everyone in my old unit would be happy to see me and catch up. I felt a little anxious about being one of those people who hung around too long after something ended, but I had only separated six months prior, so I both wanted and felt encouraged to attend. I was still part of that family.

Being home around my own family after having lived in Colorado for the six months prior surfaced a slew of emotions for me. I missed them a lot but being so far away meant I wasn't getting sucked into the family drama and cycles of co-dependency as much as if I were still there. Finally,

I had some space and distance to start seeing that what I experienced growing up was a lot more than *just the way things were*. Yet, with this realization, there was also an unfamiliar line that I was learning to walk at the time—balancing this notion of "not getting too big for my britches" and remembering "where I come from" while also carving out my own path of possibility and upward mobility through the pursuit of a doctorate degree. I was trying to reconcile my past with the future I was now creating for myself, and it was no easy feat—at school in Colorado or at home in Virginia. I was starting to feel at that time like I didn't fully belong in either place. I was struggling to understand who I was, who I was becoming, and how it all fit together. And the consequences of this struggle were very real, figuratively and literally.

Throughout my first few months in Colorado, I had kept my family, mostly my mom, in the know about the things I was experiencing at school with the tension between my classmates and me, as well as the decline of my relationship with Josh. What I didn't tell them though was how much weight I was losing from anxiety-induced disordered eating and gastrointestinal problems. I wore baggy clothes, but there really wasn't a way to hide it; I had lost around 40 pounds in the six months since I had left Virginia—40 pounds I really didn't have to lose. I was unhealthily skinny, and it was obvious. By that time, I was having panic attacks at least weekly, and I was vomiting almost daily as a result. I couldn't keep food in me, and because of this, I started to hate everything to do with food and eating. I constantly felt angry, sick, and exhausted from what I was experiencing, but I was doing my best to hold it all in.

One day in that first month of me being home in Virginia, my mom and I went to eat at my favorite Mexican restaurant for lunch. By this point, eating in public or among other people at all was very difficult for me. I was doing everything I could to try to hide what was happening. *Lower your head and drive on* was my motto. After we sat down in one of the familiar booths near the back, I ordered my usual chicken nachos. I ate a few bites and then conspicuously started pushing food around on my plate with my fork.

"This is why you're so skinny now!" my mom exclaimed once she noticed what I was doing. "Because you're not eating . . ." she went on, this time more gently.

That's all it took. I put my fork down, buried my face in my hands, and started sobbing.

"I can't eat," I choked out between tears.

48   J. R. HUNNIECUTT

"I don't know what happened. It's all so hard. I think I'm sick," I told her.

She comforted me. She told me it was okay and reminded me how strong I am and how overcoming hardship is in my blood. I told her how much the comments about my weight I was hearing from everyone since I had been home really hurt me. At school in Colorado, no one was noticing (or at least wasn't vocalizing). But since I had been home those few weeks on my winter break—the first time back home since I had moved away—it was the main thing I was hearing from my family and friends. *I was so skinny now*, they all told me. *Am I ok?* they all asked. *What was going on*, they wanted to know. I didn't know how to name or communicate about any of it. My mom assured me she would handle the comments. I didn't know what she meant, but I believed she would. I later found out she contacted every single one of my family members and close friends and asked them to not make a single comment to me about my weight and my body. I was so thankful to be home and to feel the protection and the sense of being held by the community that I came from.

Before I knew it, it was time for the 1030th annual Christmas dinner! My friend, Jackie, was going with me as my date. She had gotten out about a year or so before I did, so we were both excited to be going back to our unit to catch up and reconnect with our battle buddies. We met up at our friends' house before the dinner and a group of us—the same group that used to smoke weed together—all went together. We, of course, passed a joint around before we left. *It felt like old times. It felt like being home. I felt seen and taken care of.* Attending this dinner and being around my military family I had spent six years with caused me to realize just how much I missed that sense of community. Not only that, but it also empowered me. When it was time to go back to Colorado and face the music again, I didn't feel as alone anymore; I didn't feel as beat down and defeated. I felt plugged into and charged by my roots. Being around my family and my old unit helped me to remember just how far I had already come—how resilient and strong I was. How I had *gotten out*. How *I had served in the U.S Army.*

I headed back to Colorado refreshed and ready to make necessary changes. During my time in Virginia over break, Josh had disclosed to me via text message that I was right, he did cheat on me. So, when I got back, we were broken up and he had already moved into another room in our shared home. (It was a very large home, thank goodness!) I immediately started looking for a new place to live—on my own this time. I brought a newfound inner knowing back with me to Colorado, too. I knew that I needed community; I needed to find *my people*. Being around my old unit in Virginia again reminded me just who my people were.

So, upon returning to campus from break that winter, I looked up Veteran groups on campus, thinking maybe I would go to a meeting or event to see what it was like. Much to my dismay, however, I didn't find anything on campus for Veterans or current Service Members (SMs). There was not an active Student Veterans of America (SVA) chapter, nor was there even a Veteran services representative on campus. I found some list in a database where I could at least sign up and indicate I was a student with prior military service, so I did. It felt good to do so. I was starting, for the very first time, to acknowledge loss. Being around my unit in Virginia showed me how much I missed them—missed *it*. I still didn't consider myself a Veteran because my experience of military service did not fit the dominant narrative, but I was just starting to look inward and explore some of my feelings of loss I had that just maybe were connected to my separation from the military.

I continued to gather more tools to cope. By March of 2015, I was attending weekly sessions of psychotherapy at the counseling center on campus, I was living alone in a new apartment near campus and loved my new neighborhood, I was regularly practicing yoga, and I had started a group counseling program to learn meditation. My therapist at the time had recommended the meditation program to me, and because I enjoyed yoga so much, I thought I would give it a try. The group was small and intimate, only about six or seven of us were enrolled, and we met in a small group room in the counseling center. The instructor was another graduate student, not much older than me. He dimmed the light once we were all seated in the cozy, plush chairs and had given brief introductions. He spent only about five minutes explaining what meditation was, including how we should sit, how we should always come back to the breath when our mind wanders, and how it is a practice that develops the more we do it. He didn't waste much time, as for our very first practice, he had us all sit silently, in meditation, for 45 minutes straight!

As the minutes slowly screeched by at a painfully slow pace, I thought of the military. I could feel something rising inside of me as I sat there, silently, in the dark, amidst strangers, all with our eyes closed trying to focus on going inward. I felt an incredible urge to scream, at the top of my lungs, and release whatever it was that was rising up inside of me. The more I realized I couldn't very well stand up and scream at that moment, the more I wanted to. This is what caused my mind to drift to my military service—the feeling of needing and wanting to give voice to my emotions that I could feel so strongly bubbling up inside of me—but feeling like I was not able to. Feeling like I had to sit silently, in the dark, with my mouth shut and eyes down. As this realization came to me in that dark, quiet room, tears silently began to swell in my eyes. Through this quiet surrendering, I began to see myself for what felt like the first time.

When I look back today, I realize having us spend 45 minutes meditating at our very first (beginner) group session was a bit much, but I am immensely grateful for it because of the profound insight it brought me. That very first session helped me to see I had many feelings, buried deep inside of me, about the military and my time in it. I continued to go back to that group every week it was offered, and I tended to the hunger inside of me to know more, to see more, to name more of what I had buried deep inside. Around this same time, I got my first email from someone at the university about being a Veteran. Since I had put my name on that list (indicating my military service) a couple months prior, I had received an invitation to a dinner off campus, hosted by a university alumnus, for DU student Veterans to come network. I left the invitation in my inbox and spent a couple weeks tossing around the idea of going before I finally, with much hesitation and anxiety, decided to attend. The dinner wasn't for another month or so, so I sent in my RSVP and then filed it away for the time being.

Spring 2015: Finding Myself in the Loss

As spring begun to bloom, I had started my final quarter (DU was on a quarter rather than semester system) of that first year of my PhD program. Of all my new classes that semester, I was most excited to be taking an ethnographic research methods class with a professor who was teaching his final course before retirement. I was going to get to learn more about the ways of doing research that caused me to want to be an academic in the first place, and I felt lucky to be taking the last class this distinguished professor would ever teach.

It was a Tuesday afternoon in our second week of class when it was my turn to share my ideas and get feedback from the class for my quarter-long project I would work on in the ethnography class. At this point, all the research I was exploring was still related to family and interpersonal

2 MY VETERAN IDENTITY (CRISIS): SUICIDES AND REINTEGRATION 51

communication—I was interested in sexuality and alternative forms of relating. I shared with the class that I was thinking about doing something on BDSM (bondage, dominance, submission, masochism) culture, particularly because the 50 Shades movie had recently come out, *or* I could do something on the military, I mentioned quickly as a last-minute alternative to my main idea.

"Oh! Definitely the military!" the professor responded without hesitation. "That 50 Shades stuff is just a fad and will pass before you know it," he said with a wave of his hand.

"But the military—that's where the juice is. Is it just me, or is she lighting up just thinking about it?" he asked the rest of the class as he gestured to me.

That was it. That day changed everything. I went home that evening, and I pulled up our library journal database online and tentatively typed "Veterans" in the search box. Hundreds of articles emerged. As I scrolled through all the topics and research that was being done on Veterans—*on my people*—I felt something bubbling up inside of me that I had lost several months ago when I made my own decision to separate. It was *purpose*.

Though around this time I was slowly beginning to acknowledge that my life was different out of the military and after service, I still had nothing to attribute it to. When I began narrating my own experiences of serving in and choosing to separate from the military in my paper for the ethnography class, I kept questioning the *why*. *Why* do I feel differently? *Why* do I care so much about these topics? *I never deployed to war, I don't have PTSD, TBI, or MST. My narrative doesn't align. My experiences don't count. Can I really call myself a "Veteran" and claim that I'm reintegrating? Reintegrating from what?*

So instead, I focused on the experiences of others. *I was an ethnographer looking for field sites to collect data.* As the date for the student-Veteran dinner I had RSVPed for got closer, I decided I would go with a sort of guise. *I wasn't there as a Veteran; I was there to collect data on the real Veterans who had military experiences that I didn't have.* When the night came for me to go, I was full of anxiety as I got ready. I could feel my militarization creeping in. *Pants suit? No, that is too stereotypical. I'm out now…I can wear a dress. Hair up or down? I am not wearing a tight bun on my head. Hair half up. The dress should be longer, so it doesn't show too much skin—as modest as possible. I know wearing a dress is taking a risk because people will be more likely to think I'm a wife. I don't want to draw too much attention to myself. I want to be taken seriously. I need to look the part. What does a female former National Guard Service Member who never deployed look like?* I finally settled on a modest navy-blue dress and wore my hair half up, with less makeup than I would wear on any other day.

Walking up to the private home of the dinner host was also nerve-wrecking; it illuminated the class ladder I was climbing up. The house looked like a mansion. To me, it *was* a mansion. I felt so completely out of place. I carried a notebook and a pen close to my chest and reminded myself why I was there—to take notes for my ethnography project I was doing about Veterans. Thankfully, only a few minutes after being inside, I locked eyes with another female, and we gravitated to each other.

Her name was Jessica, and after our introductions, I learned she had been an officer—a unit commander—in the active Army. She had deployed several times. *She was exactly the kind of Veteran that I was not.* I felt intimidated, but I was immensely grateful to be standing and chatting with her; my anxiety was easing, and I felt less out of place having someone to converse with. Jessica and I stood together in a corner for over an hour, leaning against a wall, sipping on wine, and talking as if we were old friends in our own world. She talked to me about missing the connection—the *just getting it* of being in the Army. She told me she missed being able to just say something like "damn I just finished a 12-miler ruck" and the person she says it to *just gets it* without her having to explain. I nodded in complete agreement. She told me that she had come home from war, went back to college as a young 20 something and she experienced such an immense disconnect with her peers when she returned. As she spoke, I related to everything she said. *I knew exactly how she felt because I felt that way too.* I had felt completely disconnected from my peers at DU since I had started my program. *They even wanted me to take down the picture of my unit crest in my student office.* No one—not a single person in my community or peer group at school—understood the portion of my identity that was shaped by and through my military service, and I had been suffering the consequences of that hard truth ever since I had gotten there. I felt more connected to Jessica in that single hour of talking than I did with any of my peers in my PhD cohort throughout our entire first year of school together. At the end of our interaction that night, something powerful happened. Jessica gave me a hug and then *thanked me* for *just getting it.*

This connection I felt with Jessica was powerful, but it was also hard to contend, because it was further illuminating the dominant narrative of military service that I kept bumping up against. To me, Jessica represented the iconic Veteran—she was active duty, she had been deployed. Thus, she was justified to feel the way she felt now that she was separated from her service. I felt so confused because I related to everything she was feeling. *I felt that way too.* But I didn't understand why, because again, I never deployed to war, I wasn't physically injured during my service, so why did I feel so impacted by my separation?

Despite this cognitive dissonance, I kept pushing forward. I was beginning to *find my people.* I sought out and joined Veteran Service Organizations (VSOs) in the Denver community. I continued meeting new people—Veterans whose military experiences fit the narrative that I kept bumping up against. I continued in my ethnography research project and wrote about the reintegration experiences *they* were going through. The more I did this, the more I was surrounded by people who had these experiences that I had never had. Though I knew I was going through something myself and felt a renewed sense of purpose and mission when I made the decision to switch my research trajectory to focus on Veterans, it still wasn't about *me.* I still didn't fit. I was walking a line—doing this work and surrounding myself with people who had these experiences was healing. At the same time, it was wounding, because *I did not fully fit.* I felt a common thread of experience, of truth, with the Veterans I surrounded myself with. I also felt I did not belong, and my experiences of military service were not validated and did not count when talking about things like Veteran identity, reintegration, and suicides.

When I fell in love with research during my master's program, it was because I was able to find answers about myself in and through research. It was healing. So as the weeks in my ethnography class progressed and my work on my paper about Veteran experiences kept developing, I turned to the literature to find some concrete answers. I hoped to find something about myself between the lines of the articles I read. The topics to dive into regarding Veteran experiences were broad and expansive, but it didn't take long for me to know where to start. The more I had gotten involved in Veteran organizations, the more I was hearing about suicide. It seemed to be common for Veterans to know another Veteran who had died by suicide. And worse, thoughts of suicide among Veterans seemed to be *really* common.

Though I never would have admitted it at the time, during my own first six months or so out of service, the thought had even crossed my own mind once or twice. In fleeting moments between anxiety attacks, hunger pains, episodic depression onsets, and cravings for more cannabis, I would sometimes feel momentary desperation of not wanting to be here anymore, of wanting the pain to end. I never would have named or conceptualized these fleeting moments as experiencing suicide ideation at the time, but I can clearly look back now and see that's exactly what it was. William Fiegelman and colleagues conducted a study in 2018 and found that approximately 51% of U.S. adults personally knew at least one person who had died by suicide, and 35% of this group experienced moderate to severe emotional distress even up to 14 years after their loss. Other research suggests that serving in the military increases the likely of being exposed to suicide; up to 65.4% of those who serve/d know approximately three people who have died by suicide, most commonly a friend from military service (Cerel et al.). Further, Craig Bryan and colleagues even find that exposure to suicide is associated with risk for suicidal thoughts and behaviors among National Guard personnel. There were many times during my first year out of service that I thought about SGT Baker from 1030th. I sometimes tried to imagine what he must have felt when he *put a pistol in his mouth and ate a bullet*. It disturbed me to think about. He was at the forefront of my mind when I began my search for truth about my own experiences of loneliness, disconnection, and loss.

Searching for Answers: Veteran Suicides

As I dug into the literature, I found out research about Veteran suicides was both exclusive and contradictory. In 2012, the Department of Veterans Affairs (VA) published a Suicide Data Report that showed 22 Veterans died by suicide each day (Kemp and Bossarte). This number: "22 a day," became a common battle cry during those first few years of raising awareness for and attempting to combat suicide and mental health struggles Veterans experienced. Videos started popping up on my Facebook timeline around this time, of a Veteran doing 22 pushups and then issuing a virtual challenge for another to post a video doing the same, with intent to raise awareness of "22 Veterans claiming their life each day." Up to this point, the data was exclusive and not completely accurate, however, as research participants in this original report included only Veterans receiving care at the VA, and worse, not all VAs were included in the study the report was generated from (Kemp and Bossarte). Of about 21.6 million Veterans across the country in 2016, just over 8.5 million were enrolled for care from a VA provider ("Department of Veterans Affairs"). Not only

2 MY VETERAN IDENTITY (CRISIS): SUICIDES AND REINTEGRATION   55

that, but at that point, data was only collected from VAs in 21 states, missing states with large, concentrated Veteran populations such as California and Texas. What this initial report in 2012 revealed was that there was no national system in place for tracking deaths, especially suicides, across the general population of Veterans—namely, those who do not receive VA services. Subgroups of Veterans were being missed and not accounted for. As Janet Kemp and Robert Bossarte explain:

> The ability of death certificates to fully capture female Veterans was particularly low; only 67% of true female Veterans were identified. Younger or unmarried Veterans and those with lower levels of education were also more likely to be missed on the death certificate. This decreased sensitivity in specific subgroups can affect both suicide surveillance and research efforts that utilize Veteran status on the death certificate. From a surveillance standpoint, the rate of Veteran suicides will be underestimated in these groups. From a research standpoint, the generalizability of study findings for specific subgroups may be limited . . . Currently available data include information on suicide mortality among the population of residents in 21 states. Veteran status in each of these areas is determined by a single question asking about history of U.S. Military service. Information about history of military service is routinely obtained from family members and collected by funeral home staff and has not been validated using information from the DoD or VA. (p. 14)

The finding of 22 Veteran suicides a day was by no means representative of all Veteran identities and experiences. This report did trigger a multitude of studies examining Veteran suicides though—it was a national epidemic that 22 Veterans a day were taking their own lives—this was the highest Veteran suicide rate our nation had ever seen (Kemp and Bossarte). Most research following this report examined suicide susceptibility as it related to war, and more specifically, combat experience and exposure (Kessler et al.; Street et al.; York et al.). Up to this point, the dominant narrative surrounding Veteran suicides was that *it stemmed from traumatic war experiences.*

Then, in 2015, Mark Reger et al. published a groundbreaking study that challenged this narrative. Reger et al. surveyed SMs of all branches, both active and reserve components, and included and compared participants both with and without deployment experience in their study. They examined the association between deployment and suicide, including suicides that occurred after military separation from service. Their findings did not support an association between deployment and suicide mortality. Rather, they found general military separation, early military separation (<4 years), and discharge that is not honorable as suicide risk factors for this population. Notably, they found those who separated from service had a 63% higher suicide rate overall. This study was the first of its kind to examine Veteran suicides with a more inclusive and accurately representative participant sample. The results shattered the narrative of what we thought we knew about Veteran suicides.

In this study, something clicked for me. *I could have been a participant in that study.* My experience *counted.* Learning that struggling with mental health, and even suicide ideation, is common when you separate from service, even if you didn't deploy, felt *validating.* If it is not directly about deployment, maybe what I was going through at the time was, in same way, connected to my transition out of service. Maybe I *was* somehow impacted and affected from leaving an institution that I had intricately belonged to for six years. As research on Veteran suicides started to reveal the prevalence of military separation on mental health, I dove into the Veteran reintegration research seeking to understand *why.*

Though the suicide research was contradictory, with some research linking it to deployment and other research claiming it's not about deployment but general separation instead, both these bodies of research have an important commonality: *they are both about experiences of transition.* Whether the transition was about coming home from war or ending your time in service and separating from the military institution completely, these were both forms of Veteran reintegration. Thus, to learn more, I next dove into research on military separation from service—research on *reintegration.* I began to question *why* Veteran suicide was a risk factor for reintegrating out of service. I knew I was experiencing my own form of "psychological darkness"—my own identity crisis of sorts. I knew that separation from military service was a factor for suicide risk—despite not deploying. I knew I had separated from the military only a few months before my life began spiraling downward—before I, myself, experienced thoughts of suicide. But I didn't understand what about my experiences during service—if not deploying did not matter—could mean I was at a heightened risk for suicide after my separation. I looked to Veteran reintegration literature for more answers.

Conceptualizing Veteran Reintegration

I was once again disappointed to see that my experience was not represented in the existing research on Veteran reintegration. At this point, research on this topic exclusively focused on reintegration experiences of transitioning *back from war*. Overall, Veteran reintegration research covered: transitioning home *from war* into the family (Collinge et al.; Demers; "When Veterans Return"; Di Leone et al.; Hinojosa and Hinojosa; Knobloch et al.; Pfeiffer et al.; Theiss & Knobloch), transitioning home *from war* into the community (Collinge et al.; Pfeiffer et al.), and a small body of research looked at transitioning out of military service (after returning *from war*) into higher education (Kirchner). Research examining experiences of reintegration post-deployment looked primarily at the experiences of active duty SMs transitioning home from war back into their family and NG and Reservist SMs transitioning home from war back into their communities. The only bodies of research I identified at that time that examined reintegration post separating from military service focused on the experiences of student Veterans as they transitioned from the military institution into higher education. And still, the reintegration post-military service research on student Veterans focused exclusively on the experiences of *war* Veterans.

Christine Elnitsky, Michael Fisher, and Cara Blevins published an article in 2017 that systemically analyzed all research published on Veteran reintegration between 1990 and 2015, reviewing a total of 117 articles, all of which focused on reintegration post-deployment; not a single article reviewed in this study examined reintegration post-service without it still being within the context of *after a deployment to war*. This was troubling, given the prominent finding that suicide risk for Veterans increases during reintegration post-service and is *not associated with deployment to war* (Reger et al.). Reger et al.'s finding suggested Veteran suicidality may be more related to the separation from the military institution than anything else (Reger et al.). However, as articulated, *all* research on reintegration focused on transitioning back from deployment (Elnitsky et al. 2017). It is important to know and understand the struggles and challenges associated with reintegrating back from war, given that as of 2017, roughly 2.7 million SMs have been to war in the Middle East since September 11, 2001 (Zogas). Still, because we know Veteran suicidality is not directly linked to deployment (Reger et al.), it's also important to question what

58   J. R. HUNNIECUTT

we are missing by focusing exclusively on one type of military experience (returning from war).

As this research began to sink in for me, I realized something incredibly important: *the dominant narrative must change*. I realized that to progress, to heal not only myself but so many others like me, it was paramount to understand how focusing only on war Veterans in the context of reintegration creates and contributes to the dominant narrative and conceptualization of military service—a narrative that leaves little room for understanding experiences that do not fit. Focusing exclusively on reintegration *after deployment* creates a mentality that reintegration struggles and challenges are directly related to and mediated by deployment experience. This dominant narrative causes us to underestimate the overall impact of belonging to the military institution on our sense of self, our communication patterns and norms, and our relationships with others.

Erin Finley argues the military, the VA, and veterans' advocates have publicized "transition" (or "readjustment") as a language for talking about post-combat social difficulties (2011). When I separated from service, I underwent a drastic transition in my life, despite never having deployed. Conceptualizations of reintegration—both in research and in media—publicizes reintegration as being about post-war and specifically, post-combat difficulties, causing us to focus mostly on war, combat, and combat-related PTSD rather than on other variables and components of military service and the military institution that may cause social difficulties in interactions when transitioning out of service. Of relevance, as of 2016, only between 11% and 20% of post-9/11 Veterans suffer from PTSD, about 12% of Gulf War Veterans suffer from PTSD, and an estimated 30% of Vietnam Veterans have had PTSD in their lifetime ("How Common is PTSD?"). *Not all military Veterans went to war. And not all Veterans who went to war have PTSD or mental health struggles.* I realized at this point that by conceptualizing Veteran reintegration as being about war, and specifically combat difficulties, research was failing to get an accurate and comprehensive representation of the problem and of the lived realities of all types of military transitions and forms of reintegration. Anna Zogas' words resonated with me:

> These dramatic portrayals of the physical and mental health consequences of war for American troops are an important part of a larger picture but focusing primarily on the physical and emotional wounds of war survivors over-

shadows some of the other significant consequences of participating in—and then exiting—the military during these war years. (1)

The more I read the research of Anna Zogas, the more I realized *she just got it*. The more I read, *the more I felt seen*. Zogas went on to claim that "not all of veterans' post-military experiences are caused by combat-related trauma or health problems" (7). She articulated how Veterans have reported things such as "strained social relations, such as difficulty confiding in others and getting along with their spouses, children, and friends, and productivity problems, such as difficulty keeping a job and completing tasks at home, work, or school . . . feelings as if they were starting over with their career and social relationships, and feeling disconnected from the world around them, or as if they do not belong" (7). A lightbulb went on for me as I continued reading Zogas' work: "Certainly, it is possible to attribute strained relationships to unaddressed mental health concerns or drug and alcohol use, but to assume a causal connection between combat experiences and post-military stressors without also considering the experience of undergoing a disorienting shift in social identity is too narrow a view" (7). For me, that was it! *I had found my answer*. It was about *identity*! I remembered how I felt after I got home from basic training in 2009—an overwhelming feeling that I no longer belonged in my pre-military life. I felt the same way after I ended in service in 2014—like I didn't fully belong in the civilian world anymore either.

Zogas' claim that not all of Veterans' post-military experiences are caused by combat-related trauma or health problems resonated with me in a powerful way and helped to validate not only my feelings of disconnection and isolation at the time, but it prompted me to take a step forward in embodying my own identity as a Veteran. After consuming the literature on Veteran suicides and reintegration, I walked away with a new understanding of how important it is for researchers to consider and question what factors other than deployment and direct combat exposure contribute to post-military struggles and challenges. I knew we must consider the *social* implications of belonging to and separating from the military institution.

For instance, within research on reintegration post-deployment, the relevance of social relationships and interactions stands out as an integral factor shaping reintegration experiences. Michael Kirchner informs us that Veterans experience a loss of both structure and community upon transitioning out of military service. Steven Danish and Bradley Antonides

60   J. R. HUNNIECUTT

argue that reintegration difficulties are more closely tied to challenges of transitioning to a war environment and then back into *the family* rather than psychological or physical injuries from the war experience itself. They claim, "being at home requires an unlearning process to successfully acclimate" (552). They further explain, "The family, be it the family of origin or a spouse and their children or even the service member's girlfriend or boyfriend, are really the key to reintegration" (Danish and Antonides 554). Likewise, in their study examining occupation performance issues of war Veterans, Heidi Plach and Carol Sells report "The occupation of socializing and participating in relationships was identified as the most significant challenge. . . The emerging theme centered around difficulty relating to others outside of one's military peer network, resulting in isolation" (3). Finally, Jennifer Theiss and Leanne Knobloch examined communicative interactions between SMs and relational partners during reintegration post-deployment and found that relational uncertainty and interference from partners "may make it more difficult for SMs to produce positive relational messages and draw constructive inferences" (1121). How Veterans engage in relational communication during reintegration and how those relationships shape reintegration experiences are paramount to understand if we want to solve an issue as grave as Veteran suicides. Through associating reintegration challenges as being predominately about post-war/combat difficulties, we are failing to grasp the ways in which relationships and communication styles are shaped and influenced by military service as a whole; we are not accounting for a *shift in identity*. Thus, we miss opportunities for understanding how relationships and communication styles shaped by belonging to the military institution impact Veterans' lives when they separate from, then live outside of, that institution.

One of the main things I took away from my search for answers through reviewing Veteran suicide and reintegration literature was that reintegration is a difficult concept to conceptualize and define, which makes it a difficult concept to study and understand. Christine Elnitsky et al. find in their systemic review of 117 empirical articles on Veteran reintegration that the term "reintegration referred to any number of issues related to successful functioning in various facets of life," including psychological health, social interactions, physical health, employment, housing, financial, education, legal, and spiritual (5). They also articulated an important finding in their review:

After analyzing the literature, we determined, importantly, that no single article in the literature included a comprehensive conceptualization of reintegration across various levels of an ecological model (i.e., individual, interpersonal, community systems, and societal), which is a core theme that emerged from this work. (5)

Likewise, in their work on reintegration, Raun Lazier and colleagues articulated "there is no 'gold standard' of elements of life which could be incorporated into the assessment of reintegration that is applicable to all persons" (50) and further went on to articulate that

> a review of the United States Code and Code of Federal Regulations finds no common legislative language that defines "veteran reintegration" or which governs all federal veteran reintegration support programs and strategies across multiple agencies. (Lazier et al. 51)

Virginia Gil-Rivas and colleagues explain the reintegration process has an undetermined length and differs based on each family member and the family unit as a whole.

Clearly, reintegration in research has been primarily associated with deployment to war and combat exposure. This conceptualization is not working to address the problems associated with reintegration in a holistic and comprehensive way. Veteran suicide risk may not be directly related to deployment, but it is related to separating from the military institution. What then, about belonging to and participating in the U.S. Military institution—apart from deployment and combat experience—creates dissonance during and after separating from this institution? *I knew it was about identity.* Viewing reintegration both as a process and product of the Veteran identity will foster a more comprehensive conceptualization of reintegration and allow for more inclusion of varying types of military transitionary experiences.

Military Assimilation

Once I started my quest into research on Veteran suicides and reintegration, it was like opening a portal to more and more insight both into myself and into my military brothers and sisters. The more I learned, the more I wanted to know. That spring semester of 2015, I spent hours upon hours consuming literature on topics that related to Veteran experiences. I was starting to see small fractions of myself in the literature and in the spaces I didn't see myself, I knew why. I was feeling more and more motivated to shine light into and illuminate the lack of cultural and social understanding I was seeing in the research. I knew that as someone who had served in the military, I had insider status. I understand nuances of military culture in a way many of the researchers whose work I was reading did not. I was beginning to understand that many of the mental health struggles I was dealing with at that time *were* connected to my time in the military. As Anna Zogas says—there is a disorienting shift in social *identity* related to post-military service. As Smith and True explain, after we end our service, Veterans often confront identity questions such as: "How have I changed?" and "Who is my new self?" (149). In my experience, which was validated by the Reger et al. finding about Veteran suicide ideation being related to separation from military service rather than deployment experiences, this shift in social identity was all about transitioning out of the military. The dominant narrative of Veteran struggles being directly and solely about combat experiences was false. With this new insight, my inquiry began to shift; I wanted to know what it was about the military, about serving in and belonging to it, that caused such a shift in identity post-service?

I remembered my work from my master's program with my advisor who was a scholar in organizational communication. I had taught classes on communication in the workplace and had studied some of the ways in which organization culture is formed. That's what I turned to next. I knew that to fully grasp and understand Veteran reintegration in a more inclusive and encompassing way in the research (and thus in services and treatment options), we needed to first understand the organizational culture in which the Veteran is separating from. This includes both understanding more about the process of organizational assimilation, which is known in the military as Initial Entry Training (IET), and learning more about military organizational culture. We need to understand more about how we are socialized and what we are socialized into before we can understand what it truly means to separate from this institution and what challenges come with this experience.

Bernadette Gailliard and colleagues explain organizational assimilation consists of complex constructs that interrelate across many aspects of employees' organizational life, "such as getting to know coworkers and supervisors, participating in organizational activities, developing job competence, and learning organizational norms and standards" (554). In the military, organizational assimilation occurs foremost through IET, which consists of Basic Combat Training (BCT) (aka boot camp), and Advanced Individual Training (AIT) (job training). IET is where civilians are transformed into warriors. *IET is where I transformed from a cheerleader into a soldier.* As Anne Demers explains, "One of the primary goals of boot camp, the training ground for all military personnel, is to socialize recruits by stripping them of their civilian identity and replacing it with military identity" ("From Death to Life" 492). The military identity is collective. As I learned in my own experience of IET, especially the time I left my battle buddy, Starla, and was humiliated and punished for only thinking of myself in that instance, there's no room for individuality or difference in the military; *we are all Army green.*

Guy Siebold tells us two forms of social bonding occur in the military to create cohesion: primary and secondary bonding. Primary group cohesion consists of peer (those within the same military hierarchical level) and leader (military chain of command) bonding. At this level, "social control is especially based on norms and habits, with expectations of loyalty and ready assistance to other members of the primary group" (289). I.E.: *not being a "blue falcon."* Secondary group cohesion consists of organizational (between personnel and their next higher organization such as company or battalion) and institutional (between personnel and their military branch) bonding. In secondary bonding, "social control tends to be more formal and based on regulation, law, reward, and punishment" (287). I.E.: *It was against regulation for me to have a nose ring while I was in the military.*

Siebold teaches us each type of bonding has two aspects: affective (an emotional/reactive side) and instrumental (an action/proactive side). *Bonding* refers to social relationships:

> The locus of bonding is in the relationship, not the actions or interactions between the service member and the group, organization, or institution, although such actions or interactions are influenced by and feed back into the relationship. (Siebold 287)

The essence of strong primary group cohesion is about trust among group members; the essence of strong secondary group cohesion is about the trustworthiness of the organization and the institution. "As the primary group operates to prevent normlessness, the secondary group operates to prevent meaninglessness" (Siebold 288). In other words, primary bonding normalizes behavior (e.g., it's normal to be known as a blue falcon if

64   J. R. HUNNIECUTT

you leave your battle buddy behind), and secondary group bonding gives meaning to the bonding (e.g., we're all the same and we all belong, so I can't have a nose ring and look different than everyone else).

The organization and institution provide purpose, meaning, direct specific missions and information; prioritize duties; and provide necessary resources. They also set the tone for the unit culture and climate under which Service Members and their families live their lives both on and off duty. SMs are assimilated into this culture and climate:

> Generally in the military, the bonding process over time starts with institutional bonding (before entry), then leader bonding (at the start of basic training) and peer bonding within a stable group, and finally, organizational bonding as a service member's social horizon expands. Primary group cohesion generates the fighter while secondary group cohesion creates the professional service member. (Siebold 287)

During military IET, we are conditioned and taught how to interact, behave, and present ourselves in ways that generate and foster military group cohesion. For those who have not personally had these experiences of bonding within the military organization through IET, it can be a difficult concept to grasp. Ironically (or perhaps not), after an in-depth review, I failed to find a single academic article or book chapter on *how* the U.S. Military assimilates and conditions recruits. However, in a chapter entitled "Preparing and resisting the war body," Emma Newlands writes of training tactics the British Army used to socialize new recruits between 1939 and 1945.

Not surprisingly, when reading this chapter, I easily drew many parallels between the experiences of male recruits socializing into the British Army in the 1940s and my own experience socializing in the U.S. Army in 2008. The premise of Newlands' chapter was to illustrate the ways in which the military executed both control over and transformation of recruits' bodies during IET. Tactics of control and transformation included specified and mandated grooming, dress, movements such as walking, marching, and sitting as well as internal control over the body through food and substance intake regulation. Routines and rituals were also pivotal in such control and transformation and included things such as routine inspections (of both self and equipment) and rituals like chanting cadences, marching, and reciting creeds. Victor Turner claims rituals are key to understanding social structures and processes. Rituals, Turner argues, are instances that create potential for social change to manifest and be absorbed into social practices. IET is the organizational assimilation process whereby the U.S. Military institution comes to transform and control institutional members. This type of assimilation is necessary due to the nature of the military institution.

Military Culture

The U.S. Military is a "total institution," like that of "prisons or religious orders" in that members often live together in closer quarters for long periods of time and share group experiences exclusive to organizational membership (Smith and True 149). The military may also be viewed and conceptualized as a family. Leslie Baxter and Dawn Braithwaite explain whereas definitions and conceptualizations of "family" vary, there are common and core characteristics that comprise a family unit: long-term commitment; relations created through biology, law, or affection; enmeshment in a kinship organization; ongoing interdependence; and institutionalization. They explain, "'family' is a social group of two or more persons, characterized by ongoing interdependence with long-term commitments that stem from blood, law, or affection" (3). Joining the military involves signing a long-term, legally binding contract, and the military organization relies heavily on interdependence between members.

Further, the military is a collectivist society that values hierarchy, rigidity, and sameness. It functions as a sort of secret club, only sharing valuable cultural knowledge with insiders deeply embedded within the organization. It has its own laws, codes of conduct, and communicative patterns, norms, and behaviors. It is also a "greedy institution," in that it demands above and beyond from its members than that of most other organizations (Segal). In their examination of military culture, Craig Bryan and colleagues identify mental toughness, collectivism, self-reliance, self-sacrifice, and fearlessness about death as being core cultural elements of the military organization. To put it into perspective, "The military is unique in that it is the only organization sanctioned by U.S. society for members to be explicitly trained to kill other people" (Bryan et al. 98). It is important for us to acknowledge, "The unique culture of the military is, indeed, a diverse group of people in American society that must be understood as uniquely different from the civilian world" (Hall 4). As Anna Zogas explains,

66   J. R. HUNNIECUTT

When service members become veterans, they exit an institution which trained them in very specific skills, behaviors, and values: they have learned the technical skills necessary to operate weapons, technology, and machinery; they have learned to act in extremely high stakes situations; they have learned how to operate within an institutional hierarchy. Importantly, service members have learned all of these skills using an institutional language that is so specialized that it sometimes fails to translate even *between* different branches of the military. (4)

As Demers also articulated, "Military training is rooted in the ideal of the warrior, celebrating the group rather than the individual, fostering an intimacy based on sameness, and facilitating the creation of loyal teams" ("When Veterans Return" 162). Collective community and hierarchical structure are key components of military service (Kirchner).

Cultural insiders of the military institution are trained to keep our realities, challenges, and lived experiences to ourselves. *Lower your head and drive on.* Lynn Hall identified three primary psychological traits of military personnel as being *secrecy, stoicism,* and *denial. Secrecy* in that we must keep what happens at work separate from what happens at home—this is particularly relevant depending on what your Military Occupational Specialty (MOS) is and what type of experiences you have during your service. *Stoicism*—keeping up a constant appearance; in the military, we call this keeping your "military bearing." And *denial*—deny your questions to know more, deny the worry, fears, and anxieties—keep it all under wraps and *no matter the cost, accomplish the mission.* When you consider how recruits are assimilated into the military organization and then understand how being part of the military means belonging to an organization that has a distinct culture, it makes sense to think that a separation from this institution could create dissonance. *It makes to think about how when I separated from the military, I experienced dissonance around belonging, connection, purpose, and security.*

Military-Civilian Divide

When SMs transition either home from war or out of the military, we take with us all of our military conditioning and experiences into our new roles, settings, and communities. As secrecy, stoicism, and denial are key characteristics of SMs—that also means these same characteristics are part of us when we transition from a SM to a Veteran. I question, what military experiences have we had, that we keep *secret*, pretend don't bother us because we're *stoic*, and *deny* their impact on who we are and how we interact in the world? What are the consequences of such secrecy, stoicism, and denial? Mridula Mascarenhas explains, "A culture of militarism prefers the stoic veteran who is tight-lipped about the ravages of war but remains enduringly loyal to the military" (84). We are trained to not talk about it, pretend it did not negatively impact or affect us, and deny it if we feel like it did. When I was experiencing psychological darkness and my own crisis of identity my first few months out of the guard, I did not talk about it. I pretended separating from service was not impacting me, and I denied myself time and space to mourn the loss of structure and community I was undoubtedly experiencing at that time. I didn't even have the understanding, much less the language, to piece together my lived experiences of separation from service to the "psychological darkness" I was wading through at that time.

After SMs assimilate into military culture and become part of that institution, we become intricately tied to a social system, even if (such as in my case) we're not able to specifically articulate how. When we leave that institution, we find ourselves between two worlds (military/civilian) with distinctly different norms, values, structures, communicative styles, and patterns of behaviors. As Demers explains,

> It is often the case that [Veterans] find themselves living between two social contexts that offer incompatible cultural narratives and are unable to articulate an integrated personal narrative that avoids a crisis of identity. ("From death to life" 495)

Alison Lighthall painted an accurate picture of challenges Veterans (though their participants were war Veterans, this description still applies) face and how we feel once we separate from the military completely:

> When a service member is discharged from the military, it's aptly termed "separation" and it comes with all the heartbreak and disorientation that being torn from one's tribe brings. [We] just spent the last several years inextricably tied to some type of social system, whether it was a brigade, battalion, company, platoon, squad, team, or just one on one with a battle buddy. During those years, solitude was rare. Now, suddenly [we're] no longer attached to those systems, and the feeling of vulnerability can be terrifying. (82).

Reintegration is about more than reconciling post-war difficulties; it's about the merging of experiences; it is about being and feeling *understood* by those who do not have your experience. During my first several months at DU, before I "found my people" in the Veteran organizations I joined, I felt incredibly alone, isolated, and misunderstood. As of 2015, research was focused primarily on the processes and outcomes of reintegrating after a deployment. At that point we knew little, if any, about transitions surrounding other military experiences, particularly transitioning out of military service completely. I knew at this point in my own journey that we had to better understand all experiences of military transitions if we are ever to understand why reintegration after service is a risk factor for Veteran suicide. We must question, what is the process like to resume roles in families, communities, and workplaces that are situated outside of the military institution? This question necessitates a need to understand the military/civilian divide in U.S. society—we must understand that dissonance surrounding the Veteran identity and experiences of reintegration are rooted in having military organizational experiences that those outside of this organization do not understand and are unable to relate to. I was beginning to understand that my experiences with my peers and my professor who I couldn't connect with and were even unkind to me arguably because of a military symbol I identified with (the unit crest hanging in my office) were really about the military/civilian divide.

The "military/civilian divide" in U.S. society may be understood as the differences that emerge not just between the military institution and most civilian structures and organizations, but as a lack of understanding from individuals who never served in the military about the realities, challenges, and lived experiences of us who have. Many of these realities, challenges, and lived experiences go unnoticed by civilian peers and in fact, "84% of post 9/11 Veterans reported the public does not understand the problems they and their families face and 71% of the general public agrees" (Kirchner 117). This divide can be characterized by a general lack of understanding of military culture and is illustrated by media headlines that focus heavily on PTSD, TBI, and violent behavior, making Veterans susceptible to inaccurate stereotypes about our wellbeing and our abilities to smoothly integrate back into civilian society (Osborne). Nicholas Osborne asked student Veteran participants to provide examples of what they believed their professors and non-Veteran peers thought of when they heard the word "Veteran." He found student Veterans reported "images of homeless Vietnam veterans in tattered army jackets, elderly white men who served in World War II, individuals who enlisted because they were not 'college material,' and young men who are contending with post-traumatic stress" (253). Veterans are susceptible to rhetoric and narratives created in the media that produce and circulate stereotypes and archetypes about our identity. These stereotypes and archetypes shape how civilian others outside of the military institution perceive us and can negatively affect our overall mental health and perception of self. The military/civilian divide precipitates feelings of isolation among Veterans as well as civilians who seek to understand our military experiences.

Research on Veteran suicides and Veteran reintegration as it was up to that point in 2015 further contributed to the military/civilian divide in U.S. society. Though the research on suicide continues to progress since the Reger et al. study in 2015 showed there is no direct link to war deployment, the ramifications of research on Veteran reintegration exclusively examining reintegration post-deployment are concerning. The dominant narrative of military service and struggles post-service being directly about combat experiences still prevails. This conceptualization of Veteran reintegration in research has resulted in the military, the Department of Veterans Affairs, and Veterans' advocates as publicizing and framing reintegration as language for talking about post-war/combat social difficulties. If reintegration is predominantly thought of as being about war or combat, how many people hold *secret* their struggles of transitioning out of service, remain *stoic* and pretend their separation doesn't have a negative impact on them because they didn't go to war (or more likely, did not experience combat while at war), and *deny* feelings of dissonance they may be experiencing because their personal narrative is obscured by the larger master narrative? How many people struggle with or resist the Veteran identity because they feel their service was not enough, did not matter, and does not fit the dominant narrative of military service? How many of us are struggling *socially* but don't have language or conceptualizations to understand *why* if we don't have war, combat, or trauma experiences to associate it with?

My experiences of Veteran reintegration have been full of dissonance as I struggled (and continue to struggle) with embodying the Veteran identity in a way that feels honest, right, and true. I walk a constant line between recognizing and acknowledging that being in the military drastically changed my life and feeling invalidated that my service had any meaning and worth at all, because my service doesn't align with the dominant narrative of what military service looks like. I question how I was and am

70 J. R. HUNNIECUTT

wounded through leaving the military institution—an institution that redeemed me and impacted my life in such a profound way—an institution that enabled me to *get out* of adverse life circumstances in my youth. Even more than that, I question how I'm wounded through constantly feeling like I don't quite fit into Veteran communities, yet also don't always feel completely understood around civilians with no military experiences or connections. The more time I spent with research on topics like Veteran identity, suicide, and reintegration, the more motivated I became to understand the process of moving between and living in the middle of military and civilian worlds. In the next chapter, I take a break from the linear timeline of my story of military service and separation to introduce a theory of liminality that speaks to identity (Turner). I then use this theory throughout the rest of the book to continue narrating my own story of separation from service. My aim is for this theory to help us rethink the ways in which we are conceptualizing and talking about things like Veteran suicides, reintegration, and most of all, identity.

WORKS CITED

Baxter, Leslie A., ed. *Remaking Family Communicatively.* Peter Lang, 2014.

Baxter, Leslie A., and Dawn Braithwaite. "Relational dialectics theory: Crafting meaning from competing discourses." *Engaging Theories in Interpersonal Communication,* 2008, pp. 349–362. Thousand Oaks, CA: Sage.

Breland, Jessica Y., Rosemary Donalson, Andrea Nevedal, Julie V. Dinh, Shira Maguen. "Military experience can influence Women's eating habits." *Appetite,* vol. 118, 2017, pp. 161–167.

Bryan, Craig J., Keith W. Jennings, David A. Jobes, and John C. Bradley. "Understanding and Preventing Military Suicide." *Archives of Suicide Research,* vol. 16, no. 2, 2012, pp. 95–110.

Bryan, Craig J., et al. "Combat exposure and risk for suicidal thoughts and behaviors among military personnel and veterans: A systematic review and meta-analysis." *Suicide and Life-Threatening Behavior,* vol. 45, no. 5, 2015, pp. 633–649.

Caan, Woody. "Military Veteran Psychological Health and Social Care." *Journal of Public Mental Health,* vol. 16, no. 3, 2017, pp. 127–128.

Cerel, Julie, et al. "How many people are exposed to suicide? Not six." *Suicide and Life-Threatening Behavior,* vol. 49, no. 2, 2019, pp. 529–534.

Collinge, William, Janet Kahn, and Robert Soltysik. "Promoting reintegration of National Guard veterans and their partners using a self-directed program of integrative therapies: a pilot study." *Military medicine*, vol. 177, no. 12, 2012, pp. 1477.

Danish, Steven J., and Bradley J. Antonides. "The challenges of reintegration for service members and their families." *American Journal of Orthopsychiatry*, vol. 83, no. 4, 2013, pp. 550–558.

Demers, Anne. "The War at Home: Consequences of Loving a Veteran of the Iraq and Afghanistan Wars." *The Internet Journal of Mental Health*, vol. 6, no. 1, 2009, pp. 1–25.

———. "When Veterans Return: The Role of Community in Reintegration." *Journal of Loss and Trauma*, vol. 16, no. 2, 2011, pp. 160–179.

———. "From Death to Life: Female Veterans, Identity Negotiation, and Reintegration into Society." *Journal of Humanistic Psychology*, vol. 53, no. 4, 2013, pp. 489–515.

Department of Veterans Affairs. "Suicide among veterans and other Americans, 2001–2014." *Office of Suicide Prevention*, 2016, Washington, DC.

Di Leone, Brooke AL, et al. "Women's veteran identity and utilization of VA health services." *Psychological Services*, vol. 13, no. 1, 2016, pp. 60.

Elnitsky, Christine A., Michael P. Fisher, and Cara L. Blevins. "Military Service Member and Veteran Reintegration: A Conceptual Analysis, Unified Definition, and Key Domains." *Frontiers in Psychology*, vol. 8, 2017.

Feigelman, William, et al. "Suicide exposures and bereavement among American adults: Evidence from the 2016 General Social Survey." *Journal of Affective Disorders*, vol. 227 2018, pp. 1–6.

Finley, Erin P. "Fields of combat: Understanding PTSD among veterans of Iraq and Afghanistan." *Cornell University Press*, 2011.

Gailliard, Bernadette M., Karen K. Myers, and David R. Seibold. "Organizational assimilation: A multidimensional reconceptualization and measure." *Management Communication Quarterly*, vol. 24, no. 4, 2010, pp. 552–578.

Gil-Rivas, Virginia, Ryan P. Kilmer, Jacqueline C. Larson, and Laura Marie Armstrong. "Facilitating successful reintegration: Attending to the needs of military families." *American Journal of Orthopsychiatry*, vol. 87, no. 2, 2017, pp. 176.

Golub, Andrew, and Alex S. Bennett. "Substance use over the military–veteran life course: An analysis of a sample of OEF/OIF veterans returning to low-income predominately minority communities." *Addictive Behaviors*, vol. 39, no. 2, 2014, pp. 449–454.

Green, Kimberly T., et al. "Examining the factor structure of the Connor–Davidson Resilience Scale (CD-RISC) in a post-9/11 US military veteran sample." *Assessment*, vol. 21, no. 4, 2014, pp. 443–451.

Hall, Lynn K. "The Importance of Understanding Military Culture." *Social Work in Health Care*, vol. 50, no. 1, 2011, pp. 4–18.

72   J. R. HUNNIECUTT

Hinojosa, Ramon, and Melanie Sberna Hinojosa. "Using military friendships to optimize postdeployment reintegration for male Operation Iraqi Freedom/Operation Enduring Freedom veterans." *Journal of Rehabilitation Res Dev*, vol. 48, no. 10, 2011, pp. 1145–1158.

"How Common is PTSD?" *US Department of Veterans Affairs National Center for PTSD*, 3 Oct. 2016, www.ptsd.va.gov/public/ptsd-overview/basics/how-common-is-ptsd.asp.

Kemp, Janet, Robert Bossarte, and Department of Veterans Affairs. "Mental Health Services Suicide Prevention Program." *Suicide Data Report*, 2012.

Kessler, R. C., et al. "Occupational Differences in US Army Suicide Rates." *Psychological Medicine*, vol. 45, no. 15, 2015, pp. 3293–3304.

Kirchner, Michael J. "Supporting Student Veteran Transition to College and Academic Success." *Adult Learning*, vol. 26, no. 3, 2015, pp. 116–123.

Knobloch, Leanne K., et al. "Generalized anxiety and relational uncertainty as predictors of topic avoidance during reintegration following military deployment." *Communication Monographs*, vol. 80, no. 4, 2013, pp. 452–477.

Lazier, Raun L., Amy Warnick Gawne, and Nathan S. Williamson. "Veteran Family Reintegration: Strategic Insights to Inform Stakeholders' Efforts." *Journal of Public and Nonprofit Affairs*, vol. 2, no. 1, 2016, pp. 48–57.

Lighthall, Alison. "Ten things you should know about today's student veteran." *Thought & Action*, vol. 80, 2012, pp. 1.

Mascarenhas, Mridula. "Uniform to Pulp: Performance of Transformation, Critique, and Community-Building for Veteran Soldiers." *Western Journal of Communication*, vol. 78, no. 1, 2014, pp. 78–96.

Newlands, Emma. "Preparing and resisting the war body." *War and the Body: Militarization, Practice and Experience*, 2013, pp. 35–50.

Osborne, Nicholas J. "Veteran Ally: Practical Strategies for Closing the Military-Civilian Gap on Campus." *Innovative Higher Education*, vol. 39, no. 3, 2014, pp. 247–260.

Pfeiffer, Paul N., Adrian J. Blow, Erin Miller, Jane Forman, Gregory M. Dalack, and Marcia Valenstein. "Peers and Peer-Based Interventions in Supporting Reintegration and Mental Health Among National Guard Soldiers: A Qualitative Study." *Military Medicine*, vol. 177, no. 12, 2012, p. 1471.

Plach, Heidi Lynn, and Carol Haertlein Sells. "Occupational Performance Needs of Young Veterans." *American Journal of Occupational Therapy*, vol. 67, no. 1, 2013, pp. 73–81.

Purtle, Jonathan. ""Heroes' invisible wounds of war:" constructions of posttraumatic stress disorder in the text of US federal legislation." *Social Science & Medicine*, vol. 149, 2016, pp. 9–16.

Reger, Mark A. et al. "Risk of Suicide Among US Military Service Members Following Operation Enduring Freedom or Operation Iraqi Freedom

Deployment and Separation from the US Military." *JAMA Psychiatry*, vol. 72, no. 66, 2015, pp. 561–569.

Segal, Mady W., Michelle D. Lane, and Ashley G. Fisher. "Conceptual model of military career and family life course events, intersections, and effects on well-being." *Military Behavioral Health*, vol. 3, no. 2, 2015, pp. 95–107.

Segal, Mady Wechsler. "The Military and the Family as Greedy Institutions." *Armed Forces & Society*, vol. 13, no. 1, 1986, pp. 9–38.

Siebold, Guy L. "The essence of military group cohesion." *Armed Forces & Society*, vol. 33, no. 2, 2007, pp. 286–295.

Smith, James G., Ruvanee P. Vilhauer, and Vanessa Chafos. "Do military veteran and civilian students function differently in college?" *Journal of American College Health*, vol. 65, no. 1, 2017, pp. 76–79.

Smith, R. Tyson, and Gala True. "Warring Identities: Identity Conflict and the Mental Distress of American Veterans of the Wars in Iraq and Afghanistan." *Society and Mental Health*, vol. 4, no. 2, 2014, pp. 147–161.

Street, A. E., et al. "Understanding the Elevated Suicide Risk of Female Soldiers During Deployments." *Psychological Medicine*, vol. 45, no. 4, 2015, pp. 717–726.

Theiss, Jennifer A., and Leanne K. Knobloch. "A relational turbulence model of military service members' relational communication during reintegration." *Journal of Communication*, vol. 63, no. 6, 2013, pp. 1109–1129.

Turner, Victor. The Ritual Process: Structure and Anti-Structure. *Aldine de Gruyter*, 1969.

York, Janet A., Dorian A. Lamis, Charlene A. Pope, Leonard E. Egede. "Veteran-Specific Suicide Prevention." *Psychiatric Quarterly*, vol. 84, no. 2, 2013, pp. 219–238.

Zogas, Anna. "Costs of War: US Military Veterans' Difficult Transitions Back to Civilian Life and the VA's Response." *Watson Institute International & Public Affairs*, Brown University, 2017, pp. 1–14.

CHAPTER 3

Writing Through Layers of Veteran Liminality

Through my simultaneous journey of becoming both a Veteran and a scholar, I realize several truths: the military paved my path—I literally would not be sitting here writing these very words had I not enlisted in the Army when I was 19 years old. The military redeemed me and helped me to *get out* of what I was born into. The military changed me in ways I still can't fully identify—ways that are both *good and bad*. *My* truth is that the military changed my life in a powerful way, and when I separated from service, I experienced a crisis and continue to experience dissonance around the embodiment of my identity as a Veteran and what it means for how I interact in the world presently. The purpose of this chapter is to explain a theoretical framework for understanding the intricacies and nuances of *my* reintegration experience in a way that speaks to and shines light on *the* Veteran identity. I first define and explain the concept of liminality before further elaborating on two distinct conceptions of liminality: sacred liminality and institutionalized liminality (Turner). After articulating how liminality is a comprehensive and inclusive framework for contextualizing reintegration, I propose two guiding questions that shape the following two chapters (Chaps. 4 and 5). At the end of this chapter, I outline my approach (methodological tools) for answering these questions in the two proceeding chapters. Specifically, I use this chapter to illuminate the importance of critical narrative inquiry within the context of Veteran identity and reintegration; I show you that story *matters*. I

© The Author(s), under exclusive license to Springer Nature Switzerland AG 2022
J. R. Hunniecutt, *Rethinking Reintegration and Veteran Identity*, https://doi.org/10.1007/978-3-030-93754-6_3

articulate why autoethnography in the form of performance writing is the best way to answer the questions I propose and then explain how I use autoarcheology as a form of autoethnography to guide my writing throughout Chaps. 4 and 5. Autoarcheology highlights the relevance and representation of symbols during states of transition, such as reintegration; it helps us to better understand how cultural artifacts of the military impact Veteran identity and experiences of military transitions.

THEORETICAL FRAMEWORK: LIMINALITY

Liminality is about living between two different worlds, cultures, and experiences. A liminal identity is an identity of in-betweenness (Turner); it's a time, place, and space of being between cultures and social structures. Victor Turner, who was one of the first to conceptualize "liminality," explains, "Liminal entities are neither here nor there; they are betwixt and between the positions assigned and arrayed by law, custom, convention, and ceremonial" (95). Liminality is about transition, about shifting between states of being. As Veteran identity emerges through transitionary experiences, liminality is a relevant and useful theoretical framework for exploring the nuances of this identity. Literally, to shift from a service member (SM) to a Veteran, we must go through a transition between cultures and institutions. The term "liminality" was first used by A. van Gennep and then later expanded upon by Victor Turner. A. van Gennep explores rites of passage in terms of identity phases and development and identifies three phases indicative of rites of passage: (1) separation, (2) liminality, and (3) aggregation. First, *separation* is "characterized by symbols of detachment from a certain point in the social structure or from a set of cultural conditions" (Wu and Buzzanell 17); next, *liminality* is the phase of ambiguity that aligns with neither a "before" nor an "after," and finally, *aggregation* is the final phase of a newly developed, stable sense of self and belonging. Drawing from the work of van Gennep, Victor Turner expands on the concept of liminality by focusing on the second phase through understanding liminality as a rite of passage. Turner proposes two major models for human interacting: the first is *juxtaposing* as a human model of structured social positions and the second is *alternating* as the process of shifting in and out of structured positions. Turner refers to the model of alternating as "communitas" (98).

Communitas emerge within the liminal period of transitioning between social structures, and they are ignited through a sacred ritual process.

Whereas positions of structure (juxtaposing) can have the sacredness of communitas, they are not the same in that they are not always achieved through a sacred rite of passage in the form of a ritual. Communitas, on the other hand, can only emerge through a sacred rite of passage, like a ritual of sorts. Building off these two models of human interacting, Turner discusses liminality in two distinct ways: (1) sacred liminality, which is liminality as a temporary phase during a rite of passage that's achieved through some sacred ritual ("communitas"), and (2) institutionalized liminality, which is void of sacred ritual and of a final phase of aggregation— institutionalized liminality is perpetual; it never ends. The main distinctions between the two are that *sacred liminality* is temporary with a specific purpose, ritual, and an ending and *institutionalized liminality* is perpetual, ongoing, is not entered through a sacred rite of passage, and is not always an agentic choice. Let's look closer at these concepts.

Sacred Liminality: "Communitas"

Working among the Ndembu tribe in northwestern Zambia, Turner first focused his exploration of liminality in the context of ritual symbolism, also referred to as "sacred liminality." Turner describes taking off his "theoretical blinders" to understand aspects of culture that had previously been invisible and void of study within his anthropological work. His goal here was to explore the

> semantics of ritual symbols in Isoma, a ritual of the Ndembu, and to construct from the observational and exegetical data a model of the semantic structure of this symbolism. The first step in such a task is to pay close attention to the way the Ndembu explain their own symbols. (p. 12)

Like Turner, we must pay close attention to how Veterans explain our own symbols. Turner focused on the process of ritual, as practiced and described by the Ndembu, in terms of how rituals as rites of passage served as entry points into states of sacred liminality.

Both states of liminality described by Turner are similar in terms of their characteristics. Turner explains the ambiguity of liminal states when he writes, "The attributes of liminality or oflimalpmona* ('threshold people') are necessarily ambiguous, since this condition and these people elude or slip through the network of classifications that normally locate states and positions in a cultural space" (p. 96). He goes on to note,

"Thus, liminality is frequently liked to death, to being in the womb, to invisibility, to darkness, to bisexuality, to the wilderness, and to an eclipse of the sun or moon" (Turner 97). In the context of sacred liminality, you are cast into this liminal state of being through the act and performance of sacred ritual; it is "a symbolic milieu that represents both a grave and a womb" (97). There is a beginning and an end to sacred liminality. Because there is a beginning and an end to sacred liminality, it also necessitates first going low to eventually go higher (in status, in an organization or system, within a relational context, or even within the self). Sacred liminality has a purpose—it is a temporary phase one must *endure* to transition one into a higher structure.

Sacred liminality as a phase of transition during a rite of passage is characterized by cultural symbols that represent statuslessness, homogeny, reduction of self, passively obeying, and long periods of seclusion. During sacred liminality, "speech is not merely communication but also power and wisdom. The wisdom that is imparted in sacred liminality is not just an aggregation of words and sentences; it has ontological value; it refashions the very being of the neophyte" (105). This happens through both verbal and nonverbal instruction and is received in both precept and symbol. In sacred liminality, individuals go through both psychological and physiological changes; liminality is an *embodied* experience. Turner articulates,

> The neophyte in liminality must be a tabula rasa, a blank slate, on which is inscribed the knowledge and wisdom of the group, in those respects that pertain to the new status. The ordeals and humiliations, often of a grossly physiological character, to which neophytes are submitted represent partly a destruction of the previous status and partly a tempering of their essence in order to prepare them to cope with their new responsibilities and restrain them in advance from abusing their new privileges. They have to be shown that in themselves they are clay or dust, mere matter, whose form is impressed upon them by society. (105)

Initial Entry Training (IET) is the rite of passage that all military recruits must endure during their sacred liminality of transforming from civilian to service member. IET consists of both Basic Combat Training (BCT) and Advanced Individual Training (AIT), which is training for your Military Occupational Specialty (MOS), or job. As I explained in Chap. 2, Emma Newlands writes of training tactics the British Army used to socialize new recruits between 1939 and 1945 and illustrates the ways in which the military executed both control over and transformation of recruits' bodies during IET. Tactics of control and transformation included specified and mandated grooming, dress, and movements such as walking, marching, and sitting as well as internal control over the body through food and substance intake regulation. I experienced all of this during my time in BCT and AIT. The way Victor Turner describes liminality as a process of a sacred rite of passage is akin to undergoing IET in the military in terms of psychological and physiological characteristics. Turner explains:

> Liminal entities, such as neophytes in initiation of puberty rites, may be represented as possessing nothing. They may be disguised as monsters, wear only a strip of clothing, or even go naked, to demonstrate that as liminal beings they have no status, property, insignia, secular clothing indicating rank or role, position in a kinship system—in short, nothing that may distinguish them from their fellow neophytes or initiands. Their behavior is normally passive or humble; they must obey their instructors implicitly, and accept arbitrary punishment without complaint. It is as though they are being reduced or ground down to a uniform condition to be fashioned anew and endowed with additional powers to enable them to cope with their new station in life. Among themselves, neophytes tend to develop an intense comradeship and egalitarianism. Secular distinctions of rank and status disappear or are homogenized. (96)

In boot camp, we could possess almost nothing personal. The one item I had that was my own during those 11 weeks of isolated intensive training was a journal. Even then, the journal was not allowed to be kept private. It was examined on several occasions by my Drill Sergeants during barracks and locker inspections. As recruits in basic training, we were sometimes "disguised as monsters" to demonstrate our lack of status. In other words, we were often humiliated by being made to do and act in ways that demonstrated our lack of status—our lack of *humanity*. The time I was made to stand in front of my platoon and repeatedly chant, "I am a blue falcon" is an example of this.

Another example includes a time when my Drill Sergeant in basic training made two recruits in my platoon bear crawl in circles around our entire platoon on all fours while they howled like wolves (they were being punished for something I don't recall). All our civilian clothing and belongings were taken away upon arrival, including things like undergarments that were not black, white, or tan, and even our own shampoos and

80   J. R. HUNNIECUTT

bathing products because of variations in fragrance (even our scent was monitored). During our first few days at basic training we were given uniforms and taught how to dress, groom, shave, style our hair, walk, and speak. Every single thing was uniform and homogenous. I recall a phrase my Drill Sergeants used to chant when someone showed up to formation with any fragment of difference (e.g., wearing the wrong hat, not having dog tags on, and a shoelace tucked the wrong way), "Who here is not like the otheeeeer…" Another saying in the Army is "We are all green." Green represents Army green—the color of our uniform—and the saying packs a powerful ideology that dismisses and silences any identities of difference, including race, gender, class, and sexual orientation. During my time in basic, I and the other recruits were subjected to routine and regular inspections of our appearances, both in uniform and even in undergarments in our barracks (females were not allowed to shave any body hair during BCT and our legs and underarms were routinely inspected for this). As the nature of the military institution is rooted in and sustained by discourses of hyper-masculinity, cisgender women in the military must also learn to adapt and mask characteristics and performances of femininity in order to embody the warrior identity. In IET, I was literally taught how to dis-identify with femininity and occasionally punished for my performance of it (e.g., my voice being too "high pitched" when yelling cadences, my hair not being slicked back tight enough into a bun, and me moving my hips too much when I marched).

Recruits in BCT and AIT must always accept punishment without complaint, for when one person made a mistake, the entire group was punished for it. Again, I experienced this during my "blue falcon" incident in basic training when my entire platoon was made to do push-ups for several minutes while I was humiliated in front of them all. The military is a collectivist and homogenous organization. As Demers articulates, "Military training is rooted in the ideal of the warrior, celebrating the group rather than the individual, fostering an intimacy based on sameness, and facilitating the creation of loyal teams" ("When Veterans Return" 162). This is primarily how group bonding occurs. In basic training, because of our shared experiences, I formed close bonds and comradeship with the other recruits who were there with me—still to this day, over a decade later, I am friends with many of them and refer to them as my "brothers and sisters" and as "battle buddies." As shared in Chap. 1, we are assigned what is called "battle buddies" during IET; battle buddies are pairs of two and are held as accountability partners through all of the training. Battle buddies must always be together (you are never allowed to be alone in any capacity during IET) and are treated as a collective; if one of you messes up, both (and sometimes everyone within the team, squad, platoon, or unit those battle buddies belong to) get punished.

Basic training lasted for 11 weeks; I got to spend one night at home in Virginia after basic graduation, and then I shipped off to my AIT (job training) for another six weeks. I have never experienced anything in my life quite like Army boot camp; it was one of the hardest things I have ever experienced and one of the accomplishments in my life I am most proud of. Thankfully, however, it did not last forever. The liminality I experienced through IET had a point of finality and aggregation; it ended, Turner explains how within this context of liminality, the

> "sacred" component is acquired by the incumbents of positions during the *rites de passage*, through which they changed positions. Something of the sacredness of that transient humility and modelessness goes over, and tempers the pride of the incumbent of a higher position or office. (98)

Sacred liminality is a necessary state of being that precipitates growth, advancement, and evolution. It is also a very humbling experience, given all you must endure. In IET, I was reduced to a sense of nothing so I could be rebuilt into a higher position—that of a soldier. At the completion of both basic training and AIT, there was a ceremony and a graduation to mark the end of that rite of passage.

In basic training, the week before graduation, all recruits that had made it through the grueling ten weeks of boot camp underwent a week-long ritual, which took the form of a journey to "Victory Forge." This week included a ten-mile ruck march (hiking while carrying a heavy load) to a camp where we slept outside, engaged in war-fighting games, and underwent hazing rituals (at one point in this week, we were forced to stand still in a formation without gas masks while our Drill Sergeants threw tear gas grenades through our formation ranks and forbade us from moving). It was during the final ceremony of Victory Forge when we finally rose from recruits to soldiers. There was a fire, we chanted songs and cadences, and for the first time during boot camp, our Drill Sergeants looked us in the eyes and shook our hands as equitable members of the U.S. Military. The process of IET endowed me with "additional powers that enabled me to cope" (Turner 97) within my new social structure as a soldier in the U.S. Army. Once I transitioned out of the sacred liminal state of IET, I

82   J. R. HUNNIECUTT

became a full participant in the military organization. Military recruits undergo sacred liminality and experience communitas during IET. Once recruits achieve aggregation from the sacred liminality of IET, however, we then experience the other state of liminality—institutionalized liminality through belonging to and participating in the total military institution once we leave IET and merge with our assigned military units.

Institutionalized Liminality: Belonging to a Total Institution

Victor Turner went on to teach us that all social life is a "dialectical process that involves successive experiences of high and low, communitas and structure, homogeneity and differentiation, equality and inequality" (98). He explains how "each individual's life experience contains alternating exposure to structure and communitas, and to states and transitions" (100). The U.S. Military experience encompasses characteristics of both structure (institutionalized liminality) and communitas (sacred liminality), moving back and forth in a constant ebb and flow between the two. Turner articulates how within institutionalized liminality (structure), "transition has become a permanent condition" (109). Institutionalized liminality as a permanent state within an organization can be seen in what Erving Goffman calls "total institutions."

Goffman identifies five types of total institutions: institutions established to care for people thought to be incapable and harmless (e.g., senior home), institutions that care for those who are thought to be both incapable and a threat to the community (e.g., mental hospital), institutions that are organized to protect the community against dangers (e.g., prison), institutions established to pursue some technical task (e.g., military), and establishments designed as retreats from the world or as training stations for the religious (e.g., monasteries). When elaborating on the attributes of total institutions, Goffman explains,

> a basic social arrangement in modern society is that we tend to sleep, play, and work in different places, in each case with a different set of copartici- pants, under a different authority, and without an over-all rational plan. The central feature of total institutions can be described as a breakdown of the kinds of barriers ordinarily separating these three spheres of life. First, all aspects of life are conducted in the same place and under the same single authority. Second, each phase of the member's daily activity will be carried out in the immediate company of a large batch of others, all of whom are

treated alike and required to do the same thing together. Third, all phases of the day's activities are tightly scheduled, with an activity leading at a prearranged time into the next, the whole circle of activities being imposed from above through a system of explicit formal rulings and a body of officials. Finally, the contents of the various enforced activities are brought together as parts of a single over-all rational plan purportedly designed to fulfill the official aims of the institution. (314)

The U.S. Military is a total institution like that of "prisons or religious orders" in that members often live together in closer quarters for long periods of time and share group experiences exclusive to organizational membership (Smith and True 149). Military recruits undergo a temporary period of sacred liminality through the rite of passage of IET. Once the recruit transforms into a military service member, we then experience institutionalized liminality through belonging to the total institution as we carry out our contract in our assigned bases/units/platoons/squads/teams after IET. The four characteristics Goffman articulates as being representative of a total institution encompass the experiences of both the sacred liminal space of IET and the institutionalized liminal space of being a soldier.

Gloria Anzaldúa writes of liminality when she articulates her own identity as a Chicana living between two racially (and sexually) divergent cultures between the U.S. and Mexico. In this, Anzaldúa conceptualizes liminality as existing in what she calls a "borderland." The way she describes borderlands is in line with how Victor Turner conceptualizes institutionalized liminality in that there is no end state or sense of aggregation, nor is there a sacred rite of passage incorporating her into the liminal state. Gloria Anzaldúa teaches us how "borders are set up to define the places that are safe and unsafe, to distinguish us from them" (25) and further articulates, "A borderland is a vague and undetermined place created by the emotional residue of an unnatural boundary. It is a constant state of transition" (25). Note how Anzaldúa refers to this state of liminality as a "*constant* state of transition," which is akin to Turner's conception of institutionalized liminality as being ongoing with no sense of aggregation or ending. Borrowing an Aztec word, Anzaldúa names the identity of Chicanas who live in the borderlands as "mestizas" and teaches us how

la mestiza is a product of the transfer of the cultural and spiritual values of one group to another...Cradled in one culture, sandwiched between two

> cultures, straddling all three cultures and their value systems, la mestiza undergoes a struggle of flesh, a struggle of borders, and inner war. (100)

It is important to pause here and briefly discuss the sense of agency within the context of borderlands, or institutionalized liminality. In the case of Gloria Anzaldúa, she did not make an *agentic choice* to enter into a perpetual state of liminality. She was born into a borderland—into an institutionalized state of ongoing liminality.

Institutionalized liminality is existing in a "persistent societal structure" in which you do not fit. In the context of the military, an example that highlights agency (or lack thereof) within institutionalized liminality is the difference between the drafted and the all-volunteer U.S. Military. From 1940 to 1973, able-bodied men were drafted into the U.S. Military to fill vacancies that were not filled by volunteers, for the purpose of fighting in the Vietnam War. Since the draft was lifted in 1973, the U.S. Military once again is an all-volunteer military; the post-9/11 military generation is an all-volunteer force. The men who were drafted into the military during that time had little agency in having to experience both sacred and institutionalized liminality; they didn't choose to be assimilated into, serve in, and then separate from the U.S. Military during that time. When you do not choose to enter into liminality and there is no state of aggregation, then one exists in a state of liminality, suffering all the hardship of such state, without the transition into a higher state of being to look forward to; this could be seen as a perpetual state of psychological darkness.

Even within the context of choice, such as in the now all-volunteer force, reason for joining matters, especially because reason for joining impacts how closely members orient within the organizational identity (Hall). The dominant reasons people join the military are for family legacy, to escape from painful or aversive life experiences, because of patriotism, and to gain citizenship (Hall). How one experiences both sacred liminality into the military and the institutionalized liminality of serving in the military is shaped by their reason for joining. I joined the military primarily to escape from aversive life experiences and I ended up coming to see the U.S. as my redeemer, likely because the military helped me to *get out* of my adverse circumstances. Because of the U.S. Military's long history of colonization and systemic oppression and its hegemonic nature privileging masculinity, white supremacy, and heterosexism (which is further unpacked in the next three chapters), it is paramount to understand how intersectional identities (Crenshaw) shape the liminal experiences of joining and serving in the U.S. Military. For example, the experience of a black, gay, male recruit who joins for service as an escape will be drastically different from the Mexican female recruit who joins for citizenship—both of which will be even more distinct from the experience of the straight white cisgender male recruit from the U.S. Deep South who joins for patriotism or family legacy. They tell us we are "all green" in the Army. *Sure, we all wear the same uniform, but it certainly does not fit us all the same way.*

We are conditioned to fit, nonetheless. We go through a sacred rite of passage and become part of the military organization. We train to fight in war. We are psychologically and physiologically controlled and transformed into a higher state—into warriors. We go through our military service existing in an institutionalized state of liminality through belonging to this total institution. All our experiences of serving are different depending on if we're active or NG/reserve, what our job is, if we deploy and to where, how long, how many times, if we're injured, and so on. There is a saying among Veteran communities regarding reintegration: "They train you to go to war, but they don't train you to come home from war." After transitioning out of military service, we become Veterans and we reintegrate into society, culture, and structures in the civilian world. We take our militarized selves with us when we separate from the military. Our "form [was] impressed upon [us] by society" (Turner 105) of the military total institution during our IET and it was then confounded during our military service. Our psychology, physiology—our *very being*— was broken down and then molded into a warrior self. We were transformed, trained, and conditioned to fit into a uniformed and homogenized identity to belong and fit into the total military institution.

As explained in Chap. 2, current conceptualizations of Veteran identity and reintegration focus primarily on narratives of war and, more so, combat. Stereotypes and dominant narratives of the Veteran identity illustrate straight, white, cisgender, able-bodied, patriotic, stoic American men. My narrative does not neatly fit within these dominant narratives. In some ways I fit, and in other ways I don't. I fit because I'm white and from the South. I don't fit because I'm a woman and never went to war. To challenge, disrupt, and ultimately expand current conceptualizations of Veteran reintegration and identity, I suggest viewing Veteran identity through the theoretical framework of liminality as a comprehensive and inclusive framework. Using this framework, I propose two guiding research questions that I answer in the proceeding chapters. These questions are intended to disrupt, shift, and reform the dominant narrative of military service and Veteran identity:

> *Question 1*: Examining my own experiences of separating from the U.S. Military institution, what are some possible Veteran identity tensions that exist in the liminal space of reintegration?
>
> *Question 2*: How might the experiences of U.S. Military Veteran reintegration be shaped by an individual's sacred liminal experience of military initial entry training as well as their institutionalized liminal experience of belonging to the military institution?

My Research and Writing Process

As a critical qualitative identity researcher, I am committed to reflexivity and, thus, must approach these research questions first with an examination of my own experiences and assumptions. I must first understand my own experiences before I enter a dialogue with others. Paul Higate and Ailsa Cameron argue for the importance of military researchers writing [our]selves into [our] work. Dominated by empirical, post-positivist, objective research, there is an urgent, *human* need to pair story—to give face—to the quantitative research that encompasses topics such as Veteran suicides and reintegration. Veteran scholars like Miranda Hicks give a face and a story to the complexities of gender in the military through writing about her own experiences as a woman in the U.S. Army. Warren Price helps readers understand the experiential reality of living with combat-related Post-Traumatic Stress Disorder (PTSD) in his autoethnographic account of how leisure activities, such as fly fishing, can help Veterans live in the present moment and cultivate hope to drive on. These works are moving, emotive, and affective; they foster empathy and help us to grasp the complexities of military cultural discourses and narratives on an individual, experiential level. These works serve to help unite the military-civilian divide that plagues U.S. culture.

My own military story that speaks to why I joined, what my experiences serving were, and what it has meant for me to separate from the military is complex, layered, and nonlinear. My identities are intersectional; I experience them all simultaneously and they shape how I understand the world (Crenshaw). Thus, my identity as a Veteran cannot be separated from my identity as a researcher. Throughout my process and journey of writing this book (which was first written as my PhD dissertation), my own military story unfolds, fragments, complements, and leads me to a deeper understanding of my own subjective questions of "How have I changed and who is my new self [since leaving the military]?" (Smith and True 149). To explore how Veteran suicides and reintegration experiences relate to identity tensions of liminality as well as how these identity tensions are shaped by IET and time in service, I combine theories of liminality with the method of autoethnography in the form of performative writing, using military institutional artifacts as my guide.

Autoethnography

Autoethnography is comprised of three parts: *auto* (experiences of the self), *ethno* (cultural phenomenon and discourses), and *graphy* (systematic description and analysis—the research process) (Ellis and Bochner; Ellis et al.). Autoethnography works to motivate readers to consider our "social, cultural, political, and personal lives" in a different light (Jones 767). Autoethnography enables me to illustrate how my own social, cultural, political, and personal lives have all been shaped through belonging to the U.S. Military. "When researchers do autoethnography, they retrospectively and selectively write about epiphanies that stem from, or are made possible by, being part of a culture and/or by possessing a particular cultural identity" (Ellis et al. 4). Autoethnography values my cultural insider positionality as a military Veteran and is a methodological tool that can provide layered insight into the Veteran identity in a way empirical, objective, quantitative research cannot. Arthur Bochner teaches us how "narrative is used as a source of empowerment and a form of resistance to counter the domination of canonical discourses" (271). Additionally, scholars, such as Boylorn and Orbe, argue for the importance of a critical perspective in autoethnography so that we can understand how our intersectional experiences are connected to power and larger social and cultural institutions. Through narrating my individual experiences as a U.S. Military Veteran, I am intentionally challenging dominant narratives that shape how you see me and how I see myself. Further, applying a critical theoretical perspective to my own narratives allows me to illuminate an experiential reality of a liminal Veteran identity that is shaped by systems of power. This helps both me and you to understand the complexities of Veteran identity in a new way.

Guided by liminality and borderlands, autoethnography allows me to illustrate how the military organizational identity (cultural/macro/

88   J. R. HUNNIECUTT

political) intertwines with my civilian/non-Veteran identity (individual/ micro/personal) and shapes my experience of living between these two worlds. Through autoethnography, I provide a *critical qualitative and in-depth understanding* of issues of Veteran suicides and reintegration, effectively answering multiple calls from the Veterans Health Administration and the Department of Defense (DoD) to produce qualitative research in these domains (Wands; Crocker et al.). Autoethnography allows me to turn to my own challenges, realities, and lived experiences of [my] Veteran identity to both complement and counter pervasive cultural narratives about [the] Veteran identity. Autoethnography prompts me to take complex issues like Veteran suicides and reintegration and offer you "a story to think and live *with* rather than sterile facts and findings to think *about*" (Adams 190). Not only does autoethnography provide me a way to make meaning around my identity as a Veteran, but it also serves to "encourage compassion and promote dialogue" (Ellis and Bochner 748) with others regarding this identity. As Tony Adams explains, "Autoethnography thus embodies the concept of praxis—a melding of theory and practice, form and content—and, in so doing, offers engaging and accessible texts for others to easily comprehend and use" (189).

My goal of this book is to critically narrate liminal moments of [my] Veteran identity—living between military and civilian cultures—in a way that offers engaging and accessible insight into [the] Veteran identity. As I write myself into this research, I am moved to "ask the readers to feel the truth of [my] stories and to become coparticipants, engaging the story line morally, emotionally, aesthetically, and intellectually" (Ellis and Bochner 745). Autoethnographies move the researcher to understand the self as well as others better so that we may make more ethical decisions as human beings and live together in a more compassionate world. To achieve this, I recognize that "the goal is to write meaningfully and evocatively about topics that matter and may make a difference, to include sensory and emotional experience, and to write from an ethic of care and concern" (Ellis and Bochner 742). To create research that evokes connection and emotion, I use performative writing.

Writing Autoethnography Performatively
Autoethnography is the methodological tool I use to critically narrate my own challenges, realities, and lived experiences of the Veteran identity in a way that illuminates how this identity is formed and shaped through both sacred and institutionalized experiences of liminality. Performative writing

is *how* I narrate my own challenges, realities, and lived experiences of the Veteran identity. "Performance is the term used to describe a certain type of particularly involved and dramatized oral narrative" (Langellier 127). As a tool of autoethnography, performative writing is evocative and subjective, evokes perspective-taking and empathy, and expands our understandings of what constitutes knowledge (Pollock; Pelias). Performative writing seeks to connect the reader and, in some way, implicate them. *What are your perceptions of military service? Of Veterans and of reintegration?* I write performatively with the intention that in some way my stories will cause your conceptions on topics like Veteran reintegration and identity to evolve. I write my own stories of Veteran reintegration and identity to inspire you to think consciously about the language and discourses you engage surrounding these issues, especially with the military SMs, Veterans, and family members in your own life.

Guided by theories of performativity (Langellier), performative writing moves us beyond reflecting on our lived experiences to critically interrogating how power manifests in and through our reflections of lived experiences. As Kristin Langellier explains, "Personal narrative performance is situated not just within locally occasioned talk-a conversation, public speech, ritual—but also within the forces of discourse that shape language, identity, and experience" (127). Performative writing as a tool of autoethnography compels us to critically reflect on how the ways we write about our experiences have been shaped by multiple, complex, intersecting identities. Langellier argues,

> Approaching personal narrative as performance requires theory which takes context as serious as it does text, which takes the social relations of power as seriously as it does individual reflexivity, and which therefore examines the cultural production and reproduction of identities and experiences. (127)

Performative writing explicitly focuses on power and identity through critical reflection of the self.

Considering the role of reflexivity in performative writing, Bernadette Marie Calafell calls for a "more nuanced and power laden consideration of reflexivity" (7). In writing through my own experiences of military entrance, military service, and military separation, I am moved to question the ways in which I am simultaneously privileged and oppressed across my multiple identity standpoints (Crenshaw). For example, how does being a white woman from the South who joined the military for upward mobility intersect with my identity now as a scholar examining power relations in the U.S. Military? Calafell calls for me to consider "how does my story speak in relationship to larger stories of cultural Others like myself? Where do the 'I' and the 'we' separate? Do they?" (9). Through critical reflexivity in and through my research and writing process, I must consider how the "I" in my stories represents a "we" of Veteran identity. I must consider how the "I" both collides and fragments with the "we" and identify these tensions, spaces, and moments of in-between sense-making. I must question, how "my personal narrative has qualities that reverberate across cultural, social, and political contexts" (Calafell 9). *Where is the macro in my micro and how did it get there?*

Again, performativity is not just about *where* power is located, but about *how* it shapes, guides, and forces lived experiences. Critical reflection throughout the research and writing process is paramount to identify and interrogate power relations as it relates to identity. Particularly as a cultural insider, tightly woven in and through the military organization, I must remember, "there is no separation between mind and body, objective and subjective, cognitive and affective" (Pelias 418). For example, I must question, where is the military in me—how are my psyche and my physiology changed from my service? How did spending six years in the Virginia Army National Guard shape my present subjective self? How has my lived experience of separating from a total institution such as the military impacted and shaped my affective interactions in the world outside of the military organization? Bernadette Calafell suggests, "We theorize not simply through experience, but through histories, and I would argue, the relations, that are written in and through our bodies" (7).

Such as liminality is an embodied construct, performativity is a theoretical construct that also urges us to consider the materiality of the body and how it simultaneously both absorbs and produces cultural power-laden discourses (Pollock; Fox). As Ronald Pelias explains, "It starts with the recognition that individual bodies provide a potent database for understanding the political and that hegemonic systems write on individual bodies" (420). I question, how is my body "a surface on which social law, morality, and values are inscribed?" (Joyce 152). How, through narrating my liminal experiences of identity tensions living between the military and civilian worlds, can I "performatively intervene on reductive understandings of my body" and thus, my identity as a Veteran (Fox 16)? Nancy Krieger teaches us that bodies "bear the mark of both conscious and unconscious processes" (351). *How do I identify the ways in which my militarized self has been shaped, formed, and controlled? What are the military stories my now civilian body needs to tell? How does my militarized self experience liminality between military and civilian cultures?*

Autoarcheology: Military Artifacts as Symbols of Liminality
Ragan Fox describes a process of "autoarcheology" as a form of autoethnography that focuses on cultural, institutional artifacts to question and interpret how organizational power relations affect and shape individual identity. Fox claims, "Artifacts play a generative role in autoethnographic practices" (124). Lacie Marie Brogden tells us that our autoethnographic selves are positioned between "art" and "act" (858). Fox looks to Foucault's studies on disciplinary structures to understand how archeology demonstrates structure around constraining and enabling identity; institutional artifacts may indicate "ordering and exclusion in discursive systems" (Fox 124). Like Fox, the artifacts I feature in this dissertation

> are not meant to metonymically reference the experiences of all [Veterans], nor do they completely represent my individual experiences. They do, however, say something important and heuristically provocative about the culture from which they were taken. (125)

In the context of liminality, artifacts are the symbols that are representative of liminal states. The U.S. Military contains a goldmine of institutional artifacts and symbols that serve to systematically regulate and control militarized selves and experiences. Military artifacts mark liminal moments in my identity—for instance, the journal I kept during BCT, the rank I wore on my uniform, the "Army green" uniform, the dog tag chain Veterans continue to wear years after service, the Army creed that is branded into my memory, the concept of "Battle Buddies" and the list goes on. Indeed, my militarized **body** is representative of a cultural artifact of the U.S. Military. My body that was effectively trained in how to dress, walk, groom, speak, and engage in warfighting is both a process and a product of militarization. Thus, "Embodiment is a verb-like noun that expresses an abstract idea, a process, and concrete reality. Whether used literally or figuratively, it insists on bodies as active and engaged entities" (Krieger 351). How then, through examining my own artifacts and symbols representative of my liminal military experiences, may I begin to identify and describe identity tensions of liminality between cultures? How will examining my own body as an institutional artifact allow me to articulate how the experience of reintegration is shaped and controlled by my military entrance and service experiences? I will explore these questions by using performative writing as a tool of autoethnography.

Furthermore, in the act of writing and crafting narratives, I am guided by Sandra Faulkner and Shelia Squillante's as well as Anne Harris and Stacy Holman Jones' practical strategies for writing about the self performatively. For personal writing, Faulkner and Squillante suggest a set of questions to carry with you throughout the entire writing process. They first highlight purpose, asking questions such as "What are your goals of this writing?" and "What do you want your piece to do?" Considering the audience, they propose, "Whom do you want to reach?" and "What do you want the audience to do, feel, and believe after experiencing your work?" For ethics, they ask, "Are you able to write this piece now?" and "Who is implicated in the writing?" Around structure: "What structure will work and how can you include research in your writing to achieve your purpose and establish veracity? Craft considers how your voice is working in this piece and questions, 'Have you paid attention to the line, the music in the piece, form, aesthetics, voice, narrative truth?'" Finally, considering criteria, they propose, "How should your piece be evaluated?" and "How will you know if you have achieved your goal(s) for the piece?" (4).

Applying these questions as my guide, Chaps. 4 and 5 function to highlight some of my own Veteran identity tensions that exist in the liminal space of reintegration. In Chaps. 4 and 5, I pick my story back up where I left off in Chap. 2 and continue moving chronologically through my experiences of transitioning out of military service. As "artifacts play a generative role in autoethnographic practices," I rely on artifacts that represent experiences related to my military service and experiences of transition out of service (Fox 124). Following this, in Chap. 6 I move on to explore my second guiding research question and articulate how the identity tensions I narrate in Chaps. 4 and 5 are shaped by my sacred liminal experience of military IET as well as my institutionalized liminal experience of belonging to the military institution. Chapter 7 concludes by providing a new conceptualization and definition for thinking about experiences of military transitions and, most importantly, proposes a new model and conceptualization of Veteran identity.

Works Cited

Adams, Tony E. "The Joys of Autoethnography." *Departures in Critical Qualitative*, vol. 1, no. 2, 2012, pp. 181–194.

Anzaldúa, Gloria. *Borderlands: The New Mestiza/La Frontera* (4th ed.). Aunt Lute, 2012.

Bochner, Arthur P. "Criteria Against Ourselves." *Qualitative Inquiry*, vol. 6, no. 2, 2000, pp. 266–272.

Boylorn, Robin M. and Mark P. Orbe. "Introduction: Critical Autoethnography as Method of Choice." *Critical Autoethnography: Intersecting Cultural Identities in Everyday Life*, edited by Robin M. Boylorn and Mark P. Orbe (Eds.). Left Coast Press, 2013, pp. 13–26.

Brogden, Lacie M. "art ×I/f/act ology: Curricular Artifacts in Autoethnographic Research." *Qualitative Inquiry*, vol. 14, 2008, pp. 851 64.

Calafell, Bernadette Marie. "(I)dentities: Considering Accountability, Reflexivity, and Intersectionality in the I and the We." *Liminalities: A Journal of Performance Studies*, vol. 9, no. 2, 2013, pp. 6–13.

Crenshaw, Kimberle. "Mapping the margins: Intersectionality, identity politics, and violence against women of color." *Stanford Law Review*, 1991, pp. 1241–1299.

Crocker, Theresa, Gail Powell-Cope, Lisa Brown, and Karen Besterman-Dahan. "Toward a veteran-centric view on community (re) integration." *Journal of Rehabilitation Research and Development*, vol. 51, no. 2, 2014, pp. xi-xvii.

Demers, Anne. "When Veterans Return: The Role of Community in Reintegration." *Journal of Loss and Trauma*, vol. 16, no. 2, 2011, pp. 160–179.

Ellis, Carolyn, and Arthur P. Bochner. "Autoethnography, Personal Narrative, Reflexivity: Researcher as Subject." *The Handbook of Qualitative Research*, edited by Denzin and Lincoln, Sage, 2000, pp. 733–768.

Ellis, Carolyn, Tony E. Adams, and Arthur P. Bochner. "Autoethnography: An Overview." *Historical Social Research/Historische Sozialforschung*, vol. 12, no. 1, 2011, pp. 273–290.

Faulkner, Sandra L. and Shelia Squillante. "Writing the Personal: Getting Your Stories on the Page." *Sense Publishers*, 2015.

Foucault, Michel. "The history of sexuality: An introduction, volume I." *Trans. Robert Hurley.* New York: Vintage, 1990.

Fox, Ragan. "Tales of a fighting bobcat: An "auto-archaeology" of gay identity formation and maintenance." *Text and Performance Quarterly*, vol. 30, no. 2, 2010, pp. 122–142.

Goffman, Erving. "On the characteristics of total institutions." *Symposium on preventive and social psychiatry.* Washington, DC: Walter Reed Army Medical Centre, 1961.

Hall, Lynn K. "The Importance of Understanding Military Culture." *Social Work in Health Care*, vol. 50, no. 1, 2011, pp. 4–18.

94 J. R. HUNNIECUTT

Harris, Anne and Stacy Holman Jones. Writing For Performance. *Sense Publishers*, 2016.

Hicks, Manda V. "Making My narrative Mine: Unconventional Articulations of a Female Soldier." *Qualitative Inquiry*, vol. 17, no. 5, 2011, pp. 461–465.

Higate, Paul, and Ailsa Cameron. "Reflexivity and Researching the Military." *Armed Forces & Society*, vol. 32, no. 2, 2006, pp. 219–233.

Jones, Stacy Holman. "Autoethnography: Making the Personal Political." *Handbook of Qualitative Research* (3rd ed.), edited by Norman K. Denzin and Yvonna S. Lincoln, Sage, 2005, pp. 763–792.

Joyce, Rosemary A. "Archaeology of the Body." *Annual Review of Anthropology*, vol. 34, 2005, pp. 139–158.

Krieger, Nancy. "Embodiment: A Conceptual Glossary for Epidemiology." *Journal of Epidemiology & Community Health*, vol. 59, no. 5, 2005, pp. 350–355.

Langellier, Kristin M. "Personal Narrative, Performance, Performativity: Two or Three Things I Know for Sure." *Text and Performance Quarterly*, vol. 19, no. 2, 1999, pp. 125–144.

Newlands, Emma. "Preparing and resisting the war body." *War and the Body: Militarization, Practice and Experience*, 2013, pp. 35–50.

Pelias, Ronald J. "Performative Writing as Scholarship: An Apology, An Argument, An Anecdote." *Cultural Studies ⟺ Critical Methodologies*, vol. 5, no. 4, 2005, pp. 415–424.

Pollock, Della. "Performing Writing." *The Ends of Performance*, edited by Peggy Phelan and Jill Lane. New York University Press, 1998, pp. 73–103.

Price, Warren D. "I Tie Flies in My Sleep: An Autoethnographic Examination of Recreation and Reintegration for a Veteran with Posttraumatic Stress Disorder." *Journal of Leisure Research*, vol. 47, no. 2, 2013, pp. 185–201.

Smith, R. Tyson, and Gala True. "Warring Identities: Identity Conflict and the Mental Distress of American Veterans of the Wars in Iraq and Afghanistan." *Society and Mental Health*, vol. 4, no. 2, 2014, pp. 147–161.

Turner, Victor. The Ritual Process: Structure and Anti-Structure. *Aldine de Gruyter*, 1969.

van Gannep, Arnold. The rites of passage. *Routledge*, 1960.

Wands, LisaMarie. ""No One Gets Through It OK": The Health Challenge of Coming Home from War." *Advances in Nursing Science*, vol. 36, no. 3, 2013, pp. 186–199.

Wu, Min, and Patrice M. Buzzanell. "Liminalities at work: Chinese professionals' immigrant identity negotiations." *China Media Research*, vol. 9, no. 4, 2013, pp. 15–27.

CHAPTER 4

Loss of Community: Searching for and Finding Home

Michael Kirchner explains when Veterans separate from military service, we experience both a loss of a community and a loss of structure. In this chapter (and in Chap. 5), I pick my story back up where I left off in Chap. 2. I write out my stories of navigating the loss of community and structure I experienced when I separated from the military. Through these two chapters, I continue telling my story in chronological order and ground my experiences of Veteran identity tensions using artifacts. Thus, the purpose of this chapter is to illustrate the social identity tensions I felt surrounding loss of community in the years following my separation from military service. Following this, Chap. 5 illuminates identity tensions that relate to (my) loss of military structure post-separation from service.

The identity tensions throughout my story highlight both the community and the structure of the military system and show what it is like to navigate the loss of each—existing in a perpetual state of liminality. I rely on autoarcheology (Fox)—the use of institutional artifacts to guide my stories as it helps me to question and interpret how organizational power relations affect and shape my Veteran identity. Artifacts can represent "ordering and exclusion in discursive systems" (Fox 124), but they are not meant to represent my experiences completely and fully, nor are they intended to represent the experiences of others. Rather, the military artifacts I share throughout this chapter are meant to "say something important and heuristically provocative about the culture from which they were

© The Author(s), under exclusive license to Springer Nature Switzerland AG 2022
J. R. Hunniecutt, *Rethinking Reintegration and Veteran Identity*, https://doi.org/10.1007/978-3-030-93754-6_4

95

taken" (Fox 125). They are meant to *show and tell* my experiences of institutionalized liminality as I worked through my own dissonance around and embodiment of the Veteran identity.

SPRING 2015–WINTER 2016: BUILDING MY SELF COMMUNALLY

I was finally close to completing my first year of my PhD program. It was still the spring of 2015, and I was starting to become aware of a shift happening inside of me. I had scoured the literature about Veteran suicides, reintegration, and identity that was available at that time, and I had learned a lot about myself, the military, and my Veteran peers through doing so. I had learned that there wasn't a *one size fits all* when it came to reintegration, that Veteran suicides were only beginning to be understood, and that there was a great need to understand the social and identity implications of being acculturated into and then serving in the U.S. Military. I started to see at this point how there was a great need for military cultural insiders like me to write ourselves and our military stories into the empirical, objective research emerging around Veteran studies. I was also searching out and joining Veteran community groups at that time. I had attended my first student-Veteran event (the networking dinner) hosted through my school. I became involved in a nonprofit Veteran service organization called The Mission Continues, and I was actively searching for a Veteran community as well as mentors on my campus that could help guide me in my research. By this point, I had made a pivotal decision about my work— I was going to focus exclusively on military/Veteran research moving forward. Not only did it give me a renewed sense of purpose that I had lost since my own military separation, but I knew it was needed; I knew my own voice could make a difference. I was motivated to help not only myself, but my military brothers and sisters too.

Through this decision and these changes in my life, I was starting to bump against my own identity as a Veteran. For the first time since I separated from the military, I began to ask myself, "How have I changed *since I left the national guard?*" and "Who is my new self *without the military?*" (Smith & True 149). The more I asked those questions of myself, the more I began to see how intricately part of me the military was (and still is). In addition to the ethnography research methods class I was taking that quarter, I was also taking a course in family communication. About midway through the family communication course, we were learning about the potential of food to function as a form of ritual and communication within family systems. As an assignment, the professor set aside a class period for us to commune around food and we were all asked to bring in a small sample of food that represented our own family background with an accompanying short write up of what the food was and what it meant. I chose to bring in a military MRE (Meal Ready to Eat), and I wrote a poem about it:

> The MRE
> MREs are gross to eat,
> it looks like space food and smells like feet.
> It takes up too much space in my bag
> and makes going #2 a drag.
> It's supposed to sustain you all day long
> bartering crackers for pound cake around the campfire song.
> The MRE is both love and hate,
> though scoring M&Ms could get ya a date!
> With heater bombs, hot sauce, and questionable "food,"
> the MRE can and does affect the mood.
> Buffalo chicken is a sure score
> tuna fish, however, could shorten your tour.
> You gotta eat it cuz it's all that's there,
> hot food in the box is oh too rare.
> So ole' MRE you keep going strong
> feeding my brothers and sisters in arms.
> Fueling their guts and strengthening their bones
> uniting their morale
> and bringing them home!

The more I reflected on my service and what it meant to me, the more I realized that not only was I feeling a loss of community at the time, but also *why*. I was starting to understand the implications of experiencing the military as my *family*. It was in this family communication class that I learned common and core characteristics that comprise a family unit: long-term commitment, relations created through biology, law or affection, enmeshment in a kinship organization, ongoing interdependence, and institutionalization (Baxter and Brainthwaite). I had made a long-term (six year) commitment to the military, our relationship was created through law, I became enmeshed in the kinship of the organization through primary and secondary bonding, I was dependent on the military to provide me resources and to help me *get out* of situations and circumstances I was in before joining, and I became institutionalized through my participation in that total institution. The military had become my family and separating from it brought loss akin to separating from a civilian/nuclear family. I was slowly beginning to uncover this truth and what it meant. I was starting to realize how much I needed to build and surround myself with community to help cope with and heal from this loss.

Toward the end of that same quarter, the university hired a Veteran Services Coordinator on campus. I got an email about it since I had put my name on that list months prior, and as soon as he was on campus, I reached out to him to set a meeting. Damon's office was in the basement of a building near central campus; it was small with a few chairs around a single table, a microwave and coffee pot, a couple of computer stations, and then Damon's desk pushed up against a wall in the back of the room. As I walked into the office and he greeted me, he also informed me that his office was the new student-Veteran lounge on campus. "Not much to look at," he said, "but we will make improvements." I didn't care what it looked like; I was just thrilled there was finally someone at the university in charge of helping Veterans!

Damon was a Navy Veteran, and after I shared with him my service in the Virginia Army National Guard (with no deployment experience), he immediately started referring to me as a Veteran, too. I felt timid about this because I was still not really calling myself a Veteran but hearing him say it felt validating, nonetheless. As we continued to talk, I shared with Damon that I was focusing all my research on Veteran issues and that I was eager to find a mentor on campus who was military-connected and interested in the same sort of work. He vowed to do his best to help me find someone. Before our meeting ended, Damon asked me what changes I thought were needed on campus to better serve student Veterans. I immediately responded with, "community." I expressed how I had been actively searching and couldn't find any active student-Veteran groups on campus and how I thought that was a huge need for us there at DU. "We need to be around our people," I told him. He agreed and we made plans to meet again after summer break to talk more about building community there. In the meantime, he told me, there were a couple of new Veteran-related initiatives in the works on campus.

Previously known as Memorial Tower, there was an old, small brick building on campus that was built in 1917 in honor of the students who had died fighting in World War I. The tower had burnt in a fire in 1983 and had since been reconstructed. There was to be a rededication ceremony that spring, where the tower would henceforth be known at the "Buchtel Tower" and would stand as a symbol on campus for all those who serve/d in the military. The ceremony was only a week away. He urged me to attend. "I think you will really like what happens after the ceremony too," he went on. After the ceremony, there was to be a grand announcement at the reception about a new military-related program opening on campus, *The Sturm Specialty in Military Psychology.* The Sturm family was even going to be in attendance! "Sturm" is a well-known name at DU as this is an alumni family with a philanthropic foundation that gives regularly to the university. On the DU campus, we had the Sturm Law School, and my own Communication Studies department was housed in a building called "Sturm Hall." The Sturms were going to attend the reception because they gifted the university the initial funds to develop The Sturm Specialty in Military Psychology (SSMP) within our Graduate School of Professional Psychology at DU.

"You might be able to meet some professors in psychology interested in Veteran research and who knows, maybe even the Sturms," he said with a sly smile.

"Okay, I'm sold," I responded with excitement. "I'll be there!"

Getting ready for the tower rededication event and the reception felt different than when I got ready for the student-Veteran networking dinner I had attended earlier that quarter. This time, I wore a black dress, flat black boots that zipped up to my knees, and my hair completely down. I even did my makeup as per usual. I was starting to recognize how I always *militarized* my femininity when I went to any military or Veteran-related events. *Still pull my hair back in some sort of a bun, wear less make up than usual, and typically choose to wear pants with a loose-fitting blouse and minimal jewelry rather than a dress or skirt.* That time was different; *I* felt different. *I have been out long enough. If I don't "look like a Veteran," I don't care and will challenge someone on it.* Thankfully, though, they had yellow ribbons for us to put on to symbolize our military service. I was hesitant to take one as I walked into the lobby of the reception after the quick tower rededication outside, but Damon walked in with me, and I saw him watching me as I contemplated taking one or not. I looked at him before I reached for one and he gave me a subtle nod, encouraging me to put the ribbon on.

Damon sat at the front, with the Chancellor, Provost, and the Sturm family. I sat in a row near the back that was mostly empty. There was a guy in front of me and another in the row behind me that both looked around my age. They were wearing yellow ribbons too. I wondered if they were also student Veterans at DU. *I wished there was an easier way for us all to meet each other.* As the program started, the moderator began by asking Veterans to stand and be recognized. I looked around to see who else was going to stand. The guy in front of me looked back at me and then stood. I looked behind me and he was standing too. I looked down at my yellow ribbon pinned to my black dress and then stood up and folded my hands behind my back like how I would stand at the military position of parade rest, only with a little less rigidity.

As the reception was ending, a woman I recognized but couldn't remember her name spotted me from across the room and then excitedly walked toward me. I think Damon had told her about me. She worked in our university advancement office and a couple weeks prior had reached out to the chair of my department because an alumnus of our program was visiting campus. He was a Veteran who was interested in military/Veteran research and my department chair knew both that I had recently switched my research to the same and served in the military myself, so she recommended I meet with him during his visit.

"I want to introduce you to the Sturms!" she said in a loud whisper when the woman got close enough. "Who knows, they may be interested in your help with the new program." She eagerly grabbed my arm and led me over for an introduction. I didn't have much time to think or respond. *Oh my Goooood, just breathe. You ARE a Veteran. I AM a Veteran. That part doesn't even matter as much. I'm an emerging scholar getting my PhD. And I study this. I'm going to be an expert in this. Just act natural. Not like a Veteran, but not too feminine. Let them know I take this seriously. Don't smile too much! But OH MY GOD I'm SO excited! I can't believe they are opening this military psychology program. This is SO PERFECT for my research and bringing people here I can work with. Maybe we can start forming a community. OKAY be professional. Give a firm handshake.*

She leads me over to Emily and Stephen Sturm, the daughter and son of Donald Sturm. Emily and Stephen are the ones overseeing the development of this project, she tells me before introducing me, "Jeni is a PhD student in Communication Studies and her research is on military and Veteran reintegration. She is also a Veteran." My heart started beating a little faster. *Damnit, I hope they don't ask if I ever deployed.*

"My major was communication too! That's great!" Emily immediately responds.

Whew.

"That sounds really interesting, we'd love to hear more about it. Can you send me an email and maybe we can meet with you and get your perspective on some things as we work on getting this program going?" Stephen asks as he pulls a business card out of his wallet.

OH MY GOD!

"Yeah! Yeah, of course. That sounds great!" I respond with enthusiasm and take a card from each of them.

That spring of 2015—switching my research, slowly beginning to contemplate my service and identity as a Veteran, joining Veteran organizations, meeting and receiving validation from Damon, and then meeting the Sturms at this event—were all important turning points for me on my own journey of Veteran identity. I was engrossed in a whole new body of research exploring Veteran reintegration, suicides, and identity. I was learning so much about myself through the research, and it empowered me to continue exploring my own struggles with this identity. I slowly but surely started to identify as a Veteran more and more, and it was my interactions with others who perceived me as a Veteran, that helped validate me in this process and thus enabled me to work through my identity crisis I had experienced that first year after my military separation.

My first year of my PhD program finally ended and I spent most of the summer in Virginia with my family. Upon returning to Denver and to campus in the fall quarter of 2015, I began to meet with the Sturm family and informally consulted with them through some of the development of the new Sturm Specialty in Military Psychology (SSMP) program. It was affirming that this prestigious family wanted to hear *my* perspective *as a Veteran* on the development of this new military psychology program on campus. The more I felt validated in identifying as a Veteran despite still struggling with my experiences not fitting the dominant narrative, the more I yearned for community. I also became much more involved with the Veteran Service Organization, The Mission Continues, at this time. I had even been offered (and timidly, yet humbly accepted) a leadership volunteer position with the organization. I still felt like I didn't quite belong because I struggled to really see myself as a *true* Veteran, but I yearned for familiarity and belonging. And serving and being surrounded by Veterans was helping me to feel a sense of home once again within myself. Throughout that fall and the following winter quarter, I actively sought out and met other student Veterans on campus, and after talking more about it with Damon, he helped me to see I wasn't the only student Veteran who both needed and wanted to build community there. Damon introduced me to another student, Jack, and that fall, the three of us decided to build a national chapter of Student Veterans of America (SVA) at DU.

Jack was in the business school, and he was a Veteran of the Army Special Forces. He was laid back, reserved, and easy to work with. When we interacted, I could tell he cared as much or more than I did about helping Veterans. We met that fall and spent the winter working to develop the framework for setting up an organized and sustaining SVA chapter at DU. Jack and I were both motivated and willing to dedicate the time necessary to have regular meetings, recruit new members, write a mission and constitution, and set up an infrastructure for communication, events, fundraising, and leadership board elections. Jack and I worked well together but we had notably different personalities; I was more organized, communicative, and eager and Jack was more laid back, relaxed, and reserved. I struggled sometimes working with him because often I found myself wanting to take charge, but then wouldn't because I would feel intimidated. *He was Special Forces. I was National Guard and never deployed. He's a legitimate Veteran. I'm not a "real" Veteran.* As the time grew closer for the leadership elections of our new SVA chapter, I was having a hard time deciding what position I was going to run for. I wanted to run for President, but I didn't feel "Veteran enough" to do so. *It wouldn't make sense for me to be the President. Jack should be President and me Vice President. He is the real Veteran here. He should lead and I should support him.*

I kept oscillating in and out of the Veteran identity. I was slowly starting to understand more about my identity crisis and psychological darkness I experienced my first year or so out of service, and the more I interacted with other Veterans, the more I began to feel validated in this identity. However, it was like a double bind of sorts: being around other Veterans made me feel validated and gave me a sense of belonging *and* made me feel insecure and timid about my own military experiences and Veteran identity. I was still engrossed in Veteran reintegration and suicide research up to this point—research that my Veteran identity and military experiences were mostly excluded from. I was growing more and more frustrated with the research and was clearly seeing the drastic need for cultural insiders of the military institution to be doing this kind of work. I was frustrated the research was so exclusive and found myself heavily critiquing and being more suspicious of research done by people with no direct connections to the military. I questioned motive because I saw and personally *felt* the repercussions of research done on a culture and group of people by those who do not intricately understand the culture. But I knew how rare it was for scholars and academics to also be Veterans. I yearned for mentorship with my work. I longed to work with another scholar who was also a Veteran who would understand and help me to articulate and navigate the tensions I was feeling, especially as a scholar committed to social justice. I regularly asked Damon if he knew of anyone and to ask around and look for faculty on campus who did military/Veteran research. The Sturm Specialty in Military Psychology was still developing as a new program, so there were not any faculty hires there yet. Still no luck yet finding the mentorship I was craving.

My struggles continued. I was getting closer, but I didn't yet feel a sense of home or belonging in my life. I still didn't fully grasp why I was suffering so much. I didn't feel like I *fully* fit anywhere—not back home in rural Appalachia with my family and friends there anymore, not really in my PhD program in Denver with my new peers who I felt disconnected from, and not even fully with the Veteran communities and organizations I joined and built. I yearned for community and connection.

Spring 2016: Facing my Community

In the Spring of 2016, the last quarter of my second year in my PhD program, I was thrilled to take another research methods class. My cognate area of studies in my PhD program was in research praxis (translating research into action/impact), and I was eager to gather up as many tools as I could to better understand Veteran experiences and serve military/Veteran communities. The class was called "InDIGI Qualitative Research methods" and was taught by an Indigenous woman who was a professor in the Graduate School of Social Work. This course was divided into three parts, epistemology (how we know what we know), ethics, and embodiment in research. We began with epistemology, which included reading and discussing indigenous and indigenist theories and how to create subjective knowledge (Denzin and Lincoln; Foley).Then we spent the mid part of our quarter discussing the ethics and values of doing this type of work, which included learning and discussing things such as respect, reciprocity, relational accountability, witnessing, representation, obligation of taking responsibility and paving the path, and claiming/creating space for this work (Fox; Brant; Iseke). Then we ended the course with embodiment, where we centered ourselves and our experiences, articulated our positionalities, developed skills with poetry, photo voice, dance/movement, narrative, and performance, and perhaps most importantly, we embodied our decolonized subjective selves and took up space (Archibald; Furman et al.; Szto et al.; Gubrium; Joyce; Lima and Vieira). We even hosted a community event at the conclusion of our course to showcase our digital story projects we had been working on all quarter.

This class was a transformative experience for me in many ways. I was a cisgender, white, heterosexual woman from the Deep South in this class made up of mostly of queer, transgender, and students of color; I was in a space that necessitated and required me to be continuously critically reflective of my privileges. I also was in this space doing research on Veteran identity, as a self-identified Veteran, being taught and guided by an Indigenous woman. The purpose of this class was to learn indigenous tools and methods of knowing and researching—our professor was teaching us how to decolonize the way we understand and do research. In other words, I was in a space designed to *deconstruct* colonial, empiricist, objective, homogenous ways of thinking. Yet, I was there to learn research tools to help Service Members and Veterans—people who belong to a colonial institution that depends on and is rooted in empiricism, objectivity, homogeny, and collectivism.

I could feel a tension rising in me through my first few class periods as I began to use these new tools I was learning in this class to think more critically about the U.S. Military. I *knew* that Indigenous people were colonized throughout time. Aimee Carrillo Rowe and Eve Tuck articulate settler colonialism as,

[t]he specific formation of colonialism in which people come to a land inhabited by (Indigenous) people and declare that land to be their new home. Settler colonialism is about the pursuit of land, not just labor or resources. Settler colonialism is a persistent societal structure, not just an historical event or origin story for a nation- state. Settler colonialism has meant genocide of Indigenous peoples, the reconfiguring of Indigenous land into settler property. In the United States and other slave estates, it has also meant the theft of people from their homelands (in Africa) to become property of settlers to labor on stolen land. (4)

I *knew* settler colonialism creates a borderland for indigenous people and that they are colonized and placed within a persistent societal structure (institutionalized liminality) that contrasts with their own social systems. I *knew* that settler colonialism is violent. I *knew* that settler colonialism happens through militarized force. What I did *not yet see*, however, is the U.S. Military as a colonizing institution. What I did *not know* is that though it is often omitted from history, the very formation of the first forms of organized militarism in what is now the U.S. *was for the explicit purpose of colonizing Indigenous people* for the claim of power, land, and resources (Grenier). I did *not know* the U.S. Military was first formed to colonize.

I knew that the U.S. Military goes into other countries and cultures and sets up military bases, deploys troops, and "frees" people who are oppressed—or who don't have the "freedom" like we have in the U.S. However, *I did not yet see* the U.S. Military as a colonizing institution. I had not yet held together the truth that the U.S. Military—*my Uncle Sam who redeemed me*—had *colonized* Indigenous people, not just in the U.S., but all over the world. This truth stirred deep inside of me during the entire time I was in this class, but because I was molded to fit into the dominant ideologies that undergird the U.S. Military structure and system, *I could not clearly see it.* As someone who was part of the military institution, *I was molded to not see this truth* or critically consider its meaning. *I was conditioned to not see this history*—my *very being* was *formed* to perceive the military as a redeeming institution with a savior image. Though I could feel these truths bubbling up inside of me, I could not yet look at or name them. So, I attended class with anxiety and timidity and regularly reminded myself to listen and learn with an open mind.

Simultaneously, outside of class, I was working on revising a course I had proposed to teach as a special topics class within my department the following year—a course on military families. I had received feedback from the faculty in my department about the course and the overarching revisions they prompted me to make revolved around including diverse voices and perspectives in the class. "What would a Veteran of color think taking your class? What about the perspective of the military as a colonizing institution—is there room for that voice in your course?" they asked.

I had a conversation with a faculty member in my department that I had been interested in working with. He taught courses related to biopolitics and governmentality. "You might need to pick a side and decide what type of work regarding the military you want to do," he told me. "Are you for or against it?" he asked. The tension inside me grew. I wondered what student Veterans who might enroll in my course would think about me including content that critiques the military as an institution. I felt the anxiety bubble in my stomach. *Do I have to choose between a research agenda that focuses on improving the lives of those within the military institution and research that instead focuses on critiquing the military as a hegemonic system? What will my battle buddies think about that?*

I remembered a conversation I had had with Jessica—the female Veteran I had met at the student-Veteran networking dinner my first year. Jessica and I had become friends and we regularly sat together over coffee and discussed our responsibility to our work and to our people. We discussed the feelings of wanting and needing to speak for those who are still in the military because their voices can't be heard the same way while they are still within the system. We spent hours talking about how when you're within the institution, you are silenced. We reflected on what that meant for us as academics and as Veterans who are no longer within the military institutional system. Military culture fosters unity, loyalty, and allegiance—things that make it incredibly difficult to critique the military institution post-separation (Hall 2011). Patriotism and nationalism are *imprinted* into us during our sacred liminality of IET. It can't be undone. Indeed, our "bodies thus bear the mark of both conscious and unconscious processes" (Krieger 351). I felt hesitant to speak out, to speak negatively *at all*, about the military. I didn't belong to the institution anymore, but the institution still was part of me. I constantly moved in out of this military structure that was still part of me and civilian structures I now belonged to as I navigated my own liminal experiences of transition out of the military.

A few weeks into the InDIGI methods class, when we were learning about indigenous theories, an inside joke emerged within our class about the "White Supremacy Spirit." We joked about how the spirit of colonialism creeps up on us, surrounds us, enters us, moves between and within us, often without us seeing it. "It's the White Supremacy Spirit!" one of them would voice in the many instances we paused in acknowledgment of how our very conversations, discussions, ways of understanding were being influenced by western ways of knowing. Throughout my time in this course, I moved back and forth between my subjective experiences, my tensions, my privileges, and my pain. I meditated on a quote by an Indigenous writer that resonated with me, "As an Indigenous writer, I feel that the gift of writing and the privilege of writing holds a responsibility to be a witness to my people" (Brant 70). I thought about who *my* people were—my battle buddies in the military, my people in Appalachia. I thought about all the different reasons we join and how sometimes our reasons for joining (class-driven, citizenship, family expectation/legacy) can be so disconnected from what the military is, does, and stands for. I reflected more intently on my motives for doing the work I was doing. *Who is this research for?*

The more time I spent in the InDIGI class, learning about colonization and honing skills for *de*colonizing myself, the more I began to see my Uncle Sam in a different light and the more questions I had. I spent a lot of time critically reflecting on the nature of the military institution, what it stands for and represents, and what it means for me having been part of it. I revised my special topics military family course proposal I was working on and built in an integrative approach to diversity. I included a variety of content that critiques the military as an institution and illustrates its colonial nature. I found a TED talk titled, *America's Native Prisoners of War* (Huey). I read the description and built it into my course content without watching it.

As I continued in the InDIGI class, I continued to learn about colonization not only in the physical sense of violence, genocide, and stealing land and resources, but in the psychological sense as well. Settler colonialism is a "persistent societal structure" (Rowe and Tuck 4) and as explained by Victor Turner, a structure includes complex social systems. A social structure is created and maintained by and through talk, both verbal and nonverbal. I began to understand colonization as a structure that shapes our social systems, much like the military institution is a structure that shapes my social systems, sense of self, and interactions. I began to understand and see how things like my very way of *thinking* (e.g., prioritizing logic over emotion) and *being* in the world is shaped by colonialism and by militarism. In learning this, an unsettling truth kept bubbling up:

Colonialism
is violent.
Genocide.
Who conducts the genocide?
Military
soldiers
my military.

108   J. R. HUNNIECUTT

I was a soldier.
I am a Veteran.
Colonialism. Genocide. Me. Guilt.

Again, the purpose of this class was to *de*colonize ourselves and our ways of knowing and interacting in the world. "De" is the Latin root for "off, down, away". I was slowly and painfully moving *away* from and peeling *off* the conditioning of seeing the U.S. Military as a redeeming and saving institution. Part of this process was sparked through learning and embodying indigenous ways of knowing. Many of the methods we learned in this course centered on embodiment. One day in class we pushed all our desks to the wall and formed a circle and learned an indigenous dance as a way to understand and experience dance as a method of knowing and expressing. We read stories, folk tales, and poetry. We watched films, listened to music, and analyzed the meanings and messages in photos. One day our professor assigned a homework assignment using the photo voice method. We were to post a photo in a discussion thread on our course Blackboard site that represented a story we needed to tell. We were to title the photo but were instructed to include no other text. Instead, we were to "code" each other's photos by writing and posting words that we thought of when looking at their picture. I posted a picture of my bunk from basic training and titled it "Home." The photo is shown below in Fig. 4.1. *Home* followed by Table 4.1. *Photo Voice Activity*, in which I organized, grouped, and listed my *Classmates' Salient Codes* they wrote about my photo. Based on their codes, I created my own *Themes* (left column of Table 4.1) that tell a story of the photo.

I reduced my classmates' codes into the five most salient themes represented in my photo. The themes tell a story.

The following class period, we got into groups to talk about our assignments and what we discovered about each other based on the photos and about ourselves based off our classmates' codes. There was another student from my academic department in the InDIGI class, and we were assigned to the same group for this activity. Lili was an international student who stayed at my home her first two weeks moving to Denver while she worked to get situated and find a place to live. We didn't necessarily stay close friends over the course of our program together, but we had a special connection and understanding between each other because of our experience living together for those couple weeks. When Lili saw I had titled my chosen photo for this project "Home," she said something that

4 LOSS OF COMMUNITY: SEARCHING FOR AND FINDING HOME   109

Fig. 4.1 Home
Photo of a metal bunk bed with a green blanket neatly made on the bed. A piece of tape with my name on it is on the top of the bed

Table 4.1 Photo Voice Activity

Themes	Classmates' Salient Codes
I yearn for a home, a sense of belonging	Crowded but empty, community, family, dependent, just a number, silence, numbers, unison
I seek to make my own path	Ownership, follow my own dreams, be my best self, bare, individuality, private
I have neither	Space, there is no in-between, paradox, identity, transplanted, toss and turning
I am colonized	Organized, basics, sterile, in line, orderly, clean, steel, scary, not private, terrifying
I am decolonizing	Comfort, intimacy, relaxation, dreams, settled

resonated powerfully with me. "It's interesting you chose to call this home," she told me. "In the entire two years I have known you and you've lived in Denver. I've never once heard you call this place *home*. Only Virginia, where your family is from. So, I think it's really interesting and powerful that you chose to call this image, and this place, home."

I reflected on her observation. Though I named the photo "Home," the themes I generated based off my classmates' codes, suggested I was feeling a *lack* of home. I *yearned for a sense of home and belonging* while also wanting to *make my own path* but *had neither*. This photo I chose for *the story I needed to tell*, my classmates' codes, and my themes, all represented my experience of being in institutionalized liminality where I was struggling to fit and find my place *betwixt and between* two different social structures. The photo voice assignment can be seen as an institutional artifact highlighting identity tensions I was experiencing in my liminal space of reintegration. As Lili pointed out, me naming this image "Home," especially when that term was something I reserved only for my Appalachian home, reifies the impact serving in the military had on my sense of *fitting* and *belonging* in the world.

The InDIGI class neared an end, and I completed my digital story for the larger class project. My story showed pictures of me in the military, including the photo from my Photo Voice class assignment (Fig. 4.1), and included the following voice over:

Digital Story Script

I joined the Virginia Army National Guard when I was 19 years old and served a total of six years with my unit in Gate City, VA.

The military became part of who I was. It became part of my beliefs, my values, my identity.

I didn't join the military because of patriotism or family legacy. My reasons for joining were tied to socioeconomic class—I joined for the money and education benefits.

My military journey often left me in liminal—in between spaces. Woman, soldier, civilian, scholar.

The female soldier in me was well trained to always lower my head and drive on.

The other parts of me though, parts that clashed with what it meant to be soldier, motivated me to identify and unmask inequality I knew was there.

In an institution of unity, discipline, and sameness, inequality likes to hide.

I slowly worked to take notice of things. Things like how the military as an institution has colonized bodies throughout time—both the servicing bodies within it as well as civilian bodies outside of it.

>4 LOSS OF COMMUNITY: SEARCHING FOR AND FINDING HOME 111

I've examined my perspectives, ideologies, my own body—to see how I've been transformed through my training. Through the rituals, cadences, value systems.

I've also listened to the stories and experiences of diverse people and perspectives around me.

I've marched side by side with bodies that rupture the dominant narrative of what a soldier looks like. Bodies that are not white, heterosexual, cisgender, male bodies.

I question—what moments throughout my service have I seen these bodies rupture ideologies that ground military culture?

And what injustices have I witnessed as a result?

Yes, we all wear the Army green. But does it fit us the same way?

The military is a homogenous culture—it values unity, collectivism, sameness. Such unity has fostered some of the strongest bonds in my life—bonds with my battle buddies. I value such unity and sameness.

But I also value social justice. Freedom. Difference. Uniqueness.

The Veteran in me needs to stay loyal, patriotic, stoic.

But the rest of me, needs to problematize. Needs to decolonize.

What is there under the Army green? What is there when we take the uniform off? What military stories do our bodies need to tell?

I was nervous to show my digital story at our course community event. I purposefully didn't invite any of my Veteran friends on campus, because I was terrified of them seeing/hearing me critique the military. I didn't think they would understand. I imagined them questioning me, *what do I mean by what military stories our bodies need to tell?* I was in a PhD program, specializing in research methodologies and had just spent ten weeks engrossed in a course learning indigenous tools and decolonizing my way of thinking. This course was pivotal for me because the tools I learned led to my own realizations that I had been colonized—or *militarized* as I like to call it—through belonging to the military. I realized the military had a long-standing history of colonizing. I also realized that I had these tools because I had access to this education. *Could my Veteran brothers and sisters understand in the same way without having these tools too? How do I explain this realization to my people without offending them?*

As I simultaneously worked to build my military family course I would teach next spring, I was reading articles I would assign in class that critiqued the military and dominant discourses about the military. *I* was having all these realizations and beginning to see the military in a new light—but it took me a long time and a lot of education to get there. It felt *wrong* even in a way. I had access to these critical tools in the first place

112   J. R. HUNNIECUTT

because of the military giving my access to higher education. I was afraid to critique. It was different for me to critique in a course with peers who didn't serve, and it was a little bit harder but still doable to teach a class where I engage in and teach my students how to ask hard questions about the military. But—critiquing the military to other Service Members or Veterans when I was still struggling with my Veteran identity felt very scary. *What if they didn't even see me as legitimate? What if they saw me as some sort of traitor? I want to help my brothers and sisters, not turn them away from me or bash our military to them.* I even questioned if I was allowed to critique the military. *Could there possibly be any repercussions?* As I sat down in the days after to write my final paper that went along with my digital story I showed at our event, I felt both guilty and lost. Guilty for critiquing *my* military. Guilty for feeling guilty for critiquing *the* military. I didn't know what my role was in all of this anymore. I felt like I was leaving this course with more questions about my own identity as a Veteran than I had when I started. *Do I have to be for or against the military? Can't I be both?*

As I struggled through writing my final paper for the InDIGI course, I remembered the TED talk I had found to show in my military family class I would teach the following spring, "*America's Native Prisoners of War.*" I decided it was time to watch it. I pull it up on the screen and a familiar knot began to form in my stomach as the talk started. I learn about the Wounded Knee Massacre of 1890 when hundreds of indigenous people were massacred on the Lakota Pine Ridge Indian Reservation in South Dakota (Huey). *Massacred by the U.S. Military—by my beloved Army.* I learn that:

> Twenty congressional medals of honors for valor were given to the 7th Calvary. To this day, this is the most medals of honor awarded for a single "battle". More medals were given for the indiscriminate slaughter of women and children than for any battle in WWI, WWII, Korea, Vietnam, Iraq, or Afghanistan. (Huey 2010)

I thought about the heroism of receiving a medal of *honor*. I felt sick. I watched on the screen how *those white men were military heroes for massacring indigenous women and children.* The process of seeing these truths was painful. The military redeemed me and enabled me to *get out* of a scripted path of abuse, addiction, and despair. My military brothers and

4 LOSS OF COMMUNITY: SEARCHING FOR AND FINDING HOME   113

sisters are *my people*. Most people in the military are from the rural south—*my people*. I was drowning in guilt, fear, anger, a*nd* pride. I felt guilty that I was part of and complicit in an institution that was founded on white supremacy and first formed to colonize indigenous people. I felt fear that somehow voicing this Truth makes me a traitor; a bad Veteran; an angry Veteran. I feel angry that we all feel some sense of guilt, fear, and anger because no one—not even white, cisgender, heterosexual males—can ever fully adapt to fit into the military structure because the military structure is rooted in and made up of a *persistent social system* based off a false narrative of the military as a saving institution.

I ended this course sitting in this unsettling truth. I was angry and I still had so many questions. What is the military *really* about? What kind of *freedom* are we fighting for? How does being part of the military condition and colonize us to think, believe, and act certain ways? How have I been shaped—both physically and physiologically—through serving in the military? *Does it matter if I went to war or not? Is just being conditioned into the military institution and culture enough to cause struggles when we separate?* Indigenous methods taught me to look at other ways of learning and knowing—like what can our bodies and movement teach us? What can art teach us? Thinking about research through a lens of colonialism then is the opposite—it's research that values objectivity, logic, reasoning, control. *This* is what dominates the research on Veteran reintegration and suicide. *This* is what dominates military structure and culture. *This* is what has been conditioned and *imprinted* into my *very being* through the sacred liminality of IET and then confounded through institutionalized liminality of TIS: colonialism. I knew I needed to decolonize, de-militarize. I needed to find *home*.

As the end of that spring quarter neared, we held our first official SVA leadership elections. I chose not to run against Jack for the President spot; I was elected Vice President. That school year ended and through an act of self-love and self-care, I decided to take a trip to India during the summer. I had learned meditation my first year at DU when my therapist referred me to the five-week long meditation workshop. Since then, meditation and yoga had become my dominant mechanisms for coping with stress. And at the end of my second year there, I felt exhausted, lost, and broken. I desired both time and a place to simply *be* for a while. Once school released for the summer, I traveled to India and attended a five-week long course to earn my yoga teacher certification.

114 J. R. HUNNIECUTT

Works Cited

Archibald, Jo-Ann. "An indigenous storywork methodology." Handbook of the arts in qualitative research: Perspectives, methodologies, examples, and issues, 2008, pp. 371–393.

Baxter, Leslie A., and Dawn Braithwaite. "Relational dialectics theory: Crafting meaning from competing discourses." *Engaging Theories in Interpersonal Communication*, 2008, pp. 349–362. Thousand Oaks, CA: Sage.

Brant, B. "Writing as witness: Essay and talk." *Women's Press.* 1994.

Denzin, N. K., & Lincoln, Y. S. Introduction: Critical methodologies and indigenous inquiry. *Handbook of Critical and Indigenous Methodologies*, 2008, pp. 1–20.

Foley, Dennis. Indigenous epistemology and Indigenous standpoint theory. *Social Alternatives*, vol. 22, no. 1, 2003, pp. 44.

Fox, Ragan. "Tales of a fighting bobcat: An "auto-archaeology" of gay identity formation and maintenance." *Text and Performance Quarterly*, vol. 30, no. 2, 2010, pp. 122–142.

Furman, Rich et al. Expressive, research and reflective poetry as qualitative inquiry: A study of adolescent identity. *Qualitative Research*, vol. 7, no. 3, 2007, pp. 301–315.

Grenier, John. The first way of war: American war making on the frontier, pp. 1607–1814. *Cambridge University Press*, 2005.

Gubrium, Aline. Digital storytelling: An emergent method for health promotion research and practice. *Health Promotion Practice*, vol. 10, no. 2, 2009, pp. 186.

Hall, Lynn K. "The Importance of Understanding Military Culture." *Social Work in Health Care*, vol. 50, no. 1, 2011, pp. 4–18.

Huey, Aaron. "America's native prisoners of war." *TED.* 2010. www.ted.com/talks/lang/eng/aaron_huey.html.

Iseke, Judy M. Indigenous digital storytelling in video: Witnessing with Alma Desjarlais. *Equity & Excellence in Education*, vol. 44, no. 3, 2011, pp. 311–329.

Joyce, Rosemary A. "Archaeology of the Body." *Annual Review of Anthropology*, vol. 34, 2005, pp. 139–158.

Kirchner, Michael J. "Supporting Student Veteran Transition to College and Academic Success." *Adult Learning*, vol. 26, no. 3, 2015, pp. 116–123.

Krieger, Nancy. "Embodiment: A Conceptual Glossary for Epidemiology." *Journal of Epidemiology & Community Health*, vol. 59, no. 5, 2005, pp. 350–355.

Lima, Maristela Moura Silva and Alba Pedreira Vieira. Ballroom dance as therapy for the elderly in Brazil. *American Journal of Dance Therapy*, vol. 29, no. 2, 2007, pp. 129–142.

Pelias, Ronald J. *"Performative Writing as Scholarship: An Apology, An Argument, An Anecdote." Cultural Studies Critical Methodologies*, vol. 5, no. 4, 2005, pp. 415–424.

Pollock, Della. "Performing Writing." *The Ends of Performance,* edited by Peggy Phelan and Jill Lane. New York University Press, 1998, pp. 73–103.

Rowe, Aimee Carrillo, and Eve Tuck. "Settler colonialism and cultural studies: Ongoing settlement, cultural production, and resistance." *Cultural Studies↔ Critical Methodologies,* vol. 17, no. 1, 2017, pp. 3–13.

Smith, R. Tyson, and Gala True. "Warring Identities: Identity Conflict and the Mental Distress of American Veterans of the Wars in Iraq and Afghanistan." *Society and Mental Health,* vol. 4, no. 2, 2014, pp. 147–161.

Szto, Peter, Rick Furman, and Carol Langer. "Poetry and Photography an Exploration into Expressive/Creative Qualitative Research." *Qualitative Social Work,* vol. 4, no. 2, 2005, pp. 135–156.

Turner, Victor. The Ritual Process: Structure and Anti-Structure. *Aldine de Gruyter,* 1969.

CHAPTER 5

Loss of Structure: Resisting and Finding (My) Voice

For my yoga teacher training in India, I attended a school in a small town called "Rishikesh" that ran along the Ganges River among the foothills of the Himalayan Mountains. Rishikesh is the "yoga capital" of the world. I was so thrilled to be there, fully immersed in something that I loved and that felt healing to me. I was humbled to have the opportunity to be learning yoga in the place it originated by people who grew up learning and living its philosophy and values. The school was 4 weeks long, 6 days a week, 12 hours a day. Our last class every evening entailed an hour of meditation. Our meditation teacher was a middle-aged man named Sanjiv, and he had experience studying meditation across the globe, for over 30 years and had published 17 books on the topic. I was privileged to learn from him. One of the things I appreciated most about his teachings was the breadth of meditation techniques he taught us. He wanted us each to develop and grow as individuals, but also among and with each other as a collective.

One night during class, he put us into small groups; there were six people in my group. Our task was to spend the entire hour telling each other about ourselves. We were to take turns speaking, going around the circle one at a time, and spend five to ten minutes just *sharing*. When we weren't speaking, we were to *listen*. It was still early in the training and given how intense our schedule was, we hadn't gotten many opportunities to get to know each other as peers in the course yet. This exercise was intentionally creating space for that. I was the third person to speak in my

© The Author(s), under exclusive license to Springer Nature   117
Switzerland AG 2022
J. R. Hunniecutt, *Rethinking Reintegration and Veteran Identity*,
https://doi.org/10.1007/978-3-030-93754-6_5

group. Right before me, a woman named Mia shared. She spoke with a heavy Spanish accent. She was thin and toned with long, dark hair that she had pulled tightly into a bun on the back of her head. She was upbeat and full of energy and spoke for the first couple of minutes about growing up and living in Puerto Rico. Her demeanor began to change as her sharing became more vulnerable. "I am here to heal," she said flatly after sharing the basics about her background with us. "I study naturopathic medicine and I believe yoga is a great way to heal. I am in the Army..." she paused and took a breath because her voice began to crack as tears swelled up in her eyes. We were sitting in a tight circle, and she was directly next to me on my right. Our knees were almost touching. My body went tense when she said, "Army." I wanted to look over at her but looked down at the floor in front of me as she continued. I knew what was coming next.

"I have experienced a lot of pain and hurt in the Army," she said. "It is very hard for me to be a woman and to be from Puerto Rico. I don't get respect and it can be dangerous. But the military has given me so much too," she said. "I am earning my doctorate degree now and learning how to heal people," she finished.

Tears rolled down my cheeks. I took a deep breath, wiped my face with my hands, and looked over at Mia. "I was in the Army too," I said. "It's what I do now. I do research to try to help people who struggle or are hurt in some way because of the military. I love the military with all my heart, but I hate what it can do to people. Let's talk." I squeezed her hand, gave her a smile, then looked back toward the rest of the group, and continued with my own sharing.

As class that night ended, Mia walked over to me after most people had cleared out of the room. She gave me a big, tight hug and said, "I'm glad you're here, Battle," before she let go. *Battle. She called me Battle. This woman from across the world, who I have never met and don't know...here we are, both of us on similar but different journeys, ending up in the same space looking for home and healing. We know each other without knowing each other. I know her story without having to really know it, and her mine. We are battle buddies, forever connected through shared experiences of liminality. Forever daughters of Uncle Sam.*

Yoga as a practice and a lifestyle, the way I learned it in India anyway, is indigenous. It's subjective and it's about listening to and learning from your body. I did a lot of research before I chose where to attend my yoga teacher training. I chose India and specifically Rishikesh because it's known as the birthplace of yoga. Especially after taking the InDIGI research methods class and learning about decolonizing and indigenous ways of knowing, I knew when I decided to attend a yoga school that I wanted to go somewhere I would be taught by those who grew up learning and living the practice. I wanted to go to the source. I also recognized my class privilege in being able to travel to India and attend this training. Likewise, I recognize I am a white woman from the West who traveled to the East to learn a practice that is being appropriated by white Western women across the globe (Biswas; Lavrence and Lozanski; Shome; Vats).

In India, I was taught yoga by Indian teachers, who grew up learning from Indian gurus and yogis. They taught me yoga is a spiritual practice, compass, and life philosophy. My teachers brought up, on several occasions and using a multitude of examples, what yoga is *not* (cultural appropriation). "What is yoga pants?" my yoga philosophy teacher asked us with a big grin one day in class before instructing all of us to start wearing loose-fitting clothing to class so our "bodies can breathe." I learned how to chant mantras in Sanskrit, practiced meditation for hours each day, was introduced to the science of Ayurveda, took yoga philosophy classes, and participated in and witnessed spiritual ceremonies. I essentially "lived with the locals" for four weeks in a town where both meat and alcohol were banned, without Wi-Fi and hot water, and on a strict "yogic" vegan diet of mostly rice and vegetables. Then, I came back to my life in the West. I continuously work to stay true to the wisdom imparted on me in India both in my own practice and in the ways I teach yoga to others. I knew while I was there, however, how hard that would be once I was back here. I still buy and wear tight "yoga pants"; I have a mirror hanging in my own yoga space at home where I practice (in India they had ZERO mirrors in studios and always had us close our eyes during class if we were able to), and sometimes I post pictures of myself on social media in various yoga poses. Living and following an Eastern philosophy (as I was taught in India) as a Western woman living in a Western society feels nearly impossible. I tirelessly work (and fail, and then keep working) to see yoga as they taught me to see it: any experience of *unity*.

When I was in India, I learned that the word "yoga" originates from the Sanskrit word "yog," which means "union." Yoga means union of mind, body, and soul. I spent a lot of time thinking about colonial and indigenous research while learning this. These two ways of knowing felt so *opposite*. The military conditions recruits through psychological and physiological control (Newlands; Siebold). They teach us how to think and act; they *imprint* our mind and body—our *very being*. Military conditioning feels like *separation* of mind, body, and soul. We are taught how to take orders on command without question. We must mold and condition our physical bodies. We must pass height, weight, and physical fitness tests. We must groom in certain ways to meet hair and dress standards. We must get approved and report any tattoos and piercings. And we must walk, sit, stand, march, and speak in mandated ways. We are psychologically conditioned to be secretive, stoic, and in denial (Hall). We learn to suppress emotion and not show feelings.

All of this is necessary to be successful in the military as we know it; it's part of the job. If you're deployed in a war zone, in a combative situation, you must be able to take orders on command, without question, and do everything that's necessary to accomplish the mission. These conditioned behaviors serve a purpose within the military institution but are inhibiting and affect our relationships with both others and ourselves, especially outside of the military institution. Yoga, on the other hand, teaches us to be present in the moment and to sit with emotions and feelings in acceptance and nonjudgment. In India, learning yoga and meditation feel like an *indigenous way of knowing*. In my body, I knew yoga and meditation were healing something I didn't even really know was broken. I did not, however, know how to articulate this. Once again, I turned to research.

FALL 2016: RESOLVING AMBIVALENCE

Fall of 2016 arrived and my third school year at the University of Denver (DU) was about to begin. Things felt like they were looking up. It was our first official year having an active Student Veterans of America (SVA) on campus and I was the vice president. I had created a community and finally found my people. The new Sturm Specialty in Military Psychology (SSMP) program on campus was well underway and two full-time people had been hired—a clinic director who would run the off-campus community clinic where student-therapists would treat service members (SMs), Veterans, and their families, and a faculty director who would write and teach the courses and direct the research conducted in the new program. When I found out the faculty director had been hired, I was thrilled and eager to meet him. *There was a faculty member on campus now WHO DID MILITARY RESEARCH!* I emailed him immediately to meet; I told him

I was interested in talking about research and seeing if there was overlap in our work.

A few weeks before classes started, we met at a coffee shop off-campus, and he brought along one of his students in the Graduate School of Professional Psychology who was also interested in military/Veteran research. After I ordered my coffee and sat down, I began my introduction by telling him about my academic background and then shared that I was a Veteran of the Virginia Army National Guard (NG). I felt nervous sharing that. I knew he was a Marine Veteran because I had read his bio online. *Please don't ask. Please don't ask.*

"Oh great. Did you ever deploy?" It was like he just *knew.*

"No, my unit was never activated while I was in," I responded quickly. I had said that line so many times by now.

He paused for a second. Maybe he could see the intimidation in my eyes or maybe it was his psychology background. "And how do you feel about that?" he asked.

"It is what it is. Of course, I'm glad I didn't have to go to war. But you know, you train for it with the same people for so long...so there's that part too," I stumbled with my answer before changing the subject back to research.

I shared that I had recently completed my yoga teacher training and I was interested in exploring research around yoga/meditation and Veterans. He jumped right on board with it, and we sketched out a rough idea and then made plans to follow up. I went home and emailed him that night with another idea—to serve as his graduate teaching assistant for the first SSMP course, Military Culture and Psychology, he was teaching that fall. I proposed to help with teaching duties and do an independent research project for credit hours where I would do the literature review and start the IRB application for our Veteran yoga study. He accepted my proposal and we quickly got it approved.

Classes began and I was working as a graduate teaching assistant in the military psychology class and doing the independent research project on Veterans and yoga, I was vice president of our new SVA, and I was also taking a course called "Mindfulness and Trauma" in the counseling department. I used that course as an opportunity to explore more research on meditation and military/Veteran populations. I was so eager to share the tools of healing with yoga and meditation I had learned in India— tools that were semantic and connected mind and body. I had wishful thinking that the literature would reflect the truths I knew existed within these practices. On the contrary, however, literature on yoga and meditation with military/Veteran populations also felt very *colonial*. As I dove into the literature that existed on the topic up to that point, I learned the research could be divided into controlled and uncontrolled clinical trials measuring whether yoga "works" to improve and/or heal certain conditions that are highly prevalent in military/Veteran populations. Overwhelmingly, the research showed that yoga and meditation practices *work*. These practices are shown to decrease PTSD (Jindani et al.; Johnston et al.), help women Veterans decrease dependency on alcohol and drugs (Reddy et al.), reduce anxiety for people who are deployed and have combat stress (Stoller et al.), improve overall mental health and quality of life (Stoller et al.; Groessl et al.; Fiore et al.), improve chronic pain and depression and increase energy (Groessl et al.), improve hyperarousal in PTSD and sleep quality (Staples et al.), and improve spiritual wellbeing, acceptance, and social functioning (Fiore et al.). The research showed that practicing yoga/meditation helps service members and Veterans in a variety of ways. However, the research didn't know *how*. The biggest "problem" with the research on yoga at that point was that we couldn't standardize, quantify, and prove it. The absence of a coherent, standardized yoga program specifically tailored to this population was inhibiting the work being done in this domain (Patwardhan; Jindani et al.). All the existing studies used different types, styles, and durations of yoga; mostly, the studies were not replicable. Because the studies were not replicable, it couldn't be "proven" that yoga/meditation works to heal issues impacting military/Veteran populations.

Yoga has been used as a form of healing for thousands of years (Iyengar). Yoga was helping to heal *me*. I *knew* this in my *mind, body, and soul*. I also knew that this truth had not been "legitimized" using Western, empirical research tools and modes of inquiry. Further, for it to be considered a "clinical" practice widely accepted, offered, and funded in military/Veteran settings (like the VA), the standards of "legitimacy" were even more stringent. I felt defeated uncovering these "truths" in the Veteran yoga/meditation literature. Nonetheless, per the independent research as part of my graduate teaching assistantship, I worked to develop a framework for a study that would contribute something new—that would be true to the embodied and subjective practice of yoga as I had been taught it in India while also being considered "legitimate," empirical, objective research for military/Veteran populations.

I struggled as I felt boxed into using objective, empirical, quantitative, *colonial* tools to generate knowledge about a practice that felt so sacred, spiritual, subjective, social, and *decolonizing*. I felt like we needed *new* knowledge. We needed a *new* way to understand what was happening with Veteran suicides and reintegration. The research paradigms dominating this work needed to expand. The InDIGI research class and my experiences and lessons in India with yoga taught me to think outside of the paradigm of logic, reasoning, and "proving" right or wrong, legitimate, or false. I started to open more to things like sensory intelligence and knowing through emotions and intuition ("Innsaei").

I felt defeated almost before I began however, because these ways of knowing are not valued or considered *legitimate* in the military I know or the research system I was learning through and within. It's the opposite. I wanted to find a way to resist, for myself, for Mia, for all my brothers and sisters who suffered. I wanted to contribute something *new* that accounted for all sorts of truths. *How do I work to change the system? I am privileged to have access to higher education and to have these tools to think critically and to learn these new ways of knowing and experiencing the world. With privilege comes responsibility. The military gave me access to this privilege. But then, who is my responsibility to?*

That same fall quarter, a student Veteran at DU attempted suicide. I didn't know this person that well at the time, but they were part of my community—part of the SVA that I built and was now leading. Jack called me and told me about it. I didn't know what to do. "Should I call?" I asked Jack. "Nah. He is checked into a hospital now and Damon knows. We're just gonna keep checking in," he said. A couple of months later I reached out and connected and then brought this student Veteran along with me to an event with The Mission Continues, the Veteran Service Organization that I was a leadership volunteer with. Community is what we both needed.

Winter 2017: A New Redemption

It was December and The Mission Continues event was an ugly Christmas sweater party. We had fun and met a lot of new people, and as the night came to an end, we walked together toward our cars in the chilly Colorado air. I felt a sense of pride about being a good SVA leader and reaching out to this student Veteran on campus who needed support. "I'm glad you came tonight, Battle," I said with a big grin as I looked over at him.

"You can't call me *battle*. We didn't serve together. You were National Guard! You didn't even deploy! Come oooooon!"

I felt a knot in my stomach. I brushed it off. *Deny. Stoic.* I was beginning to feel more confident identifying as a Veteran, but still felt hesitant and intimidated doing so around people who had military experiences of war and combat that fit the dominant narrative I kept bumping up against. I wanted to resist. *I am a Veteran too. It doesn't matter if I was National Guard and didn't deploy. I served too! My service matters. I would have gone! I still signed up and was always ready and prepared. The military changed me too. I get to have permission to feel the consequences of those changes too.* I kept quiet. I couldn't find the words. I was *so* eager to find a way to articulate this. I was *so* eager to find research that *validated* this. I also questioned—why did I need proof, logic, and reason to *validate* what I *feel* and know to be true? *Was this part of military conditioning too?*

A couple of days later I was at home browsing social media when I saw a post recruiting for Veterans to volunteer to "deploy" to the Dakota Access Pipeline protests in North Dakota that were happening at that time. Organized by Michael Wood Jr., former Baltimore police officer and Marine Corps Veteran, the campaign for this assembly read, "We are veterans of the United States Armed Forces, including the U.S. Army, United States Marine Corps, U.S. Navy, U.S. Air Force and U.S. Coast Guard and we are calling for our fellow veterans to assemble as a peaceful, unarmed militia at the Standing Rock Indian Reservation on Dec 4-7 and defend the water protectors from assault and intimidation at the hands of the militarized police force and DAPL security." The tagline for this call was as follows: "We swore to support and defend the Constitution of the United States against all enemies, foreign and *domestic*."

I knew that line. It was from the oath I swore when I officially raised my right hand and enlisted: "I, Jeni Hunniecutt, do solemnly swear (or affirm) that I will support and defend the Constitution of the United States against all enemies, foreign and *domestic*; that I will bear true faith and allegiance to the same; and that I will obey the orders of the President of the United States and the orders of the officers appointed over me, according to regulations and the Uniform Code of Military Justice. So help me God." They were taking *the enlistment oath*—a *core* military institutional artifact—and using it as *a form of resistance*.

I pulled up the news and read that the North Dakota NG was mobilized to Standing Rock to support the state police. I was both horrified and inspired. I was both angry at and sympathetic for the NG SMs. *Did they have a choice to be there? Were they allowed to say no?* I knew what the likely answer was to that. *Did they want to be there? Did they know what they were protecting? Do those SMs know the community members—the water protectors—they are their pointing weapons at? How could they participate in things like putting people in cages, shooting pellet bullets, and using tear gas against civilians there—against the people they swore to protect? Could I have done that? What about when the group of Veterans show up to protect and defend the water protectors? Will the NG SMs point their weapons at their— our—own Veteran brothers and sisters?* The call for Veterans to deploy to protect the water protectors felt so inspiring to me, especially after having just learned these indigenous tools and truths in the class I took. *They were using the oath as resistance, and it was so powerful. I wanted to resist.* I contemplated going but opted not to because I had an important job interview coming up.

The Sturm Specialty in Military Psychology (SSMP) was hiring! By winter of 2017, I was at the point in my PhD program where I was finished with my coursework, taking comprehensive exams, and beginning my dissertation research. I was almost finished teaching, with only my military family course left to teach in the Spring. I had been working as the graduate teaching assistant for the SSMP faculty director for a few months now and once I learned they were hiring a full-time outreach specialist for the program, I lept at the opportunity. I had spent enough time engrossed in research on military/Veteran suicides, research, identity, and Complementary and Alternative Medicine (CAM) (Wahbeh et al.), like yoga, to know most of this work came out of the mental and behavioral health disciplines. This was an opportunity for me to embed myself deeper in the Denver military/Veteran communities, continue to help develop infrastructure for building a military/Veteran community at DU, learn more about military psychology, and earn extra income while writing my dissertation! I applied for the job, passed a first-round phone interview, and set up a day/time for the in-person interview.

Two days before the interview a friend was over at my apartment, and I was showing her what outfit I planned to wear for my upcoming interview. I knew I had to once again, *militarize.* It was a below-the-knee length navy blue dress with nude tights and shoes with a small heel. My nails were painted a light beige color, and I would wear minimal make-up, dainty jewelry, and my hair half up. "It's perfect. Navy and beige colors are neutral. It's not too feminine but also not too masculine. The heels are not tall, and the dress is conservative. Minimal make-up is good. But what about your nose ring?" she asks me.

I stop what I'm doing and look at her with wide eyes. "No," I said shaking my head.

"You have to take it out! They want you to be the *face* of the organization. The *face of a military psychology program*. You *can't* have a nose ring. Could you have that in the military?"

"But I'm *not in* the military anymore," I explain. "I GOT OUT!" She raises her eyebrows at me. "It's my freedom ring!!"

Getting my nose pierced was the *very first thing* I did after I went home and changed out of my uniform for the last time after my very last drill with my NG unit. I wanted my nose pierced for so long but couldn't have it done for six years while I was in the military. So, after I finally got out and took my uniform off for the very last time, I practiced my own small form of resistance and immediately went and had it pierced. It was one of the ways I "took my freedom back" from Uncle Sam when I got out. I leaned in close to the mirror and looked at my nose ring and then back at my friend. I let out a big sigh.

"Damnit. You're right," I say to my friend. *This is a military psychology program and that means being engrossed somewhat in military/Veteran culture. It means still being somewhat militarized. I'm sure they wouldn't say anything if I kept it in...but would I be taken as seriously going on bases meeting with high-ranking military officials and leaders? Do I look less like a Veteran with my nose pierced? I hesitantly and painfully took the ring out.*

The interview was in the Buchtel Tower. It felt a little strange, but also a very *full circle*. Two years earlier I had stood outside that tower when it was rededicated to student Veterans on campus, then went on to build an SVA for DU student Veterans, attended the reception when they announced the SSMP was opening and met the Sturms and then went on to give input and perspective on the program as things got off the ground. Now, I was there interviewing in that symbolic place, with the people who had helped guide me to the place I was at in that very moment. I knew almost everyone there on the interview committee—the new clinic and faculty directors for SSMP, Damon—our Veteran services coordinator I worked to build the SVA with, and Emily and Stephen Sturm. I got the job and I let my nose hole close indefinitely.

Spring 2017: Duality and Liminality

Spring arrived and it was finally time to teach my special topics undergraduate course I had been working on for the past year: *(Re)making the U.S. Military Family.* The students were so eager, and we were learning so much together. About mid-way through the quarter, we spent a week talking about acculturation into the military organization. We watched and unpacked military marching cadences and read about the tactics of control and transformation that are employed in training to effectively adapt the civilian body for military utilization (Newlands). After we unpacked the ways in which the words, body movements, and collectivism inherent in military cadence drills function to transform civilians into soldiers, a student raised his hand with an observation and questions, "This," pausing for a moment before continuing, "is *brainwashing.* How is this allowed?"— he asked with a look of disbelief.

The class became silent. Everyone shifted their eyes to me, waiting for my response.

I paused for a moment, frozen with a rush of thoughts and emotions about my role in and responsibility to this truth. There I stood before my class, my "brainwashed," militarized self, here to guide my students through a complexity of truths about the U.S. Military, about Veterans, about my *self.* My goal for this class weighed heavy on my heart: *critique the military as an institution AND create space for empathy, understanding, and compassion for those who have served.* I had decided I didn't want to—I *couldn't*—choose either/or. I was going to do both. I made eye contact with my only student in the class with official military ties: she was a Reserve Officers' Training Corps (ROTC) cadet and would contract into the Army as an officer once she graduated from school. Her reciprocated gaze challenged me: *"are you going to let him say that about us? That we're brainwashed? What side are you on here?"* I could hear her thinking. I took a deep breath and repeated to myself a familiar phrase of perseverance, *drive on, soldier, drive on.*

"It makes sense to come to that conclusion," I finally said. "I don't know that I would call it *brainwashing* necessarily." I glance over at my ROTC student before continuing, "but, yes, we're conditioned, acculturated, taught...to think and act in certain ways. To believe certain things. We must respond, act, take orders without questioning. This is necessary for some of the situations SMs find themselves in. In a life-or-death situation, there isn't time to think. This type of training is necessary for these types of situations. But the question then becomes, how does this *brainwashing*, or conditioning, fit into life after service? The same training that could save our life while you're at war can hinder the way you live your life outside the context of war and the military generally. How do we reconcile this?" I continued with the lesson.

I was beginning to feel more comfortable identifying as a Veteran at this point. Working as the outreach specialist for SSMP helped a lot because I was constantly embedded in military/Veteran communities and organizations. I was constantly hearing stories that had parallels with my own and I was constantly receiving validation about my Veteran identity through others' perceptions of me as so. I was also getting more comfortable feeling like I was in a position where I both could and should openly critique the military as a hegemonic institution. I was decently well versed in research on military/Veteran experiences at this point and felt determined to use my PhD dissertation as an opportunity to shift paradigms and perceptions around these experiences and topics. Despite feeling like I had finally made it through my own identity crisis as a Veteran and had found a new sense of community and home, I was still struggling with structure. *How do I move forward with these new critical tools I have? How and where do I try to make a change? What is my mission now? How do I critique the system and try to change it and help my brothers and sisters at the same time?* I sat with these questions as the final quarter of my third year ended and throughout the summer as I began preparations for my dissertation work that I would start the following fall. I wrote a poem late that summer as an attempt to make sense of what I was feeling and struggling with at that time.

The Green
We don't know how to answer these questions.
I struggle in knowing how to piece it all together.
The military became part of me.
I joined as an escape
from a system that did not serve me.
I became one who serves.
And my place in that system changed. It elevated. More respect. More financial freedom. More opportunities. More experiences. More control over that life.
This and that, up and down, black and white. The green.
More control over that life meant less control

over this new life
where I must stand ready
to deploy, engage, and destroy
my enemies.
Enemies that want to *control* my *freedom*.
A freedom that ironically
doesn't feel so free
as I serve the people of the United States, and live the Army values.
Who's controlling what freedom?
Wait, who is the enemy again?
Just switched systems.
Don't question. Do what you're told.
Drive on, soldier, drive on.
Experiences good and bad. A love-hate relationship, I used to say.
When the time came,
I chose freedom again
from an institution that saved me and then constrained me.
Screw you, Uncle Sam.
Caught me, broke me, built me, trained me, kept me.
And then sent me on my way
with a heroic future glimmering on the screen.
A new road before me
a new self only meant to discover
the old self was still there. The old system intact.
Under six years of enlisted escape.
Six years of enlisted experiences.
Only to find
this life doesn't fit with that one.
This and that, up and down, black and white. The green.
In between.
How does this fit with that?
Where is freedom?
What is worth defending and protecting?

I wrote this poem the night after the Unite the Right rally in Charlottesville, Virginia, on August 12, 2017. This rally happened in my home state, where I served in the National Guard. I knew that NG units had been activated to the scene there—units I served with. It was a Sunday evening and I had spent the day working on my dissertation. I was distracted though, as my mind was preoccupied worrying about the state of the nation on a large scale *and* about my brothers and sisters in arms who might be on the ground there. I worried not only about them being surrounded by violence, but also about them being in a morally conflicting situation. I messaged Shawn, my friend who had helped recruit me into the NG many years earlier. Shawn was still in, serving in the same battalion that I was assigned to in 1030th. I sent him a text and asked him what he knew and if our unit had been activated to help with the riot.

"Nah we weren't but 229 MP [Military Police] company from our battalion was on the ground from the beginning at the request of state police. This is the first time in my 16 years [in the military] a unit has responded to a riot with weapons and ammo. It's bizarre. 116th infantry is on standby if it doesn't calm down soon," he told me.

"Wow and 229 has a lot of black soldiers. Could you even imagine? I wonder if they were given the option to not go," I typed.

"They're all green, friend," he responded with a laughing face emoji.

I roll my eyes to myself and then text back, "They got fucking militia there and shit."

"Yep it's ridiculous," he responds.

"Read militia as: likely a bunch of vets. So we got veterans fighting current service members and black NG members breaking up Nazi white supremacy rallies. WOW," I say.

"Those 'vets' in the militia are likely a bunch of turd soldiers mixed in with a bunch of racist air soft playing soldier wannabes. Still dangerous though," he replies.

I pause for a moment. "They actually had ammo? 229...was issued ammo? WTF," I exclaim.

[Note: "Ammo" is live ammunition—live rounds—real bullets as opposed to "blanks," which are rounds that make the loud noise but do not release an actual bullet from the weapon when fired.]

"Well yeah, as you pointed out the militia was carrying guns and riot shields don't stop bullets. Plus, Antifa was threatening to Molotov cocktail riot control. They're mixed in with the State Police it's not like they're operating on their own. The MPs train with them 4 or 5 times a year on this. They're very good at their job," he tells me.

[Note: a "Molotov cocktail" is essentially a homemade bomb.]

"That's good to hear," I said back.

"The state police requested the weapons and ammo, we denied the request that they bring m4s and only allowed m9s," he continues.

[Note: m4s are automatic rifles and m9s are pistols.]

"Wow that they requested automatic rifles," I say.

5 LOSS OF STRUCTURE: RESISTING AND FINDING (MY) VOICE   131

"When in a civil defense scenario, they're outfitted with a block that prevents the weapon from being switched to burst so just one round per trigger pull. But they ended up not taking them."

"You've not been out that long have you?" he asks me.

"Three years. Yep," I reply.

"You've forgot your roots."

"Noooo…" I texted back in defense.

"Don't start thinking we're blood thirsty to kill protesters," he says.

"Of course I don't think that," I tell him. "It's complex."

"229 doesn't want to be there either," he says.

"No I sympathize with 229. Not think bad of them."

"Good. They're good people."

"Heartbroken of the realities people there are confronting," I say.

"I know, it's terrible."

"I know they're good people. I just can't imagine being a black soldier asked to show up at a riot like that," I go on.

"True. But hopefully they do it with pride knowing what they're protecting," he says.

"That's the thing though. Do they know what they're protecting?" I reply.

"Freedom!" he says in a final text before we end the conversation.

About a week later my friend from school was over again and we were sitting in my living room, listening to Nora Jones, drinking watered down coke, and browsing through our Facebook newsfeeds. We were taking a break from working on our dissertations. She was writing about race, and I was writing about the Veteran identity.

"Hey did you see this video I posted?" she asked me. She pressed play and handed me her phone. It was the *Vice* documentary called "Charlottesville: Race and Terror." Scenes of violence flash across the scene. Riots. People screaming. People in "full battle rattle" with guns, shields, and bulletproof vests. Nazi flags. Confederate flags. Black people, white people, rainbow flags, crosses. The landscape I saw on the screen was familiar to me on so many levels. I grew up in southwest Virginia, a few hours south of Charlottesville. I felt a pit in the bottom of my stomach. *This is my homeland. These are the people I grew up with, went to high school with, went to church with, served in the Army in rural Virginia with.*

I focused on the scene and felt paralyzed as I absorbed what I was seeing. I was mortified at how much I recognized on the screen. How much I could see. How familiar it all was.

"There's so many Service Members and Veterans there," I said blankly as I stared into the screen with a glossy gaze.

"What?! Really? How can you tell?" my friend asked.

The clothes, the backpacks, boots, hats, black watches on the left wrists, dog tag chain peeking out from his shirt collar, the haircuts and beards, equipment and gear. The way he is walking with a purpose, the tone of his voice. He speaks with authority. He has a mission, and he will accomplish his mission at all costs. The military is intricately a part of who he is and because I was in the military and I study this now, I can see it in me, and I can see it in him too.

We were taught how to dress, groom, walk, talk, *be*. Belonging to and serving in the military affect us psychologically and physiologically. *The military is intricately part of who we are.* When we separate from service, or when we're on "civilian time" and not "on duty," the military is *still part of us*. The structure and community that makes up the social system of the total military institution is *still part of us*. Living life outside of the military system (having a civilian life), then, means existing in a place *between* systems—a place of liminality. As Victor Turner explained, "Liminal entities are neither here nor there; they are betwixt and between the positions assigned and arrayed by law, custom, convention, and ceremonial" (95). To shine a light on the experiences of Veteran liminality, the purpose of Chaps. 4 and 5 was to *show and tell* my own lived experiences of reintegration from military service. In doing so, I aim to highlight some tensions that can exist in the liminal space of Veteran identity.

The tensions embedded within my narratives illustrate the loss of both community and structure I felt when separating and how I struggled to embody the Veteran identity as my experiences of service did not fit the dominant narrative. I drew from artifacts that emerged during my experiences of reintegration post-service to illustrate my loss of community as I searched for a sense of home (family food and the InDIGI class projects). As I took an indigenous research methods class designed to decolonize my ways of thinking and behaving, I began to *look within* at the ways in which my *very being* had been militarized and colonized through belonging to and participating in the U.S. Military institution, *whether I ever went to war or not*. With the tools I gathered in that class, I started to *see within* as I traveled to India and engrossed myself in indigenous practices and continued my own process of demilitarization.

When I returned to school the following fall, I began to feel a *loss of structure*, which illustrates tensions I was feeling around the loss of purpose and mission. Who was I if I was no longer *a guardian of freedom?* What was I to do if I no longer bought into *the American way of life?* Who *was my loyalty to?* My stories illuminate the loss of structure I felt as I explored and embodied new critical ways of thinking and adopted new paradigms to guide my behaviors. I struggled between tensions of military conditioning around discourses of freedom, patriotism, and nationalism and commitments as a social justice scholar. I needed community and purpose and I was in a constant back and forth adapting to find each. I wanted to blend and fit into the Veteran identity, but I also wanted to resist. I moved toward a new redemption as I worked to resolve the ambivalence I was feeling *between* staying forever true and allegiant to my Uncle Sam and reclaiming agency over my life while finding a way to change to the system that *saved me and then constrained me.*

Am I *brainwashed?* Can I *undo* the conditioning? Can I *re*integrate? Can we go *back?* "*How* have I changed?" and "*Who* is my new self?" (Smith and True 149). I was in liminality. I didn't know where I belonged, and I didn't know what my new purpose was. "The attributes of liminality or oflimalpmona* ('threshold people') are necessarily ambiguous, since this condition and these people elude or slip through the network of classifications that normally locate states and positions in a cultural space" (96). In this and the previous chapter, I illustrated "attributes of liminality" surrounding my experiences of reintegration and the Veteran identity by narrating my stories, anchored in institutional artifacts. The artifacts throughout Chaps. 4 and 5 included class projects related to my military service, the military enlistment oath, my nose ring, and a poem I wrote. The artifacts helped me to question and interpret how power relations affect and shape my Veteran identity. In the next chapter, I also employ autoarcheology (Fox) as I explore how my sacred liminal experiences of military Initial Entry Training (IET) and my time in service shaped my experiences of transition after service and my negotiation into and embodiment of the Veteran identity.

Works Cited

Biswas, P. "Social sutra: Yoga, identity, and health in New York's changing neighborhoods." Health, Culture and Society, vol. 3, no. 1, 2012, pp. 95–111.

Fiore, Rachael; Rhonda Nelson, and Eric Tosti. The use of yoga, meditation, mantram, and mindfulness to enhance coping in Veterans with PTSD. *Therapeutic Recreation Journal*, vol. 48, no. 4, 2014, p. 337.

Fox, Ragan. "Tales of a fighting bobcat: An 'auto-archaeology' of gay identity formation and maintenance." *Text and Performance Quarterly*, vol. 30, no. 2, 2010, pp. 122–142.

Groessl, Erik et al. Yoga for Veterans with chronic low-back pain. *The Journal of Alternative and Complementary Medicine*, vol. 14, no. 9, 2008, pp. 1123–1129.

Hall, Lynn K. "The Importance of Understanding Military Culture." *Social Work in Health Care*, vol. 50, no. 1, 2011, pp. 4–18.

InnSaei: The Power of Intuition. Directed by Kristín Ólafsdóttir, performances by Hrund Gunnsteinsdottir, 2016.

Iyengar, Bellur Krishnamukar Sundara. Light on yoga: Yoga dipika. *HarperCollins*, UK, 2001.

Jindani, Farah, Nigel Turner, and Sat Bir Khalsa. A yoga intervention for Posttraumatic Stress: A preliminary randomized control trial. *Evidence-Based Complementary and Alternative Medicine*, 2015, pp. 1–8.

Johnston, Jennifer et al. Yoga for military service personnel with PTSD: A single arm study. *Psychological Trauma: Theory, Research, Practice, and Policy*, vol. 7, no. 6, 2015, pp. 555–562.

Lavrence, Christine, and Kristin Lozanski. "'This is not your practice life': Lululemon and the neoliberal governance of self." *Canadian Review of Sociology/Revue canadienne de sociologie*, vol. 51, no. 1, 2014, pp. 76–94.

Newlands, Emma. "Preparing and resisting the war body." *War and the Body: Militarization, Practice and Experience*, 2013, pp. 35–50.

Patwardhan, Avinash R. "Yoga research and public health: Is research aligned with the stakeholders needs?" Journal of Primary Care & Community Health, 2016, vol. 8, no. 1, 2017, pp. 31–36.

Reddy, Shivani et al. "The effect of a yoga intervention on alcohol and drug abuse risk in Veteran and civilian women with Posttraumatic Stress Disorder." *The Journal of Alternative and Complementary Medicine*, vol. 20, no. 10, 2014, pp. 750–756.

Shome, Raka. Diana and beyond: White femininity, national identity, and contemporary media culture. *University of Illinois Press*, 2014.

Siebold, Guy L. "The essence of military group cohesion." *Armed Forces & Society*, vol. 33, no. 2, 2007, pp. 286–295.

Smith, R. Tyson, and Gala True. "Warring Identities: Identity Conflict and the Mental Distress of American Veterans of the Wars in Iraq and Afghanistan." *Society and Mental Health*, vol. 4, no. 2, 2014, pp. 147–161.

Staples, Julie, Michelle Hamilton, and Madeline Uddo. "A yoga program for the symptoms of Post-Traumatic Stress Disorder in Veterans." *Military Medicine*, vol. 178, no. 8, 2013, pp. 854–860.

Stoller, Carolyn et al. "Effects of sensory-enhanced yoga on symptoms of combat stress in deployed military personnel." *American Journal of Occupational Therapy*, vol. 66, no. 1, 2011, pp. 59–68.

Turner, Victor. The Ritual Process: Structure and Anti-Structure. *Aldine de Gruyter*, 1969.

Vats, Anjali. "(Dis)owning Bikram: Decolonizing vernacular and dewesternizing restructuring in the yoga wars." *Communication and Critical/Cultural Studies*, vol. 13, no. 4, 2016, pp. 325–345.

Wahbeh, Helané, Angela Senders, Rachel Neuendorf, and Julien Cayton. "Complementary and alternative medicine for posttraumatic stress disorder symptoms: a systematic review." *Journal of evidence-based complementary & alternative medicine*, vol. 19, no. 3, 2014, pp. 161–175.

CHAPTER 6

You Can't Go Back

To be a Veteran is to constantly live with conflicting emotions; it is to exist in a perpetual state of liminality between military and civilian social structures and systems. The purpose of this chapter is to tease out and illustrate how this perpetual liminality is formed through both military Initial Entry Training (IET) and Time in Service (TIS). Specifically, this chapter addresses the second guiding research question proposed in chapter three: *How might the experiences of U.S. Military Veteran reintegration be shaped by an individual's sacred liminal experience of military initial entry training as well as their institutionalized liminal experience of belonging to the military institution?* Like in Chaps. 4 and 5, in this chapter I also rely on Fox's method of autoarcheology. Doing so allows me to elicit stories related to military institutional artifacts that represent my experiences of transitioning out of service and making sense of my identity as a Veteran. This chapter illustrates how the struggles and experiences related to military transitionary experiences are not solely about war and post-combat difficulties but more so are related to social conditioning and organizational assimilation that occurs during the sacred liminality of military IET and institutionalized liminality of TIS.

In this chapter, I rely on three dominant military institutional artifacts to navigate my points: 1) The Soldier's Creed, 2) the term/concept "Army Greens," and 3) the term/concept "Battle Buddy." Additionally, I incorporate artifacts such as journal entries, more class projects, and photos of myself in and out of uniform to exemplify and complement points I

© The Author(s), under exclusive license to Springer Nature Switzerland AG 2022
J. R. Hunniecutt, *Rethinking Reintegration and Veteran Identity*,
https://doi.org/10.1007/978-3-030-93754-6_6

137

make about ideologies and discourses encompassing the Soldier's Creed, Army Greens, and Battle Buddies. The purpose is to show how these military institutional artifacts represent dominant organizational ideals. These artifacts function to both physiologically and psychologically mold members to fit into military structure—affecting our social identities and experiences during transitions.

The specific journal entries, class projects, and photos I included have two purposes: 1) they correspond with and reify specific moments in time: IET, TIS, and separation from military service, and 2) they illustrate how the micro (my personal lived experiences) interacts with the macro (ideological power structures and systems) in a way that impacts and shapes Veteran identity. Of note, this chapter does not flow in the same linear chronological order of the two previous chapters. Rather, I intentionally jump back and forth between moments in time during this chapter to make points about sacred (IET) and institutionalized liminality (time in service and separation after service) that Veterans experience. Thus, this chapter is organized in the following way: I first share and unpack The Soldier's Creed—an Army institutional artifact containing an ideograph functioning to position the U.S. Military and those who serve in it as redemptive. Following this, I share stories and artifacts of "Army Greens" and "Battle Buddies" from my IET, time in service, and reintegration out of service. Through sharing these artifacts and stories, I illustrate how social conditioning during these liminal (sacred and institutional) experiences affects Veteran identity positioning and military transitionary experiences. These stories and artifacts allow me to examine the micro and the macro surrounding Veteran identity. More specifically, it allows me to ask, "How does my story speak in relationship to larger stories of cultural Others like myself? Where do the 'I' and the 'we' separate? Do they?" (Calafell 9).

FREEDOM: "GIVE ME LIBERTY OR GIVE ME DEATH!"

It was week seven of basic training. We were in old barracks that had been emptied and cleaned out and the Drill Sergeants in my platoon had set up different stations all around the room, each one a different test we had to pass. Basic training was divided into three phases—red, white, and blue phase. Each was three weeks long and before advancing on to a next phase, we had to pass tests to prove we were ready. I stood tall at attention. My legs were straight with my heels touching and my toes pointed slightly outwards on each side. My arms were straight down my sides, with my fingers curled making a small cusp around the seam of my Army Combat Uniform (ACU) pants on my outer thighs. My shoulders were back and down, my spine straight, my head pointed forward and my gaze fixed straight ahead. My face stoic—like a rock, showing no emotion. One of my Drill Sergeants sat in a medal folding chair directly in front of me. He had a clipboard with a rating sheet in one hand and a black pen in the other. "Begin," he ordered once I was ready at the position of attention. I took a deep breath and then with the volume and enthusiasm of a new soldier, proclaimed:

> *"THE SOLDIER'S CREED...*
>
> *I am an AMERICAN SOLDIER. I am a WARRIOR and a member of a TEAM. I serve the people of the United States and live the Army values. I will ALWAYS place the mission first. I will NEVER accept defeat. I will NEVER quit. I will NEVER leave a fallen comrade. I am DISCIPLINED, physically and mentally TOUGH, TRAINED and PROFICIENT in my warrior tasks and drills. I ALWAYS maintain my arms, my equipment, and MYSELF. I am an EXPERT, and I am a PROFESSIONAL. I stand ready to DEPLOY, ENGAGE, and DESTROY the ENEMIES of the United States of America in CLOSE COMBAT. I am a GUARDIAN OF FREEDOM and the American way of life. I am an AMERICAN SOLDIER."*

The Soldier's Creed is an artifact of Army culture that demonstrates structure around constraining and enabling identity (Fox). The more I chanted it during my IET, the more it became part of my "very being" (Turner, 105) and helped to prepare me for my new responsibilities as a soldier in the U.S. Army. During my time of sacred liminality in basic training, "form [was] impressed upon [me] by society" (Turner 105). The "society" of the U.S. Army become part of my very *form and being* through conditioning tactics such as being made to memorize and repeatedly recite (in a very specific way that entailed my physical body positioning) The Soldier's Creed.

The history and story of The Soldier's Creed has many layers. When the U.S. Military first invaded Iraq in 2003, we faced a new form of warfighting. No longer was the enemy in a specific place wearing a specific uniform, but they could be anyone and anywhere. In 2003, six American soldiers were taken POW (Prisoner of War) by Iraqi forces. One of these soldiers, Private First Class (PFC) Jessica Lynch, received widespread media coverage. I remember hearing about PFC Lynch in basic training.

Don't be like PFC Lynch, they told us when teaching us land navigation. *Don't be like PFC Lynch,* they'd whisper in your ear when you wanted to quit. The story goes, this group of soldiers belonged to a Maintenance Company; they were mechanics. They were driving somewhere in Iraq to a specific location and got lost (because they were from a Maintenance Company and were not adequately trained in land navigation). When they got lost, they found themselves in enemy territory, were attacked, and six soldiers were captured and taken POW (including Jessica Lynch). They say Lynch never fired a single round.

The military analyzed this situation and concluded that our current system (both during IET and in permanent duty stations) fostered more of an "I" then "we" mentality. The argument was that our training structures emphasized specialized job training more than Basic Combat Training (BCT), including things like land navigation (which keeps you from getting lost and ending up in enemy territory) and marksmanship (Loeb). This then led to an individualist versus collectivist mentality among troops—*I have a specific job and that's all I need to know how to do.* For example, thinking of oneself as a "mechanic" rather than a "soldier." This then inhibited military group cohesion, which consequently hindered military effectiveness and lethality.

The solution to this problem was the Warrior Ethos Program. A task force was developed, and the Soldier's Creed was written. The Warrior Ethos consisted of four lines embedded within the creed: *I will always place the mission first. I will never accept defeat. I will never quit. I will never lead a fallen comrade.* This ethos was intended to strengthen every level of military group bonding: primary, secondary, organizational, and institutional. The creation of The Soldier's Creed kicked off a campaign known as the "Task Force Soldier." This campaign was a commitment from military leadership to ensure soldiers are adequately trained to be efficient in basic combat skills and to embody the warrior ethos contained within The Soldiers Creed. The Warrior Ethos emphasize prioritizing mission about all else, never quitting, and never leaving someone behind. This new set of ethos, creed, and campaign went on to influence training tactics employed through IET and TIS.

Tactics used to control and transform recruits' bodies during military training includes things such as specified ways to move/stand and routines/rituals like chanting cadences, marching, and reciting creeds (Newlands). The Soldier's Creed, Army Greens, and Battle Buddies were all tactics used to control and transform my body and psyche during

6 YOU CAN'T GO BACK 141

military Initial Entry Training. The Soldier's Creed is the creed for the U.S. Army; each branch has its own creed. However, despite each creed having differences reflective of branch missions, they all have commonalities. Each creed positions the U.S. Military as a *saving* and *rescuing* organization and each creed highlights the *defending* and/or *guarding* of *freedom* and/or *country*. Though each military branch is unique and has its own cultural elements, the military organization in the U.S. functions as a social structure and system that centers on homogeny and collectivism. Army Greens make sure I see that I'm green before I'm anything else so *I will always place the mission first, never accept defeat*, and *never quit*. Battle Buddies helps ensure *I will never leave a fallen comrade*. These institutional artifacts help enforce the Warrior Ethos contained in The Soldier's Creed.

During IET, the Soldier's Creed became part of me, and I chanted it with pride and conviction. Yet, that pride and conviction faded as I moved out of sacred liminality into institutionalized liminality once I graduated IET and joined my regular NG unit. The creed and all it stands for continued to be a part of me through my time in service (and inevitably is still part of me now), but the more time I spent in the total military institution, and especially the more time I spend *now* outside of that institution, the less I believe in what the creed stands for and what it means. The more time I spend separated from the military institution, the more I question what it means for me to have this creed and what it stands for *imprinted into my very being*.

My positionality now, over a decade after I stood in front of my Drill Sergeant and recited this creed from memory and with unfettered conviction, is a much more *skeptical* and *critical* one. Since that day, I have changed and grown. I have earned a bachelor's degree in Technical and Professional Communication, a master's degree in Communication Studies, and a PhD in Communication Studies, I have traveled the world, I have studied and become certified to teach yoga and meditation, and I have lived outside of my "box" of "white isolation" (DiAngelo) in central Appalachia. I served my six years in the Army NG and was exposed to and experienced inequitable social structures during my service. I have focused tirelessly since my own military separation on not only negotiating my own identity as a Veteran but serving in multiple capacities as a military/ Veteran advocate in the educational and professional organizations I inhabit and as well as within my local communities. The military gave me

142   J. R. HUNNIECUTT

access to higher education and served as my bridge between that day I recited the creed to my Drill Sergeant in basic training, and now.

Now, I know how to think critically. *What is "freedom" anyway? What is the "American way of life" I pledged my life to guard?* Now, I recognize my privileges that have granted me tools to learn how to think critically. Now, I have a responsibility because of those privileges. Now, the conviction I feel about being *a guardian of freedom and the American way of life* is much different from the conviction I felt then. Then, I thought the *American way of life* was about having freedom to chase your dreams and build a life that you want for yourself. I thought it was about opportunity, liberty, and prosperity; this is what I learned. I was taught this by my white, heterosexual, monogamous, middle-class, Christian parents, at my predominately white elementary, middle, and high schools, in my church, in my Appalachian community, and in the military. But now, after filling my toolbox full of ways to think critically—after placing social justice at the forefront of all I do—I think about the *American way of life* a bit differently.

The *American way of life* becomes something else when you consider how the systems undergirding U.S. American society (and the *American way of life*) were established. These systems were established (i.e., our country and our military were founded) by white, heterosexual, able-bodied, middle/upper class, Christian men. These systems were created *by* people of these identity standpoints and perspectives *for* people of these identity standpoints and perspectives. This means that anyone who doesn't have these identities must learn to adapt in a world undergirded by a system that was not created by them or with them in mind. My perspective now is that the American Dream represents a system that oppresses a lot of people, a lot of *others*. When it comes to having freedom to chase your dreams and build a life that you want—it's much easier to do that if you live within a societal and structural system built by people that look like you, for people like you.

The inherent assumption in the American dream *is that we all have equal access to it*—that we all have the same amount of freedom to live our lives the ways we choose. We don't. If I was alive and tried to join the military before 1948 when Congress (white men) passed the Women's Armed Services Integration Act, I wouldn't have had the *freedom* to do so. Actually, when I joined the military in 2008, Don't Ask, Don't Tell was still in place—a policy that dishonorably discharged anyone in the military who revealed (intentionally or unintentionally) a non-heterosexual identity. Those discharged from the military with any type of discharge other than honorable have a higher risk of suicide (Reger et al.). More so, I was limited to the jobs I could enlist into when I joined in 2008. It wasn't until 2013 that the Combat Exclusion Policy barring women from direct combat jobs in the military was lifted (by men) and not until 2016 when it finally began to go into effect. If I was a black man serving in the military before 1948 when Executive Order 9981 (signed by a white man) went into effect, I likely would have been serving in an all-black unit in a job that had me directly on the front lines of combat action.

We do not *all* have the same amount of freedom to live our lives how we choose. We do not *all* have the same amount of access to the American way of life. So *now*, when I think about being a *guardian of freedom and the American way of life*, I realize I don't want to be a guardian of *this* American way of life. Sure, we've "come a long way" in that now as a woman I can join the military and black people serve alongside white people. But the reverberations of this system are still felt today. One in four women in the military experienced severe and persistent sexual harassment or gender discrimination in 2016 (Brignone). *I am one of those women*. Black people in the military *today* experience bias in getting promoted, discrimination in the military justice system, and poorer healthcare if they experience Post-Traumatic Stress Disorder (PTSD) (Burk and Espinoza). *Blinded by my own conditioning of white supremacy growing up, I contributed to that racialized bias as a white woman in the military*. The U.S. Military was first founded and organized to colonize indigenous native people. *What is the freedom and American way of life we're guarding?* Now, I'm much more reflective of my role in maintaining the oppressive and hegemonic systems that undergird our society.

Alas, with this *new* perspective, I also fully recognize that it is *because of the military* that I now have these tools to think critically *about the military*. Uncle Sam *got me out of* where I come from. But what did he bring me *up into*? And *what did it cost me to get here? What did Uncle Sam take from me, and what did he give me?* I continue to walk the line between two oppositional modes of thinking:

> I am *for* the military
> or
> I am *against* the military.

144   J. R. HUNNICUTT

Freedom Isn't Free

I cringe a little when I read the Soldier's Creed now. And yet, despite cringing, I could still stand up right now, over ten years later, snap to the position of attention, recite this creed from memory, *and still feel a sense of pride* while doing so. *Pride and shame? Confusion?* I don't know any more—what *freedom* did I guard? What does *freedom* really mean?

Michael Calvin McGee says the terms "freedom" and "liberty" are *ideographs*. *Ideographs* are words/phrases that are "the basic structural elements, the building blocks, of ideology"; they are intricately linked to culture (McGee, 7). Ideographs are words/terms that incite community and shared meaning. Driven by the need to explain human collective consciousness (or political consciousness), McGee seeks to understand how and why collective groups of people think and believe the same things in the same ways. He is guided by the assumption that human beings think and behave differently in isolation than in a collective. Following this assumption, collective consciousness, then, is composed of a falsity, a mistruth, a manipulation. The idea here is that we are conditioned/taught/ socialized from birth to think/behave/act in certain ways that are culturally bound and as such, "pure thought" does not exist. The "falsity" is in the conditioning/teaching/socializing. The essential question McGee seeks to answer is how such conditioning happens to incite political consciousness. *What causes/drives/shapes collective thinking?* McGee explains how within the dominant scholarly inquiries seeking to explain such collective consciousness, two primary modes of thought exist: 1) Materialists argue collective thinking/behaving is formed by/through *ideologies*; 2) Symbolists believe collective thinking/behaving is formed through *myth*— through the stories told and passed down through time and culture. McGee, however, argues collective consciousness is formed not necessarily through ideology *or* myth—but through *both*. McGee goes on to explore the differences between ideology and myth before describing how an *ideograph* is a word/term in which symbolism (myth) supplements, rather than competes with, ideologies shaping political consciousness. Ideographs contain both.

McGee explains how viewing collective thinking as being formed by ideology necessitates taking a moral stance with the goal being to reveal the falsity of the ideology and move toward a "true consciousness" (i.e., closer to social justice/equality). On the other hand, viewing it as myth is amoral because myths are stories with lessons of redemption and therefore do not require taking a moral stance. Both forms contain a falsity, but myths don't drive us to want to make change in the way that unmasking ideologies do. The difference is in the rhetoric—both ideologies and myths condition/shape the ways we think and behave. For example, *Veterans who have gone to war are broken and have PTSD*. This is an ideology—it's a dominant/common way people think about Veterans in the U.S. This ideology often incites taking a moral stance—*not all Veterans who went to war are broken or have PTSD*.

However, this way of thinking is also influenced through myth—we watch movies about and see reports in the media about Veterans who went to war and are now broken and have PTSD. We don't necessarily feel incited to take moral stances with these movies and media because they are presented through story and often related to historical events in time. In this example, when broken war Veterans with PTSD is presented as myth, I don't question it because it's rooted in story/history/time. However, when *Veterans who went to war are broken and have PTSD* emerges in a conversation I'm having, I work to reveal the falsity of that ideology: *not all Veterans who went to war are broken and/or have PTSD*. The rhetorical form the conditioning takes *matters*. The point is that whether it appears through myth or ideology dictates whether I am motivated to take a moral stance or view it as amoral or not. What McGee teaches us about collective thinking, however, is that there are words/phrases in our language that are indeed ideologies that contain a falsity but are presented only as myth through story/history/time/place. These *ideographs* are thus powerful ideologies, rooted in discourse yet clouted in myth, and so are rarely thought of as something to contest.

Ideographs are "building blocks" of ideologies, blanketed in the rhetorical language of myth; *ideographs are ideologies told through stories*. Because ideographs are both—they become powerful ideologies which are positioned as amoral because they are rhetorically used to story history (you don't have to take a moral stance and prove it's false because it's understood through story rooted in time/history/place). An ideograph is bound within the culture it defines. The nature of an ideograph is being a common denominator in usage throughout time. An ideograph should be understood vertically, in history, related to events in time. In other words, if I wanted to understand how the word "freedom" came to mean what it means within the U.S. (and became an ideograph), I would look back through dictionaries and encyclopedias to find the earliest usages and references of the word within U.S. historical context. I would come to understand the word and its meaning through understanding how it was used to describe cultural events throughout time and history. McGee explains,

> To learn the meaning of the ideographs "freedom" and "patriotism," for example, most of us swallowed the tale of Patrick Henry's defiant speech to the Virginia House of Burgesses: "I know not what course others may take, but as for me, give me liberty or give me death!" These specific words, of course, were concocted by the historian William Wirt and not by Governor Henry. Wirt's intention was to provide a model for "the young men of Virginia," asking them to copy Henry's virtues and avoid his vices. Fabricated events and words meant little, not because Wirt was uninterested in the truth of what really happened to Henry, but rather because what he wrote about was the definition of essential ideographs. His was a task of socialization, an exercise in epideictic rhetoric, providing the youth of his age (and of our own) with general knowledge of ideographic touchstones so that they might be able to make, or comprehend, judgements of public motives and of their own civic duty. (14)

We understand what freedom is and means through how we have learned about it in history, related to time and events, namely within education systems. In my middle school social studies classes, I learned about Christopher Columbus and how he "discovered America." I learned about Thanksgiving and about how the pilgrims and "Indians" broke bread over a shared table. I learned about how the U.S. Military formed to fight for our freedom against the tyranny of Great Britain! I learned the phrase, "Give me liberty or give me death!" I was taught that the Civil War was about *freeing* the slaves and about when woman gained the *freedom* to vote. I was told how we fought in WWII to defend our *freedom* after the attack on Pearl Harbor and to help *free* the Jews from the Nazis. I learned about the Vietnam War differently, because of how much it was protested and how the Veterans were treated when they returned home—*freedom* feels more absent from this what I remember of the rhetoric of this war compared to others. Rhetoric surrounding the post-9/11 wars, however, centers on *freedom* from terrorism, especially since the attack on U.S. mainland in 2001.

We understand freedom both through its ideographical form in culture and through our own our social identities. Freedom as contextualized within U.S. culture, and especially within U.S. Military culture (the two are not mutually exclusive), represents the "American way of life." *I am a guardian of freedom and the American way of life*. Again, the inherent assumption is that we have a choice to *freely* live life. Freedom is an ideograph, though; it gains its meaning through how it is recorded/told throughout history related to events in time. In the U.S., we understand freedom through the lens in which it is written. As a white woman in the south, I grew up reading about and learning that the U.S. Military formed to fight for our freedom against Britain. I did *not* learn *that the very formation of the first forms of organized militarism in what is now the U.S. was for the explicit purpose of colonizing Indigenous people for the claim of power, land, and resources* (Grenier).

Further, unaware of my white, Christian, cisgender, heterosexual, able-bodied privileges, I always understood that having *freedom* meant being able to live my life the way I want, *freely* (rhetoric of the *American way of life*). The only inhibitions on my individual *freedom* I ever remember feeling was related to being a woman and growing up in a low-income family within intergenerational trauma. Joining the military gave me access to redemption for the latter two. The military *freed* me from my adverse life circumstances. I learned that freedom redeems and that the U.S. Military—*my* Uncle Sam—fights for and represents such freedom, *not* takes away freedom. The point is that during military IET—when being imprinted with creeds that contain ideographs such as *freedom*—there is an assumption of shared meaning. This shared meaning and purpose of being a "guardian of freedom and the American way of life" is a "building block" of military culture and the military institution. This shared meaning is conditioned and becomes part of our *very being* through sacred liminality, especially through training tactics such as Army Greens and Battle Buddies.

But this meaning is false. The shared meaning *is false*. The shared meaning assumes we all experience these concepts in the same way—it assumes *we are all the same*. It promotes collectivism and homogeny rather than recognizing individuality, perpetuating powerful ideologies of color and gender blindness (DiAngelo). The U.S. Military first formed to colonize indigenous people, not fight for our freedom against Britain. We formed because of settler colonialism. Settler colonialism is a "persistent societal structure" (Row and Tuck, 4). So, *does being a guardian of freedom and the American way of life really mean being a guardian of the persistent societal structure of settler colonialism?*

148   J. R. HUNNIECUTT

> I continue to walk the line:
> I am for the military
> or
> I am against the military.
> *This*
> is liminality.

Indeed, for me to claim the U.S. Military is a colonizing institution—especially as a Veteran of the U.S. Military—feels inherently unpatriotic. It *feels* like a *betrayal*. At the same time, as I continue to apply critical tools to understand the military institution and my experiences related to it, it *feels like Uncle Sam betrayed me*. This way of thinking critically about the U.S. Military is incredibly hard to do when the military is rooted in the ideograph of freedom because its power is in its ability to disguise as myth and therefore be positioned as amoral. *The military exists to defend, guard, and protect freedom.* Freedom has a shared meaning and that meaning is conditioned to *not* be critically questioned and assessed. Thus, the military is positioned as having a righteous mission of being a guardian of such freedom and the American way of life. *The military both redeems those who serve in it through sacred liminality of advancing into a higher structure, and those it serves through providing guardianship of freedom. Are part of the tensions of Veteran liminality about consistently molding and adapting to fit into an identity rooted and based in a falsity?*

My final point regarding freedom as an ideograph in the Soldier's Creed is to explain how this ideograph also functions to create a sort of hierarchy within military/Veteran culture. Again, we understand ideographs as they are written in history. As McGee explained regarding the ideographs of "freedom" and "patriotism," most of us learned the tale and associated phrase, "give me liberty or give me *death*." We are taught that freedom *is worth dying for*. The military conditions all recruits that the *ultimate sacrifice* for country is the sacrifice of one's *life* fighting for *freedom. I will always place the missions first. I will never accept defeat. I will never quit.* As part of the U.S. civilian and especially military culture, fighting and *dying* for freedom is redemptive. The military gives out medals, we have "gold star" military mothers and families, holidays, and national memorials and structures to honor our fallen heroes. The ultimate *hero* is one who *gave their life* for country. If one doesn't die fighting for freedom but was physically wounded fighting, they are also revered as *hero*—our wounded warriors (Blair). Beyond this, we have Veterans with invisible wounds and moral injuries—they are broken inside but physically unscathed (Litz et al.). However, because the military conditions us to be *disciplined, physically and mentally tough, trained, and proficient*, those with invisible wounds are not positioned as heroes as much as they are seen as mentally weak, broken, or angry and violent. This sets up a binary that many Veterans find themselves living between as we navigate this liminal identity: *we're heroes or we're broken. But what if we're neither? What if we're both?* Perhaps all of us who fall short of the ultimate sacrifice—loss of life fighting for freedom—feel some layer of guilt, shame, or regret for not having done enough. For those of us who served and did not die fighting for freedom, do we fall short of redemption? *Did we accomplish our mission? What did I ever do during my service to guard freedom and the American way of life? I never went to war. I was never wounded. The military did not break me; it redeemed me.*

FREEDOM?: GIVE ME LIBERTY (OF SELF) OR GIVE ME (PSYCHOLOGICAL) DEATH!

In the first part of this chapter, I highlighted how the military institutional artifact, The Soldier's Creed, works to shape perceptions of the military institution and service as redemptive and heroic, based on a shared cultural and historical meaning of *freedom*. The purpose of articulating freedom as an ideograph is (1) to articulate how a shared meaning and identity around the U.S. Military exists and to challenge it through revealing its falsity—we are *not* all the same and our intersecting identities such as race, gender, sexual orientation, ability, and class (Crenshaw) all impact our relationship to *freedom*; and (2) to highlight how freedom as an ideograph functions to create a type of Veteran identity hierarchy (this concept is further articulated in Chap. 7). *True heroes gave their life defending freedom. True Veterans have gone to war and been in combat.* As explained in Chap. 2, reintegration is mostly conceptualized as being about *post-war* struggles rather than social and identity implications of belonging to and separating from the military institution (Zogas). However, during IET and time in service, we are conditioned to embody a collective identity with a collective mission and shared meaning about such mission. During IET, we go through sacred liminality and are imprinted with this identity, mission, and shared meaning. Throughout institutionalized liminality during TIS, conditioning continues to happen as we consistently work to

150   J. R. HUNNIECUTT

embody such identity, mission, and meaning, sometimes also finding ways to resist. Finally, during military transition experiences, we carry with us the identity, mission, and shared meaning of the U.S. Military institution into the Veteran identity, which is situated between military and civilian societal structures and systems.

In the next half of this chapter, I center institutional artifacts of the "Army Green" uniform/concept and "battle buddies" as a concept to further illuminate how such conditioning happens in IET, TIS, and then shapes Veteran identity tensions during experiences of transition, particularly transition out of military service. Starting with IET, I first show how the concepts of "Army Green" and "battle buddies" function as powerful discourses in Army culture that condition us to see, think, and act as if we are all the same and dismiss difference (race, gender, sexual orientation). I show how I was formed to be Army Green but nonetheless still felt and saw difference in myself and in my battle buddies. Next, I illustrate how during TIS, we adapt to mold into Army Green, or resist, and either way—suffer the consequences and loss of individual *freedom*. Finally, I explain how this tension continues through the transition from Service Member to Veteran identity during reintegration post-separation, illuminating how you *can't go back* once imprinted with the persistent social structure of the U.S. Military institution during sacred liminality of IET and institutionalized liminality of TIS. Throughout each section, I rely on additional artifacts such as journal entries from IET as well as my own body as an artifact to further illustrate identity tensions rooted in conditioning surrounding the artifacts of The Soldier's Creed, Army Greens, and Battle Buddies.

Assimilating

When I was in BCT, the Drill Sergeants used to tell us we were all "Army Green." They told us that when we wear the uniform, we're not male, female, black, or white—we're *soldiers*—we're all *green*, which is a rhetoric of color and gender blindness and erases all issues of power. In another book chapter where I write about my experiences of militarizing my femininity, I share my memory the first time I received my Army Green uniform during my IET:

> I remember when I was first issued my uniforms in BCT. I stood in an assembly line, with both male and female soldiers, waiting to step forward

so my size could be determined and then I could be issued uniforms. I remember stepping forward and standing in front of a male Drill Sergeant who was seated at a desk in front of me. I waited to be asked my size, which I knew for this particular uniform was a small, as I had uniforms back home I had worn for months during my recruit sustainment training I went through before shipping out to BCT—uniforms that were a comfortable size small. "What size?" he asked without looking up. "Size small, Drill Sergeant" I replied with the volume and enthusiasm of a new soldier. He looked up. He looked me up. And then he looked me down. Up and down. "Medium," he called over his left shoulder. And the female supply Sergeant from the back brought me size medium uniforms. I tell this story to illuminate a way in which the military worked to dis-identify my femininity during the socialization process into the US Army. Having pants that were too big served to be one of my most annoying experiences in all of BCT. I wore those too-big of pants everywhere and every single time I pulled my belt tighter or held my pants up with my hands as marched, ran, or crawled, I was reminded of what I am and what I am not—of what I was trying to become. I remembered that I am not to show my body—the body of a female. What is the message? We are all soldiers and we all wear the same uniform—a uniform that when put on, dismisses any identities that may serve as a contradiction. (Hunniecutt 50).

The Army Green uniform is the actual ACU, but the term "Army Green" represents more than the physical uniform itself. I will *always* maintain my arms, my equipment, and my *self*. Not *just* while in uniform and not just my arms and my equipment. I will *always* maintain *my self*. During my sacred liminal experience of basic training, it was the militarizing of my femininity as a cisgender woman where I felt the most tension in *maintaining my self*. I felt how my female-ness did not fit. I knew that we were *all the same* and that I wore the uniform just like the males there—but I could noticeably feel how my gender did not fit into the Army Greens. During my TIS, putting the uniform on became a sort of monthly ritual for me. A day or two before drill, I would remove any nail polish or jewelry I had on, and I would make sure my hair color was within regulation (and cut if it was too short to be pulled back into a bun). There's an entire manual of Army regulations that tell us how to dress and groom ourselves.

The morning of drill, I would put on about 1/3 of the make-up that I wore every other day. I even had specific underwear and bras that I reserved only for my ACUs; they were black, white, or tan—the only colors we were allowed to wear in basic training. The uniform fit terribly; it's not made for a woman's body. Once I heard the Army was researching a uniform for women that would fit us better, but I never actually saw one (and I worked in supply and had access to all the new gear and uniforms we routinely got). The size small pants fit me the best, despite being a little snug around my hips. The waist was always too big … but there was never enough room for my hips. The fabric was starchy and itchy. I didn't mind the patrol cap we wore (only when outside) though. *I always felt a little bit like a badass when I had my patrol cap on.* Putting the uniform on was like stepping into another identity. When drill weekend rolled around, I would tell my civilian family and friends it was time for me to go "play Army." I never felt *feminine* wearing the uniform. I didn't feel confident *as a woman* when I had the uniform on. I felt like "woman" was something my uniform was designed and intended to hide. I did feel something else when I wore it, though. I felt *elevated* in another way. Like I was stepping into an identity that was redeemed, heroic, and savior-like. To feel this way though, I had to adapt; I had to constantly shift in and out. I couldn't be both; *I couldn't be feminine and be soldier.*

As Brownson (2014) explained, "females in the military consciously adopt gender strategies to manipulate other actors' perceptions of them" (p. 783). In my experience of IET, I was directly taught to dis-identify with femininity in order to fit. Brownson (2014) found "failure or misuse of a female's biology in any of the three categories of physical fitness, personal/sexual relationships, and professional/occupational obligations separates her distinctly from male [Marines]" (p. 773). Through IET and during my TIS, I regularly and routinely managed my femininity. As a woman, I had to wear long spandex under the shorts of my physical training uniform (the males did not). In basic training, my Drill Sergeants confiscated the female recruits' razors and regularly inspected our body hair to make sure we were not shaving; *my body no longer belonged to me.* I was disciplined in basic for having a "high pitched voice," for moving my hips when I walked, and for smiling too much. All the while, my sexuality was always heightened because I was a woman in a man's military. My male peers (and leadership) flirted with me, objectified me, and urged me to still model cultural norms of femininity. On average, one in two women in the U.S. Military reports unwanted sexual harassment during their TIS (Wilson). *Me too.* Though I wouldn't have named it as sexual harassment at the time, the story I shared in Chap. 1 about SGT Kaye making a sexually inappropriate comment to me during an Annual Training with my unit is a concrete example of this. This experience of sexual violation has an impact.

For me to always *maintain my self* and to be an *expert* and a *professional* in the U.S. Army to fit into the Army Greens, I had to adapt and mold my performance of femininity to fit the institutional military identity—a hyper-masculine identity that dismisses difference consistently and intentionally. They tell us we are all Army Green—but I both felt that I was different because I'm a woman. Further, I still saw difference in others; I still saw *black and white*. As a 19-year-old girl raised under the shadow of the rebel flag in the U.S.' Deep South, in basic training, *I still saw race.*

March 18, 2009

Journal from Basic Training

Today was a shitty day. Homesick. The girls in my platoon were all being bitches. Honestly I just really felt kind of alone all day. Being upset with the people here I guess triggered the homesickness. What is it with black girls? I've been sheltered for too much of my life. It's like they come in packs. And they're loud and rude and but into other people's business they have nothing to do with. The white girls here don't act like that. I feel like I'm so much more mature in that sense. There's a way to go about everything. I dunno, like I said, I'm not even used to being around black girls at all really. Maybe it's just how they are. Fuck it though, I'm here for three more weeks. I don't want to make enemies in my platoon and be miserable for the next three weeks. Just gotta finish it out. I'll be home soon enough. Then I'll have to adapt again. Find my new place in my old world. I hope it's not as hard as adapting to this, here. I hope I've changed for the better. I wonder how I've changed. I know that I have a greater appreciation for the little things in life. I'm more patriotic, I'm happy to be part of something serving my country. Before I came here, the American flag didn't mean nearly as much. I have more self-respect now too. I think also that I'm not gonna be nearly as lazy. Hopefully I'll be more motivated in every aspect of my life, school, work, fitness, my relationships.

I was a white girl from the south who grew up in white isolation (DiAngelo) embedded in discourses of white supremacy, conservatism, and patriarchy. *My grandfather wouldn't let my biracial black cousin come to the family cookouts, the black high school student at my school always got in trouble, and now these black girls in basic were being "loud and rude" and butting into my business.* Before I had the tools to think critically about race, I read black bodies as unruly and undisciplined (Yancy). Despite spending several weeks in basic training being conditioned with the ideology of color blindness as we were all *Army Green,* I was *still a prejudiced white girl from the south.* This journal entry is saturated with discourses of white supremacy and my perception then was that my way of interacting in the world (as a white person) was superior (*The white girls here don't act like that*). We were supposed to all be green—but I still saw *black* and *white.* I note throughout the entry things like, "I've been sheltered for too much of my life," and "Like I said, I'm not even used to being around black girls at all really." I recognized that I come from an area that is 90% white ("ARC study") and have been "sheltered" from diversity but made no attempt to think critically about my thoughts and behaviors as a white woman. *We were all Army Green.* Instead, I dismissed it (*Fuck it though*), and then highlighted the necessity of having to communicate across difference so that I was not *miserable for the next three weeks,* again centering myself. I was aware at this point of how being a woman in the military meant you had to modify yourself to fit. I, if even on a subconscious level, knew that the Army Green uniform did not fit me like it fit the men there. I was not yet aware, however, of my expected performance of *white* femininity both in larger society and in the military space in particular. I did not yet realize or understand, that for people of color—and for transgender or LGBTQ SMs—the Army Green fit *even less* than it did on me.

The second part of this journal entry reflects the ideological assumptions that underlie the Soldier's Creed. *I see difference but ignore it because it prevents me from succeeding.* "Just finish it out." *I'm being redeemed to something better.* This mirrors rhetoric of the American Dream—*just work hard and you can achieve;* it ignores and erases structural barriers. I knew that I was "changed for the better" somehow. But I wondered *how.* I felt purpose, patriotism, and pride for "serving my country." The *flag now meant more to me* than it did before I experienced the sacred rites of passage of IET into the U.S. Army—sacred liminality. I knew that I was moving up and out of my "old world." I was moving into a *higher* structure and system. Simultaneously, I wrote of struggle in this entry. I recognized I would have to "find my new place in my old world" and hoped it would not be "as hard as adapting to this, here." What I did not yet see or understand was how "changing for the better" meant sacrificing and losing my individual self, outside of what I was experiencing during that time in the sacred liminal space of IET. I was dismissing and ignoring structural barriers. There, it was worth it for me to mold and sacrifice my sense of self because I was being "endowed with additional powers to enable [me] to cope with [my] new station in life" (Turner 96). The suppression of self then felt worth it. It didn't feel like a loss—it felt like a *gain*. However, as I aggregated from the sacred liminal space of IET and transitioned into institutionalized liminality when I joined my NG unit, I started to see and feel the structural barriers; I became much more aware of how much of my individual self I was sacrificing to be a *guardian of freedom and the American way of life*.

Serving

August 19, 2009

I HATE being here. Being home, back in school. What the hell's wrong with me?! When I was there I absolutely could not wait to get home and now that I'm home I don't want to be here. I'd rather be there. Without all of this. None of this matters. I feel depressed. I want to cry. I want to be with my Army friends. I want to go to Afghanistan with them. Would I be happy in Afghanistan though? It'd be worse than this when I got home. And it's like no one understands. I don't even understand. I can't even explain it. I'm miserable. So unhappy. I want to be happy. I'm trying. Maybe I should just have a better attitude. It's hard. They should tell you this when you enlist. That the transition back to civilian life is harder than the transition to Army life.

This second journal entry was written a few months after I had completed IET and illustrates a state of psychological darkness—an identity crisis of sorts—related to a shift in social systems and consequently feeling a lack of belonging overall. I felt this way after *returning home from being in IET* for nearly five consecutive months. It's important to point out this way of feeling isolated, misunderstood, disconnected, and unhappy *is not isolated* to transitioning home from war or even out of military service altogether—it's prevalent during *any type* of transition between military structure and an outside system. Although, type of service does matter: Active duty SMs are sent to a duty station upon completing IET and NG/ Reserve return to their home state and begin monthly drilling with the unit they signed up to join. In other words, active duty SMs transition from IET to another full-time, all-encompassing military structure and NG/Reservist SMs transition from IET back to their civilian systems. NG

156   J. R. HUNNICUTT

and Reserve SMs constantly move between civilian and military structures, acting as sort of "transmigrants" in the form of social hybrids bridging the civilian/military worlds (Lomsky-Feder, Gazit, and Ben-Ari).

This journal entry represents a social process and outcome that encompasses transitioning between the structure of the U.S. Military institution and an outside system as a National Guard soldier still maintaining a civilian life. Though one form of reintegration cannot be applicable to all persons/experiences (Lazier et al.), there is a commonality of adaptation among all forms of military transitionary experiences—specifically, *social* adaptation. Both this entry and the previously shared journal entry when I was still in basic training speak to adapting and modifying the self to fit into a new structure. They both also represent structural barriers I faced: during IET, I had to mold my civilian feminine self to fit the military identity; during TIS, I had to continue to mold my civilian feminine self to fit the military identity while simultaneously adapting my now militarized self to fit into my civilian life outside of the military. I was always "neither here nor there … betwixt and between the positions assigned and arrayed by law, custom, convention, and ceremony" (Turner 95).

In the first journal entry I wrote, "I hope it's not as hard as adapting to this, here" when thinking about being home again. I noted how I had to adapt to the military system there at basic. Likewise, in the second entry from after I had returned home, I felt anger, guilt, and shame for my inability to adapt back to my old social systems. I was struggling to modify my new militarized self to fit into my old civilian social structures. I perceived this struggle to be something I should not have been experiencing, as illustrated in how I wrote, "What the hell's wrong with me?!" This sentiment that something was wrong for me for struggling with this adaptation is in line with military psychological traits of secrecy, stoicism, and denial (Hall). I felt I was in "a vague and undetermined place created by the emotional residue of an unnatural boundary … a constant state of transition," what Anzaldúa refers to as a "borderland" (25). *This* is institutionalized liminality—a constant state of transition—a perpetual process of modifying the self to fit into social structures.

September 12, 2012
    Public note I wrote on my Facebook profile
    Cost of FreedomI'm wondering right now about freedom, about the
    cost of freedom, about who is really free. After my ex-boyfriend and I broke
    up I swore to myself I would never date anyone in the military again. I

decided I was done competing with Uncle Sam, as silly as that may seem. But for those of you who have never been with someone who belongs to some branch of the military or have never seen a military relationship up close and personal, there are sacrifices that have to be made that civilian couples don't typically have to encounter. With my ex-boyfriend there was a constant, underlying, never ending fear. Fear of when he would have to go. Fear of if and when he did go, would he come back. Fear of having to go days and weeks without talking to him, without knowing where he was or if he was safe. In a sense I felt like I never really had him, had all of him, wholly and completely. Because he didn't have all of himself to give to me. I'm in the same boat myself though, as part of the military. You see, when you join the armed forces, you sign part of your self away. The government owns you, in a sense. Make what you want of it, but it's true. I could get a call right now, right this very second, and have to leave. Have to drop out of school, have to leave my job, have to hug my parents and my friends and my boyfriend goodbye and go somewhere, to a foreign land, to "defend" the freedoms we're all so leisurely enjoying. What does that mean, though? What does it mean for those whom I commit myself into a serious relationship with? It means I can't really give all of my own self to them. Because, well, I don't own all of that self to give. The government compensates us for our time and our service, yes. But can they really compensate us for the ownership of our self? Hell, in a drastic light, it's a form of prostitution. The government pays me and when they want and how they want, I will do exactly what they want. At the cost of others, of all the others who know and love me. Could you sign? Give you give up ownership of your very self to "defend" the freedoms we all enjoy here in the United States? If you ever consider joining, be sure you can answer these questions.

At the time of writing this, I had been part of my NG unit for roughly three years. I was living within institutionalized liminality and drastically feeling the loss of freedom of individual self. My tone in this writing is very different than my tone in the journal entry from Basic Training. This reflection does not indicate feelings of freedom and redemption. Rather, this entry illustrates how I was struggling with the *costs* of being a *guardian of freedom and the American way of life*. I was still at this point conceptualizing freedom as something we are "so leisurely enjoying" and seeing it as something that we all have equal access to here in the U.S. As indicated by the quotation marks around the word "defend," however, I was beginning to question the nature of the military I belonged to as being redemptive. The focus, tone, and purpose of including this artifact is primarily to exemplify the extreme loss of self I felt being part of the military during my TIS of institutionalized liminality. This artifact is an example of how the macro was interacting with the micro for me. The more I felt the constraints of my own freedom to live my life how I chose, the more I began to question, "Who is really free?"

And the more I questioned, the more I wanted to do something about it. Michel Foucault teaches us that where there is power, there is resistance. I found miniscule ways to resist during my TIS—or at least *tried* to. I got my nose pierced about a year or so before my ETS (End of Time in Service) date. As I shared previously, that didn't go over so well. I was made to remove it at the first drill I attended after I got it pierced (my nude-colored nose ring didn't work) and it closed up immediately. It seems menial, but this is one small example of the many "little things"— the choices of individual expression of self—that I had to sacrifice during my TIS to adapt and fit into the Army Greens. I could try to resist as much as I wanted when I was on civilian time and not at drill, but nonetheless, what I did in my civilian life was still dictated by my military identity. The military was all-encompassing, even as a NG civilian-soldier.

Separating

I question sometimes if making an active choice to end your time in service and separate from the military institution is the ultimate form of resistance for SMs. They did everything they could to keep me in. It costs the military less to keep us once we are trained than it does to replace us with someone new. They dangled large cash bonuses and more student-loan repayment money in front of me. I was offered a promotion, a list of schools I could attend for more training, and the option to change jobs and even advance from enlisted to officer. I turned it all down. I was done. I reaped the benefits I initially joined to get, and I was done living my life with Uncle Sam breathing down my neck.

During IET and my first couple of years in my unit, the uniform was uncomfortable to wear, yes, but it felt worth it because the uniform made me feel redeeming, heroic, and like I was doing something honorable and courageous. *I was willing to go to war to be a guardian of freedom and the American way of life.* The more time I spent within the institutionalized liminality of TIS, however, the more I felt the inequity inherent in the military social structure. As a NG SM, I constantly wove in out of military and civilian systems and the more time I spent in this liminal space, the more uncomfortable and intolerable the Army Green uniform became for me. I felt dissonance being a woman in the U.S. Army. I had to sacrifice my own individual expression of femininity to be part of the military institution. When I chose to get out, I knew I was giving up both the structure and the community the military provided me, but it was worth it to have the "freedom" once again to be whoever I wanted to be. When I was in sacred liminality of IET, the self-sacrifice was worth it because I was working toward something—a higher structure—I was going to be a soldier. However, after spending time in institutionalized liminality as a soldier during TIS, I came to feel the *little things*—freedom of choice to be who I wanted to be—were no longer worth sacrificing for the community and structure the military provided me. The more I saw and felt the inequities within the military system, the more I wanted to resist. One way I did that was through seeking ways to reclaim my body.

Nancy Krierger teaches us that bodies "bear the mark of both conscious and unconscious processes" (351). As Ronald Pelias explains, "individual bodies provide a potent database for understanding the political and that hegemonic systems write on individual bodies" (420). Turner suggests that "the wisdom that is imparted in sacred liminality is not just an aggregation of words and sentences; it has ontological value, it refashions the very being of the neophyte" (105). I could feel the military *owned* me and I wanted to find small ways to reclaim agency over myself, my body and my *very being*. In addition to my *freedom ring*, I also reclaimed my body by getting a tattoo after I finished IET.

My sister and I wanted to get our first tattoos together, but we didn't decide on what we wanted to get until a couple months before I shipped out to basic training. I couldn't get a tattoo because my body had to be in the exact condition it was when I shipped to basic as it was when I went through the Military Entrance Processing Station (MEPS) and signed my enlistment contract. It was out of regulation for me to get a tattoo then. *My body wasn't my own to do what I pleased with anymore. Uncle Sam was all-compassing.* So, we had to wait. The second day I was home after I graduated from my job training in AIT, my sister and I went and got our tattoos (Fig. 6.1).

When SMs and Veterans are on long periods of leave or separate from service completely, we're known to do things like get tattoos (Pionke and Osborne) or especially for men, grow beards (Vest). This isn't just limited to when we return home from combat. Given the social implications of joining and belonging to the military institution, this desire to mark, reclaim, and ritualize our self and bodies can be seen throughout all

Fig. 6.1 Body
Two photos side by side; photo on the left is of me saluting while in the Army Combat Uniform and photo on the right is of me in civilian clothing and pulling up my t-shirt to reveal a fresh tattoo of a flower on my hip

military transitionary experiences, including after completing IET and between drills as a NG Service Member (Vest). It's not just about experiences we may or may not have at war—it's about how being in the military intricately becomes part of who we are—our minds, bodies, and souls. Thus, during periods of transition when we're between the military and outside systems, we find small ways to take our bodies back. But because *we can never go back*, there will always be traces. I never felt like I could ever be fully one or the other. I was always stuck *in between*. After I joined the Army, I drastically altered my performance of femininity in my civilian identities. I never again felt like I could completely and totally embody femininity without there still being this underlying, nagging layer of militarization. *I was militarized*. The military was in my *very being*. Likewise, I could never fully fit into the military identity either because I was a woman. It was about the *little things* for me; how Uncle Sam (the macro) wove into every area and component of my life (the micro)—from what underwear I wore to how many days of my life I walked in fear and guilt.

I believed that once I separated from service, these "little things" would instantly go away. I was a NG soldier, not active duty. I constantly shifted between the military and civilian life and so was in a constant ebb and flow. Even when I wasn't physically at drill—I had to always be mission-ready and available. Uncle Sam came first in my life over everything and everyone else. I felt it both psychologically and physiologically. *My body wasn't my own anymore.* I separated from the service fully realizing all it had given me, happy to leave behind what I was tired of giving, and confident I would not be negatively impacted since I never deployed or experienced military-related trauma (at the time, I didn't yet understand the impact of the sexual harassment I had experienced during service). Once I separated, I thought I would take the redemption with me and leave behind the constant back and forth of having to adapt between *who I wanted to be* and *who I had to be* in the military. Yet as illustrated in Chap. 2, once I got out, I experienced an identity crisis and an array of psychosocial struggles that many Service Members and Veterans face during periods of transition. I did not associate any of my challenges of that time as having to do with separating from the military though. On the contrary, when I initially separated from service, I viewed my time in the military as the most redemptive experience of my life.

As shared in Chap. 1, in my first quarter of my PhD program I took a class where I was assigned to create a visual narrative of a time in my life I experienced a form of redemption. I created an artifact (Fig. 6.2) representative of my military service.

That day in class, we sat with our tables arranged in a square, so we were all facing each other, and one by one had a "show and tell" with our Visual Narrative of Redemption artifacts. When it was my turn, I held up my paper for the class to see (Fig. 6.2). "My redemption is about my military service," I began.

"First, the background paper for the whole thing I like a lot because I think it looks like rays of light, which is a good image for redemption. On the left here is my old crest from my National Guard Unit in Virginia. The motto of the crest is 'Construct and Conquer.' We wore this crest as a patch on our uniform. Over the crest, I wrote the Soldier's Creed," I shared before reading the creed aloud.

"Wow, that doesn't leave much room for failure," my professor said once I finished.

Fig. 6.2 Visual Narrative of Redemption
Picture of tan stock paper with white lines on it resembling sun rays. A military crest cutout is on the left side of the paper and shows a red background with a spear breaking through a chain. The crest has handwriting over it. Two cut out drawings of people are on the right; one is of me in military uniform and the other of me in cheerleading uniform

"That's the Army," I shrugged my shoulders and then continued to describe the rest of my artifact.

I drew two versions of myself here on the other side—me as a college cheerleader, which is what I was before I joined, then me as a soldier. In the military, you are part of a collective and we don't use our first names. So, I wrote my rank and last name under that version of myself and wrote 'civilian-soldier' because I was National Guard not active duty. Under the cheerleader

6 YOU CAN'T GO BACK   163

version, I wrote my first and last name and wrote 'college student, cheerleader, civilian' because those were my primary identities before I joined. In the cheerleader me, I used my favorite color—purple—as background paper and drew myself as feminine with my hair down, a big bow and smile, and my hands gently folded in front of my body. In the soldier version, I used green—the color of the Army—and drew myself in uniform, with my hair back, a stoic look on my face not showing emotion, and my hand on my hip indicating a sense of redemption, heroism, and pride.

I had gone from being a college cheerleader at a private, Christian college in rural Appalachia—an epitome of white femininity—to wearing Army Green as a soldier and *guardian of freedom and the American way of life*. It's interesting that I chose to depict myself as a cheerleader in the civilian image (Fig. 6.2), as this is perhaps the most drastic opposition in my social identity that I remember feeling. I used to joke about how I "traded in my pom-poms for combat boots and an M16." I also felt very disconnected from my college friends when I returned home from IET (as reflected in the journal entry from 8/19/09)—college friends that I was on the cheerleading team with. I believe this represents the way I felt about femininity at this time and is a consequence of military conditioning to minimize and suppress performances of femininity in order to mold into the hyper-masculine soldier identity. This was because, before even officially signing the dotted line and joining, I felt both the need to hide *and* the heightened visibility of my femininity in the military.

This artifact (Fig. 6.2) was made after I had separated from service, however. I chose to leave the military to regain freedom of self-expression; I assumed I would not feel a need to ever militarize my femininity again after the final time I wore the Army Green uniform. I had left all of those "little things" behind me when I separated, *I never went to war and wasn't wounded*. During my sacred liminal experience of IET, I felt redeemed—both redeemed personally because of what the military was giving me (community, structure, upward mobility), and redeemed within my social structures as I was now a *guardian of freedom and the American way of life*. I served our country and was therefore perceived as a *hero*. During my time in service, however, I did not feel like a hero, nor did I feel redeemed; I started to feel the inequities—I felt like I was giving up *my freedom* to be *a guardian of freedom*. After I separated, I believed that feeling of sacrificing my own freedom would go away. I knew I was no *hero* because I never went to war. I also knew I was not *broken*, because I never went to war.

The only way I knew how to reflect on my military service was through the lens of redemption—through the color of *Army green*. What I did not realize then, and what research on military/Veteran suicides, reintegration and identity fails to capture, is that once we put the Army Greens on, *we can never fully take them off.*

The purpose of this chapter was to explore how experiences of U.S. Military Veteran reintegration might be shaped by an individual's sacred liminal experience of military initial entry training as well as their institutionalized liminal experience of belonging to the military institution. I relied primarily on the Army institutional artifact of The Soldier's Creed to question and interpret how organizational power relations affect and shape my individual identities (Fox). When we go through military IET, we're imprinted with hegemonic discourses of nationalism, patriotism, and stoicism. Deep-rooted ideographs of "freedom" perpetuate a dominant way of thinking about the U.S. Military as a type of "savior" and idolized institution that *serves the people and guards the American way of life.* As ideographs are the "building blocks of ideologies," they contain a falsity. The U.S. Military originally formed for settler colonialism. Therefore, characteristics of the soldier and the Veteran identity are rooted in ideologies of settler colonialism—that is, white nationalism. The U.S. Military originated and formed to colonize people of color, like indigenous people and slaves (Grenier). With this history often hidden, however, discourses of pride and "service to the people" dominate the way most people think and talk about the military, especially in the post-9/11 era. *Give me freedom or give me death.* This ideograph undergirding military structure creates a Veteran identity hierarchy where dying fighting for "freedom" is revered as the highest level of heroism. *What freedom are we dying for?* We're conditioned to be loyal and to not question orders; to *always accomplish the mission.* To *never accept defeat.* To *never quit.* To *never lead a fallen comrade.*

One way this *imprinting* happens is through teaching concepts like Army Green and Battle Buddies (which perpetuate color and gender-blind ideologies and erase issues of power). As "artifacts play a generative role in autoethnographic practices" (Fox 124), my journal entries, notes, images, and class project all reflect the liminal spaces I moved between throughout my military transitionary experiences of IET, TIS, and separation after service. Further, they demonstrate structure around constraining and enabling of my identities *among and between* the military and outside systems. These artifacts "are not meant to metonymically reference the experiences of all [Veterans], nor do they completely represent my individual experiences" (Fox 125). They do, however, show how dominant ideologies surrounding [the] Veteran identity and reintegration causes tensions in [my] daily lived experiences.

I am No Hero, nor am I Wounded

Or am I? Within my first six months of separation from service, I suffered an identity crisis and experienced physiological darkness. I never deployed to war, I never served in combat, and I was never physically injured, and I *still* suffered an identity crisis when I separated from the military institution. Reintegration is not solely about post-war or combat difficulties; it's about the social implications of serving in and belonging to the military social structure. Veteran identity is a process and product of living among and between systems in a perpetual state of liminality (Turner). During sacred liminality of IET, we're imprinted with structure (The Soldier's Creed, Army Greens) and with community (Battle Buddies). The structure conditions us both psychologically (to view the military as a savior and guardian of freedom and our service in the military as personally redemptive) and physiologically (molding our bodies and performances of self-expression to fit Army Greens). We are socialized to be blind of difference: to suppress our own and to not see others. We're taught this is a good thing, as in the military, "who you are entirely depends on your willingness to surrender who you are" (Junger 176).

IET is when this socializing and imprinting primarily happens and then when we transition into our TIS, we shift into institutionalized liminality. Turner articulates how within institutionalized liminality, "transition has become a permanent condition" (109). During our TIS, because the U.S. Military is a total institution (Goffman), transition between the military system (structure and community) and outside systems *becomes a permanent condition.* As the military system is rooted in an ideograph of "freedom," it contains an inherent falsity. Therefore, *the Veteran identity is essentially a permanent condition of adapting to fit into a system that you will never fully fit into* (because of its falsity). Gloria Anzaldúa similarly refers to this state of institutionalized liminality when she writes about *borderlands:*

166 J. R. HUNNIECUTT

la mestiza is a product of the transfer of the cultural and spiritual values of one group to another ... Cradled in one culture, sandwiched between two cultures, straddling all three cultures and their value systems, la mestiza undergoes a struggle of flesh, a struggle of borders, and inner war. (100)

Finally, at some point, we all separate from service, which is when Veteran suicide susceptibility is highest (Reger et al.). It's not necessarily about what we did or didn't do during our time in service; it's about the loss of *structure* and *community*. This is a loss *we all feel* regardless of what our experiences of service entailed. It often manifests as *little things* as we find ways to resist and reclaim a sense of agency in our lives—our minds, bodies, and souls. But *halt*—we *can never go back*. The military is *intricately part of who we are*; it's part of our *very being*.

> We're *imprinted* to see it
> as *redemptive* and *heroic*.
> If we don't
> it's because we're *angry* or *broken*.
> If we're angry or broken
> it's from *war* and/or *combat*.

The military system is never addressed, never critiqued. The social implications of joining and belonging to the military social system are rarely accounted for. To create effective policies and programs to foster military transitionary processes that are not riddled with "psychological darkness," we need to better understand the *process* and *product* of reintegration—we need to understand it is NOT solely about war and combat experiences; it is *social*, and it is *communicative*. We need to view and conceptualize reintegration as a process of *social identity transformation*. We need new language and new conceptualizations of this experience. We need to *adapt* our understandings to *overcome* the barriers that prevent us from healing. We need *awareness* and we need *union*.

WORKS CITED

Anzaldúa, Gloria. *Borderlands: The New Mestiza/La Frontera* (4th ed.). Aunt Lute, 2012.
"ARC Study: Disproportionately High Rates of Substance Abuse in Appalachia." *Appalachian Regional Commission*. August 2008. www.arc.gov/news/article. asp?ARTICLE_ID=113

Blair, Elizabeth. "It's Not Rude: These Portraits of Wounded Vets are Meant to be Shared." *National Public Radio,* 2015. www.npr.org/2015/05/25/408505821/its-not-rude-these-portraits-of-wounded-vets-are-meant-to-be-stared-at?utm_source=facebook.com&utm_medium=social&utm_campaign=npr&utm_term=nprnews&utm_content=2

Brignone, Emily, et al. "Differential risk for homelessness among US male and female veterans with a positive screen for military sexual trauma." *JAMA Psychiatry,* vol. 73, no. 6, 2016, pp. 582–589.

Brownson, Connie. "The battle for equivalency: Female US Marines discuss sexuality, physical fitness, and military leadership." *Armed Forces & Society,* vol. 40, no. 4, 2014, pp. 765–788.

Burk, James, and Evelyn Espinoza. "Race relations within the US military." *Annual Review of Sociology,* vol. 38, 2012, pp. 401–422.

Calafell, Bernadette Marie. "(I)dentities: Considering Accountability, Reflexivity, and Intersectionality in the I and the We." *Liminalities: A Journal of Performance Studies,* vol. 9, no. 2, 2013, pp. 6–13.

Crenshaw, Kimberle. "Mapping the margins: Intersectionality, identity politics, and violence against women of color." *Stanford Law Review,* 1991, pp. 1241–1299.

DiAngelo, Robin. "White fragility." *The International Journal of Critical Pedagogy,* vol. 3, no. 3, 2011.

Foucault, Michel. "The history of sexuality: An introduction, volume I." *Trans. Robert Hurley.* New York: Vintage, 1990.

Fox, Ragan. "Tales of a fighting bobcat: An "auto-archaeology" of gay identity formation and maintenance." *Text and Performance Quarterly,* vol. 30, no. 2, 2010, pp. 122–142.

Goffman, Erving. "On the characteristics of total institutions." *Symposium on preventive and social psychiatry.* Washington, DC: Walter Reed Army Medical Centre, 1961.

Grenier, John. The first way of war: American war making on the frontier, pp. 1607–1814. *Cambridge University Press,* 2005.

Hall, Lynn K. "The Importance of Understanding Military Culture." *Social Work in Health Care,* vol. 50, no. 1, 2011, pp. 4–18.

Hunniecutt, Jeni. "Stroking my Rifle like the Body of a Woman: A Woman's Socialization into the U.S. Army." *Organizational Autoethnographies: Our Working Lives,* edited by Andrew Herrmann. Routledge, 2017, pp. 37–52.

Junger, Sebastian. Tribe: On homecoming and belonging. *Hachette,* UK, 2016.

Krieger, Nancy. "Embodiment: A Conceptual Glossary For Epidemiology." *Journal of Epidemiology & Community Health,* vol. 59, no. 5, 2005, pp. 350–355.

Lazier, Raun L., Amy Warnick Gawne, and Nathan S. Williamson. "Veteran Family Reintegration: Strategic Insights to Inform Stakeholders' Efforts." *Journal of Public and Nonprofit Affairs,* vol. 2, no. 1, 2016, pp. 48–57.

Litz, Brett T. et al. Moral injury and moral repair in war veterans: A preliminary model and intervention strategy. *Clinical Psychology Review*, vol. 29, 2009, pp. 695–706.

Loeb, Vernon. "Army plans steps to heighten "Warrior Ethos."." *The Washington Post*, 2003.

Lomsky-Feder, Edna, Nir Gazit, and Eyal Ben-Ari. "Reserve soldiers as transmigrants: Moving between the civilian and military worlds." *Armed Forces & Society*, vol. 34, no. 4, 2008, pp. 593–614.

McGee, Michael Calvin. "The "ideograph": A link between rhetoric and ideology." *Quarterly Journal of Speech*, vol. 66, no. 1, 1980, pp. 1–16.

Newlands, Emma. "Preparing and resisting the war body." *War and the Body: Militarization, Practice and Experience*, 2013, pp. 35–50.

Pelias, Ronald J. "Performative Writing as Scholarship: An Apology, An Argument, An Anecdote." *Cultural Studies ⟺ Critical Methodologies*, vol. 5, no. 4, 2005, pp. 415–424.

Pionke, J. J., and Nicholas J. Osborne. "Symbols of service: Oral histories of veterans tattoos as outreach." *College & Undergraduate Libraries*, 2018, pp. 1–9.

Reger, Mark A. et al. "Risk of Suicide Among US Military Service Members Following Operation Enduring Freedom or Operation Iraqi Freedom Deployment and Separation from the US Military." *JAMA Psychiatry*, vol. 72, no. 66, 2015, pp. 561–569.

Rowe, Aimee Carrillo, and Eve Tuck. "Settler colonialism and cultural studies: Ongoing settlement, cultural production, and resistance." *Cultural Studies↔ Critical Methodologies*, vol. 17, no. 1, 2017, pp. 3–13.

Turner, Victor. The Ritual Process: Structure and Anti-Structure. *Aldine de Gruyter*, 1969.

Vest, Bonnie M. "Citizen, soldier, or citizen-soldier? Negotiating identity in the US National Guard." *Armed Forces & Society*, vol. 39, no. 4, 2013, pp. 602–627.

Wilson, Laura C. "The prevalence of military sexual trauma: A meta-analysis." *Trauma, Violence, & Abuse*, vol. 19, no. 5, 2018, pp. 584–597.

Yancy, George. "Black Bodies, White Gazes: The Continuing Significance of Race in America." *Rowman & Littlefield*, 2016.

Zogas, Anna. "Costs of War: US Military Veterans' Difficult Transitions Back to Civilian Life and the VA's Response." *Watson Institute International & Public Affairs*, Brown University, 2017, pp. 1–14.

CHAPTER 7

Adapt and Overcome

Throughout this book, I have shared my story. I joined the military for access to a life better than what I knew as a 19-year-old girl living in rural Appalachia. I served for six years in the Virginia Army National Guard (NG), never deployed, and then chose to get out when my time was up. When I got out, I didn't expect to experience the psychological darkness, or psychosocial difficulties that I found myself in. I experienced a loss of both structure and community when I separated from service but didn't have the language or understanding around why this mattered and what it meant for my functioning, my relationships, and my mental health. I went through an identity crisis but didn't contribute it to separation from military service because I didn't consider myself a Veteran when I separated. My story of service didn't fit the dominant narrative of what I thought a Veteran was. Because I didn't identify, I didn't seek out help—I didn't look for, nor was I offered or even had access to resources that could have been helpful to me at that time.

As an academic who believes in the power of healing through writing, I turned to research for answers. I was guided by mentors and friends who could see in me what I could not yet see in myself. With their help, I found answers. I looked to research on Veteran suicides first—I sought to understand *why* so many Veterans were taking their own lives. *I sought to understand more about why SGT Baker died by suicide.* This research shocked me because of its incoherence at that time—there was no organized tracking system for Veteran suicides in place, the research was inconclusive and

© The Author(s), under exclusive license to Springer Nature Switzerland AG 2022
J. R. Hunniecutt, *Rethinking Reintegration and Veteran Identity*, https://doi.org/10.1007/978-3-030-93754-6_7

169

contradictory, and only war Veterans were included as participants in most of the research. It was the study by Reger et al. and their finding that suicide risk is not related to deployment but is about separating from service that shifted the direction I took in my own research.

If Veterans weren't committing suicide because of trauma from war, then what was going on? *I never deployed, so maybe the psychological darkness I experienced after I separated was related to my military service?* I realized that coming home from war and separating from service had one major thing in common: they were both forms of Veteran reintegration, so I turned to that research next. Much to my dismay, I found Veteran reintegration mirrored Veteran suicide research—it was exclusive and wasn't offering up many answers. *I did not see myself or my experiences of military service and reintegration represented in this research either.* Focusing exclusively on the experiences of reintegration post deployment from war, this body of work was also missing an important part by not exploring experiences of reintegration post separation. I especially knew this was true after reading Mark Reger and colleagues' finding that Veteran suicide susceptibility was related to reintegration post *separation* from service, *regardless of deployment experience or not.* I saw a big problem: both bodies of research attributed Veteran suicides and reintegration challenges as being about war and, specifically, combat experience. Even in research that highlights the importance of family and social relationships in reintegration, research participants were *exclusively war Veterans* and most of the research inquiries centered on coping with *war* experiences. If we only recruit *war* Veterans for *all* research done on Veteran suicides and Veteran reintegration, then inevitably the main conceptualizations and understandings of these phenomena will center on *war* and combat. At large, the research in these domains was failing to account for the social implications of joining, serving in, and then separating from the social structure of the U.S. Military institution; we have been missing *identity.*

A notable finding in the research on Veteran reintegration has been the lack of a coherent conceptualization, definition, and framework for reintegration. The commonality seems to be that there cannot be one single cohesive way to explain or understand reintegration because it is such an individuated, circumstantial, subjective experience. My goal for this book, then, is to present a new way of thinking about Veteran identity and experiences of military transitions. *Military transitions entail a shift in social identity.* To understand how reintegration is a process of identity transformation, we must understand how military organizational assimilation and conditioning occurs, we must be well versed in military cultural norms and behaviors, and we must acknowledge the impact of living between the societal military-civilian divide in U.S. culture. We must account for power and for relationships. An identity framework of liminality is useful here, as liminality is about living between social structures.

Turner teaches us that there are two types of liminality: sacred and institutionalized. Sacred liminality has a purpose; it functions as a space that breaks us down so we can be rebuilt to fit into our higher position in our new structure. Sacred liminality is temporary. Military Initial Entry Training (IET), including Basic Combat Training (BCT) and Advanced Individual Training (AIT), is a period of sacred liminality whereby recruits are transformed from civilians to warriors; this is where institutional, leader, and peer bonding primarily take shape (Siebold). Once recruits graduate IET, we join our assigned military units and transition into our Time in Service (TIS), or institutionalized liminality, where organizational bonding develops (Siebold). Institutionalized liminality is a perpetual state of liminality with no finite ending or aggregation into a higher state; institutionalized liminality is not always chosen. Not all U.S. Military Veterans chose to join the service (Vietnam draft) and not all of us choose to get out—sometimes our service gets cut short, sometimes we actively choose to separate, sometimes we choose to make a career of it and separate in our later years, and sometimes we die fighting. Choice matters and the reasons we choose to join the military matters, especially as reason for joining impacts how closely members orient within the organizational identity (Hall) and, thus, establish organizational bonding necessary for military group cohesion (Siebold).

Our level of organizational bonding impacts our experiences of institutionalized liminality. When I separated from service I saw the military only in a redemptive light, despite choosing to separate because of the lack of individual freedom I felt serving cost me. My reason for joining directly shaped my organizational bonding, which then directly shaped my perception of the military post separating. *I joined to be redeemed, and when I got out, I saw the military as my redeemer.* Before I joined, I saw the military in a "savior" light because this is how U.S. culture and the socializing I received as a white woman in the rural South taught me to see it. During my TIS, however, my perception shifted. Army Green didn't fit that well; it was uncomfortable, and it was no longer worth the tangible structure (resources) and community it provided me. I got out and, then once

172   J. R. HUNNIECUTT

again, saw the military as a redemptive, saving institution, despite the individual loss of freedom and self expression I experienced while I was in.

My military conditioning taught me to be secretive, in denial, and stoic (Hall). *I still have a tint of Army Green on my lenses and can't seem to completely wash it off.* It doesn't matter if I ever deployed or not—I served, was imprinted, and adapted and molded myself to fit the best I could. If the military is part of my *very being*, it's part of how I see the world. It's part of my self-perception, part of my composition, part of my relationships with others, part of my career, and part of all my life paths. Overwhelmingly, current research methods and participant criteria in most studies on Veteran reintegration do not account for this; it misses my social experiences surrounding identity. At large, military/Veteran research reflects the military institution; it's rigid, controlled, empirical, cold, and colonial. Thus, I chose to employ critical qualitative tools for this book and write out my stories to allow you to see, feel, and understand how reintegration is a process and product of Veteran identity. I wrote performatively, relied on institutional artifacts as my guide, critically reflected on the Veteran identity tensions I experienced during my liminal space of military transitions, and then illustrated how these tensions were shaped by my IET and TIS.

I wrote through my own loss of community and search for a sense of home. I showed you my own process of looking and seeing within as I navigated my responsibilities as a critical scholar and to my people. I revealed my emotions, thoughts, and behaviors confronting truths about my Uncle Sam that were hard to swallow, hard to say aloud, and hard to share with others. I uncovered my own loss of structure as I questioned how serving in the military had changed me and what it meant for my life now outside of the military. I engaged in resistance and illuminated my challenges in doing so. I found my voice and I'm using it to tell you that Veteran suicides are so high because we don't understand military transitionary experiences; we don't understand Veteran *identity*. We aren't giving SMs tools they need to navigate a drastic shift in social identity they experience during periods of military transitions between systems. The military is intricately part of who we are—it's part of our *very being* and it's been there since we advanced from the sacred liminality of IET. Military social structure has been *imprinted* in our being. *It's all about identity.*

The societal structure undergirding the military system is rooted in the ideograph of freedom and positions the U.S. Military as being a type of "savior" institution that *guards freedom and the American way of life.*

Thus, those who serve in the military (especially the all-volunteer military of post-9/11) are seen as socially responsible, heroic, and redeemed. *Give me liberty or give me death;* freedom is worth fighting and dying for. Those that die fighting for their country as seen as gold-star heroes who make the ultimate sacrifice. This discourse of *self-sacrifice in the name of freedom* functions to establish a type of invisible hierarchy within Veteran culture and identity and I argue causes many Veterans to experience dissonance and psychosocial difficulties around their identity and their service. *All of us feel a tinge of not having done enough.*

The ideograph of freedom undergirding the U.S. Military social structure incites community and creates a shared meaning among all of us who serve (and reverberates into the civilian community). We are assimilated into believing that *freedom is worth fighting and dying for.* We have this belief *imprinted into our very being* when we go through the sacred rite of passage (IET) and become part of the military organization. We understand this belief through *story. Ideographs are ideologies told through stories.* Since September 11, 2001, we have understood the ideograph of freedom through the story that *terrorists want to take our freedom.* So, we train to fight in war—*to fight the terrorists who want to take our freedom.* We train and prepare to make the ultimate sacrifice for freedom; *give me liberty or give me death!* We believe the ideograph that *freedom is worth fighting and dying for* because we understand it through a story, that is situated in a place and time (the 9/11 terrorist attacks in this example). Because we understand it through story, or myth, we accept it; we do not resist it. We adapt to assimilate this ideograph into our *very being.* Our "form [was] impressed upon [us] by society" (Turner 105) of the military total institution during our IET and it was then confounded during our military service. Our psychology, physiology—our *very being*—was broken down and then molded into a warrior self that is a *guardian of freedom and the American way of life.* Under the guise of this ideograph of freedom, we were transformed, trained, and conditioned to fit into a uniformed and homogenized identity to belong and fit into the total military institution *that protects freedom and the American way of life.*

We can all wear the Army Green, *but we are still white, black, brown, straight, queer, man, woman, transgender, Appalachian, immigrant, cheerleader.* Our social identities *matter.* Ironically, to accept and assimilate this ideograph of freedom into our *very being,* we must sacrifice our own freedom of self. *Who you are in the military entirely depends on your willingness to surrender who you are.* If actively choosing to separate from service is an act of resistance against the military institution, perhaps that means we've realized *Army Green doesn't fit us*. Perhaps we've picked up on the inherent falsity in this ideograph of freedom, even if we don't have the consciousness, much less the language, to understand or articulate it. Yet still, even if we do realize it—even if we do find ways to resist it—the reality is that regardless of whether Army Green ever fully fits the right way or not, *we will never be able to completely take it off*. We already underwent the rite of passage; we were already imprinted. The structure and community of the military have been engrained into us, and thus, when we separate, we experience an extreme loss of each as we struggle to understand who we are and how we have changed once we're back in civilian systems as a self that has been militarized.

We lose the military structure and community we had, but we never lose the militarization of our selves we experienced during IET and TIS—we take that militarization with us back into our civilian systems after service. Sebastian Junger tells us that

> brotherhood has nothing to do with feelings; it has to do with how you define your relationship to others. It has to do with the rather profound decision to put the welfare of the group above your personal welfare. In such a system, feelings are meaningless. In such a system, who you are entirely depends on your willingness to surrender who you are. Once you've experienced the psychological comfort of belonging to such a group, it's apparently very hard to give up. (276)

In the military, *who you are entirely depends on your willingness to surrender who you are*. *This* is what reintegration is about: understanding who you were, who you surrendered, who you became, and who you will be now. As Tyson Smith and Gala True explain, when Veterans transition out of service, we confront questions such as "How have I changed?" and "Who is my new self?" (149). Our conceptualizations and understandings of military/Veteran reintegration need to account for these questions.

If we understand that the military is *intricately part of who we are* and *we cannot ever return or go back* (because we've been *imprinted* during sacred liminality of IET) to our old civilian systems with the same sense of self, world view, and communicative patterns and behaviors, then how can conceptualizing "reintegration" with new language help? How can a new definition and framework of Veteran identity help us to create a new self that, in a cohesive, unified, pluralistic way, is able to live *among and between* differing structures and communities? How might finding a new way to talk and think about "reintegration" and Veteran identity shatter the hero/broken binary and move away from exclusive and misleading associations of war and combat? How can we label, define, and conceptualize these experiences in a way that creates room for difference, resistance, and movement toward union? As a Veteran and a scholar who wants to help improve the wellbeing and quality of life for military service members, Veterans, and their families, this is my mission—*my new redemption.*

> *Drive on,*
> *soldier,*
> *drive on.*

Rhetoric shapes our collective understanding of a concept (McGee). In the following sections I first review frameworks, concepts, and definitions that inform the new language and definition I propose for Veteran identity. It's necessary at this point to note the tension between employing autoethnography in this book—a method that centers subjectivity and is not about generalizability—and then proposing a general theoretical framework/model in this final chapter. Narrating my own tensions and experiences surrounding the Veteran identity and reintegration has led me to develop a framework that accounts for both the macro and the micro. In the following sections, I articulate both a model and reconceptualization of Veteran identity that considers "how does my story speak in relationship to larger stories of cultural Others like myself? Where do the 'I' and the 'we' separate? Do they?" (Calafell 9). The framework is designed to center *identity.* It claims space to understand how dominant narratives and power systems undergirding the military institution (the macro) intersect with the lived experiences of *differential,* individual identities in conflict with the military system (the micro). The new model and language I propose is based on differential experiences, which is at the core of autoethnography itself. What is general about differential experiences is that we all have them.

Building Blocks

In the following sections, I propose a new conceptualization for military/Veteran identity. First, however, I review frameworks and concepts that inform my proposed model and reconceptualization of Veteran identity. I review Nancy Schlossberg's Model for Analyzing Human Adaptation to Transition, which provides a useful, comprehensive definition of "transition" and outlines characteristics influencing the process of adaptation. Next, I draw from Antonio Tomas De La Garza and Kent Ono's theory of differential adaptation, which calls attention to problematic assumptions with current conceptualizations of "adaptation" before pointing out how through adaptation processes, individuals also have the capacity to employ forms of resistance against assimilation that functions to disrupt and change the host culture. Finally, I explore the ecological framework (Bronfenbrenner), complimented by family systems theory (Bavelas and Segal), to illustrate the importance and interdependence of proximal relationships in the process of reintegration. Following this, I propose a new model and reconceptualization of Veteran identity and military transitionary experiences.

Model for Analyzing Human Adaptation to Transition

Nancy Schlossberg proposed a Model for Analyzing Human Adaption to Transition, which attempts to explain the following: "What determines whether a person grows or deteriorates as the result of a transition," and "why do some people adapt with relative ease, while others suffer severe strain?" (3). She explains that people continually experience transitions throughout life that result in new networks of relationships, behaviors, and self-perceptions and that we all differ in our abilities to cope with change. Schlossberg defines transition as "an event or non-event that results in a change in assumptions about oneself and the world and thus requires a corresponding change in one's behaviors and relationships" (5). She explains adaptation to transition as a being a process of shifting from being completely preoccupied with the transition to integrating it into your life.

The Model for Analyzing Human Adaptation to Transition, then, identifies three major sets of factors that influence adaptation to transition: (1) characteristics of the transition, (2) the pre- and post-transition environments, and (3) the individual. First is characteristics of the transition, which include the following: (a) *role change* as being a gain or a loss (when I separated I lost my military community and tangible structure but gained individual freedom over self); (b) *affect* as positive or negative (I felt good about getting out and was sure it would not negatively affect me); (c) *source* as internal or external (I decided to get out rather than being non-voluntarily discharged); (d) *timing* as on-time or off-time (it was on time for me because I had been accepted to a PhD program and had a plan moving forward); (e) *onset* as gradual or sudden (I had time to make my decision to separate and process it was happening); (f) *duration* as permanent, temporary, or uncertain (Could I get back in? Should I get back in? Is there an end to the liminality of reintegration?); and, finally, (g) *degree of stress involved* in the transition, which is dependent on all the previous factors.

Next, Schlossberg outlines the characteristics of pre-transition and post-transition environments: (a) *interpersonal support system* (I experienced a loss of my military and civilian communities when I got out and moved to Denver); (b) *institutional support* (I do not qualify for most Department of Veterans Affairs benefits and never received any support for reintegration from my unit when I separated); and (c) *physical setting* (cohabitating with my ex-partner that I had an unhealthy relationship with when I moved to Denver did not help). Finally, the model articulates the characteristics of the individual experiencing the transition: (a) *psychosocial competence*, including self-attitudes, world attitudes, and behavioral attitudes (my self, world, and behavioral attitudes all improved through practicing meditation and yoga); (b) *sex and gender* (I never should have taken out my *freedom ring* for that job! Will I ever stop militarizing my femininity?); (c) *age*, including life stages (my age allowed me to blend in with my graduate peers in school); (d) *state of health* (my psychological health negatively affected my physical health—I developed disordered eating as a result of anxiety my first few months out); (e) *race-ethnicity* (I was a white woman who grew up in white isolated rural Appalachia—Army Greens fit me a little better than SMs of color); (f) *socioeconomic status* (I had somewhat of a financial sustainability plan moving forward); (g) *value-orientation*, to include religious, spiritual, and moral commitments (I was conditioned to see the military as redemptive, yet I grew to be committed to social justice); and (h) *previous experience with a transition of a similar nature* (the only basis of comparison I had was returning home from IET). According to Schlossberg, all three sets of characteristics interact and determine whether one can adapt or fails to adapt. "Ease of adaptation to a transition depends on one's perceived and/or actual balance of resources to deficits in terms of the transition itself, the pre-post environment, and the individual's sense of competency, well-being, and health" (8).

This model is useful in understanding reintegration as a process of transitioning that Veterans adapt through or fail to adapt. Further, we can apply this model to the transitionary experience of joining the military. You either adapt or quite literally fail to adapt. There is, in fact, a specific type of military discharge called "Chapter 11," which entails and names a "failure to adapt to the military environment." A Chapter 11 discharge can only occur during one's first 180 days in the military. Applying Schlossberg's model, joining the military, returning home from a deployment, and separating from service are all transitions that ignite a change in assumptions about our self and the world; we either adapt our relationships and behaviors to accommodate the transition/change or struggle in maintaining preoccupied with the transition and "fail to adapt." This model is significant because it includes social identity factors in the individual characteristics, accounts for environmental influences, and prioritizes the importance of relationships and institutional support. Yet, the way this model positions the lack of adaptation as a "failure" is problematic, particularly as it applies to transition out of the military, which is an identity experience of navigating institutionalized liminality.

The Veteran identity is not fixed; because of institutionalized liminality, the Veteran identity is a perpetual, ongoing negotiation of self attempting to adapt between military and civilian worlds. To be a Veteran is to perpetually exist between civilian and military systems, including structure and community. *We cannot ever fully fit into one or the other because we are both.* The transition from civilian to service member happens through sacred liminality—through the rite of passage that is initial entry training (which happens during one's first 180 days of belonging to the military). Not adapting to the assimilation that occurs during IET can result in a "failure to adapt" and one can literally be discharged from the military for this. The Veteran identity is different, though, as it is a form of *institutionalized* liminality; there is no summation or aggregation—there is no end to the transition. Framing this transition out of military service as "adapt" or "fail to adapt," then, only re-establishes the hero/broken hierarchy inherent in Veteran culture. *Army Greens don't fit us all the same way.* But there is no "failure to adapt" discharge option when Army Green doesn't fit after you've reached a state of institutionalized liminality in the military and especially once you separate from the military. Schlossberg's model moves us closer to seeing and understanding the social implications of belonging to and transitioning out of military service, yes, but it's still not accounting for the *institutionalized liminal* experience of belonging to a *total* institution.

Theory of Differential Adaptation

Antonio Tomas De La Garza and Kent Ono articulate the same problem with most scholarly conceptualizations and theoretical approaches to "adaptation." When discussing adaptation in the context of immigration, they first point out the problem in an inherent assumption that all experiences are similar enough to create a reliable generalized model. *One size does not fit all.* The same has been true for reintegration conceptualizations—they fail to account for the inconsistencies in lived experiences. *Army Greens do not fit us all the same way.* De La Garza and Ono went on to explain how "traditional adaptation theories also assume a unidirectional relationship between the individual and society. The society changes the individual, not the other way around" (274). They argue that this assumption of a unidirectional relationship leads to equating *adaption* to *assimilation* as being the same thing (which they are not) and, further, assumes that assimilation is both desirable and inevitable. Agency, again, matters here in that if the transition is not chosen, then it may not be desirable. Yet sometimes, it is still *inevitable.* Like the Model for Analyzing Human Adaptation to Transition, dominant conceptualizations of adaptation assume that not adapting to transition results in failure or preoccupation with the inability to adapt. This sets up a binary: you adapt, or you fail to adapt and suffer the consequences and any efforts to resist are a hindrance to adaptation. Within this conceptualization of adaptation, in the context of Veteran identity where one adapts back into the family after war or back into civilian society after service separation, this binary emerges: You sacrificed as much of your individual self as you could and then you remained tight-lipped, stoic, and loyal to the military about it. *Or* you didn't sacrifice all of yourself that you could (maybe because Army Greens didn't fit you the same way and thus you didn't have access to the same opportunities of self-sacrifice) and/or you didn't remain quiet, stoic, and loyal. Thus, *you're a hero or you're broken.*

De La Garza and Ono point out that within this dominant conceptualization of adaptation, "no thought is given to the ways that the destination society may adapt to the immigrant, the immigrants' culture, or the immigrants' expectations" (272). For example, in the mid-1970s many Vietnam Veterans were returning home from war and experiencing agitation, irritability, hostility, hypervigilance, flashbacks, fear, anxiety, depression, loneliness, isolation, insomnia, and nightmares. These Veterans were socially perceived and positioned as being hindrances to society, as *failing*

180   J. R. HUNNIECUTT

to adapt. They were not heroes; they were broken, angry, and dangerous war Veterans. It wasn't until 1980 that this thinking shifted, however, when civilian society adapted to the influx of Vietnam Veterans rejoining civilian culture. Eventually, physicians realized the issues these Veterans were having were related to external factors, like exposure to traumatic events during war, rather than an inherent internal weakness. They weren't failures to adapt; they needed medical attention. Post-Traumatic Stress Disorder (PTSD) was officially added to the American Psychiatric Association's *Diagnostic and Statistical Manual of Mental Disorders* and the symptoms became diagnosable ("PTSD History"). Veterans influenced the host culture.

A more recent example includes Military Sexual Trauma (MST) in the military. I learned early during my time with my unit in 1030th that if I ever experienced any unwanted sexual comments or advances from anyone in my unit, that I had better be tight-lipped about it or there would be consequences. *I did not want to be seen as angry or broken.* So, when I did experience it, I didn't report it. *I suffered in silence.* As I became a researcher of Veteran studies, I learned that on average, one in four women in the military experience it (Wilson). Over time, I have seen more and more women report their experiences. Recently, through being surrounded by other women with experiences of MST, I have begun to identify, name, and report my own experiences of unwanted sexual comments and advances (i.e., sexual harassment) I experienced during my military service. Enough women *resisted* until finally something was done. Recently, the current presidential administration (Biden) convened a 90-day Independent Review Commission on Sexual Assault in the Military ("Recommendations"). This committee has made recommendations related to accountability, prevention, climate and culture, and victim care and support. *The host culture is changing because enough of us resisted.*

De La Garza and Ono's "theory of differential adaption" is a "nonuniversalist framework that acknowledges the radical diversity of immigrants' experiences, immigrants' agentic efforts to navigate pressures to assimilate, and the potential they have to reshape subjectivities, culture, and society" (De La Garza and Ono 270). This theory accounts for the diversity of lived experiences and holds space for resistance. It "recognizes the ways immigrants resist pressure, and even foment or make gradual (perhaps initially imperceptible) changes to their host culture" (De La Garza and Ono 275). Though this theory was developed for the context of immigration, it directly applies to military/Veteran transitionary experiences, notably because it distinguishes between assimilation and adaption:

> The primary distinction we draw between adaptation and assimilation is the role of the subject. People do not assimilate; they can be assimilated and can tacitly or actively participate in their own or another's assimilation. Assimilation, therefore, is pressure applied by a State and its associated culture to individual subjects to conform. (De La Garza and Ono 276)

What De La Garza and Ono are arguing is that we are active subjects who *chose* to adapt *or resist* cultural assimilation; we are not assimilated—we *choose* to adapt or to resist assimilation. Instead of adapting to fit, we may find ways to resist and change our host culture. They propose that "the space between assimilation and adaptation continually produces new conditions of possibility for subjectivity" (276). The "space between assimilation and adaptation" sounds a lot like the space of liminality, in that it's uncertain, ambiguous, and challenging and represents existing *between* social structures and systems.

In the context of the military (in the all-volunteer force, that is), we join the military and enter into the sacred liminal space of IET; this is where we adapt or "fail to adapt" to assimilation into military structure and culture. In IET, if you do not assimilate, you are literally discharged for a "failure to adapt." Entering into and completing IET contains a transition, and we either adapt to or resist the assimilation. Resisting can result in consequences and/or in incremental changes to military culture from a bottom-up approach. Some people adapt easier than others; *Army Green fits some of us better than it does others.* Differential adaptation theory assumes "society has the potential to limit attempts to adapt and be accepted" (277). This is where other social identity factors become most relevant. As a cisgender woman in the U.S. Military, my attempts to adapt and be accepted into military organizational and institutional structure were limited. Now as a Veteran outside of the military institution, my attempts to adapt to civilian societal assimilation are also limited—my experience of military service doesn't fit the dominant narrative. During my TIS, I perpetually and habitually adapted myself to fit into the military identity. Now that I'm out, I continue to perpetually adapt myself to fit into the Veteran identity. *And no matter how long I've been out of the military, I just can't seem to completely wash off the Army green.*

182   J. R. HUNNIECUTT

During IET, our level of adaption of self is temporary and contextual. We then aggregate sacred liminality and transition again into institutionalized liminality when we join our units and serve our time as *guardian of freedom and the American way of life*. Here, we must continue to adapt or find ways to resist throughout TIS. When we separate from service, we once again transition, and this time out of military structure into civilian society as our now militarized selves. Now, we must assimilate into civilian society taking with us all the military assimilation or "militarization" we've adapted to during IET and TIS. The military is a total institution and is composed of communication patterns, norms, and behaviors distinctly different from civilian society. When we separate from service, we can adapt or resist the pressures of being stoic, loyal, and patriotic and always viewing Uncle Sam as redemptive. We can be heroes, we can be broken, *or we can reject both and attempt to change the culture rather than adapt to assimilate*. However, society has the ability to limit our efforts to both adapt and resist (De La Garza and Ono). The military-civilian divide in U.S. culture limits Veterans' attempts to adapt to life without military structure and community. Mridula Mascarenhas explains, "A culture of militarism prefers the stoic veteran who is tight-lipped about the ravages of war but remains enduringly loyal to the military" (84). The "military/civilian divide" in U.S. society encompasses the lack of understanding between individuals who never served in the military about the realities, challenges, and lived experiences of us who have. Many of these realities, challenges, and lived experiences go unnoticed by civilian peers and, in fact, "84% of post 9/11 Veterans reported the public does not understand the problems they and their families face and 71% of the general public agrees" (Kirchner 117). As pointed out in much of the literature on Veteran reintegration, this is where the importance of interpersonal and familial relationships emerges.

Ecological Framework and Family Systems

Virginia Gil-Rivas and colleagues relied both on the ecological framework (Bronfenbrenner) and on family systems theory (Bavelas and Segal) to describe reintegration in an article that summarizes influential factors of reintegration and recommends research and practice ideas to promote wellness for military families. The ecological framework positions adaptation as happening "within and between the multiple systems in which individuals and families are embedded" (177). Like liminality, this framework highlights the nature of being *within* and *between*. More so, the ecological framework accounts for individual, proximal, and distal influences on adaptation (Gil-Rivas 177). *Individual* influences include things such as age, gender, education, race/ethnicity, and history. *Proximal* factors are our interpersonal relationships—those with a direct influence on the individual such as spouses, caregivers, coworkers, and friends—and *distal* factors are things with an indirect influence, like organizations, institutions, and culture. Gil-Rivas points out how family systems theory compliments the ecological framework because it accounts for interdependence within the family system.

When we separate from the military, we experience a loss of structure and community. We lose our military family—our brothers and sisters in arms, our Uncle Sam. Leslie Baxter and Dawn Braithwaite claim the core characteristics of a "family" include long-term commitment, relations created through biology, law, or affection, enmeshment in a kinship organization, ongoing interdependence, and institutionalization. They explain, "'family' is a social group of two or more persons, characterized by ongoing interdependence with long-term commitments that stem from blood, law, or affection" (3). In the military, *we are a family*. We gained this community and formed closed bonds with our Battle Buddies because of the structure of the U.S. Military institution. It's a total institution (Goffman; Smith and True). "In such a system, who you are entirely depends on your willingness to surrender who you are" (Junger 276). In the military, *who you are depends entirely on* your *ability and willingness* to *adapt to assimilation*; it's about *identity*. Yet again, *Army Green doesn't fit us all the same way*. It is much easier to adapt to assimilation for some than it is for others.

Research on military/Veteran reintegration and suicides as is, overwhelmingly, has been missing this. The ecological model and family systems theory are useful in theorizing reintegration as a concept, especially because they illuminate the influences of relationships and culture. Yet alone, they fail to comprehensively capture the nature of adaptation. Christine Elnitsky and colleagues incorporated the ecological model into their proposed universal definition for reintegration: "*MSMV [Military Service Member and Veteran] reintegration* is both a process and outcome of resuming roles in family, community, and workplace which may be influenced at different levels of an ecological system" (2). This definition is the most inclusive I have seen and is able to be applied to various types of military adaptive transition experiences, such as transitioning in and out of IET (sacred liminality), transitioning home from war, transitioning back and forth for drills and trainings, and transitioning out of the military institution completely.

However, *family*, *community*, and *workplace* are all types of *social* systems and I think it's paramount to explicitly include "social" in the definition. Particularly as Anna Zogas explains how reintegration challenges are currently associated almost exclusively with post-war/combat difficulties, it is paramount to shift conversations to centering the *social* implications that stem from belonging to and participating in the military institution as a whole. This argument parallels the findings of Mark Reger and colleagues that show Veteran suicides are correlated with reintegration post separation from military service and not with reintegration post deployment to war. Even in the current reintegration literature as is, the concept of reintegration is framed as being about reintegrating back into the family (Collinge et al.; Demers; "When Veterans Return"; Di Leone et al.; Hinojosa and Hinojosa; Knobloch et al.; Pfeiffer et al.; Theiss & Knobloch) and/or into community (Collinge et al.; Pfeiffer et al.). These are *social* experiences and highlight the urgent need for *social* implications of military IET and military service to be at the center of our conceptualizations and definitions of reintegration. Likewise, "family, community, and workplace" encompass some proximal and distal factors, but not all (i.e., romantic partners, friendships, media, and culture at large).

Further, using the word "resume" as it is in Elnitsky et al.'s definition limits the way we think about the experience of reintegration. "Re" is the Latin root for "back." *The military intricately becomes part of who you are.* You become *impressed upon* by military structure and society (Turner). *There is no going back* once you go through the sacred liminality of IET, become endowed with additional "powers" (Turner), and become part of the total military institution. We do not *re*sume roles in our families, communities, and workplaces. Perhaps some of us, some of the time, *re*turn to our same physical families, communities, and workplaces; perhaps we go back to the same people and places. Physiologically and psychologically, however, we do not *go back*. We do not *re*sume. We are anew. Socially, our *very being* has been modified to fit into a new system. Therefore, we may find ourselves back in the same social systems in which we left, but our lenses through which we perceive those same systems have become militarized; they have become the color of *Army Green*. We need space to recognize that we have been socially impacted by service and that we have no tools or language for understanding, and much less articulating, how. I suggest the idea of "resuming roles" sets up us for failure. Language shapes our reality and our perceptions.

Likewise, the same logic applies to the term "*re*integration." The word means to integrate *back*. Conceptualizing this process and experience in a way that inherently means *to go back* creates unrealistic expectations and does not allow space for recognition that military service changes a person, especially socially. *Where is room for resistance in our adaptation process? Where is recognition that we also impact and change the cultures working to assimilate us?* Further, not only is this experience (of "reintegration") social (it's about our family, community, and workplace roles and communicative interactions), but it's fluid and sometimes it reaches a state of aggregation (graduating from IET or having a welcome home ceremony after deployment) and other times it does not (separating from service). Because the U.S. Military is a total institution, even once you reach a state of aggregation from the sacred liminality of IET, you aggregate *into* a state of institutionalized liminality through being a full member of the total military institution. Understanding this experience through language that inherently implies "going back" does not leave space (or give us tools) to navigate the perpetual and liminal space that is Veteran identity. I propose we no longer use the term "reintegration" to name or explain the experiences of military transitions; it's doing more harm than good. It is not about going back; it is about the creation of something new that exists in the in-betweenness.

Once you become a part of the military institution—once military ideologies are imprinted into your psyche and physiology—you can never go back. It is perpetual liminality. There is no way to undo imprinting that occurs during sacred liminality. There is a way to resist adapting to assimilation, however. It's important here to highlight the distinction once again between sacred liminality and institutionalized liminality. Sacred liminality is a temporary period that functions to imprint the very being of a person to mold them to fit into a higher structure. Sacred liminality is "a symbolic milieu that represents both a grave and a womb" (Turner 97). It is not just a grave—it is also a *womb*. Sacred liminality signifies and fosters a type of rebirth; you sacrifice self to gain status. *Who you are entirely depends on your willingness to surrender who you are.* Institutionalized liminality, on the other hand, does not always follow sacred liminality. Institutionalized liminality is *the grave without the womb*. In the context of immigration, it is unlikely immigrants experience a period of sacred liminality whereby they are "fashioned anew and endowed with additional powers to enable them to cope with their new station in life" (Turner, 96). Rather, they are cast into institutionalized liminality where they are pressured to assimilate and seen as a "failure to adapt" or "broken" if they don't. Therefore, in the context of military/Veteran adaptation and identity, because all SMs must graduate IET, we all experienced IET; we all experienced sacred liminality and were "born again" as *guardians of freedom and the American way of life*. We cannot return to the womb—not during TIS and not after we separate from service. We do not *re*integrate; we do not *go back*. We *adapt and overcome. Drive on, soldier, drive on*.

Veteran Identity: A New Consciousness

In the time that has passed since I separated from the military, since I started exploring literature and research on Veteran suicides, transitions, and identity, and in writing this book, both little and much have changed. I successfully finished my dissertation project, which is how this book originated. I moved to the Midwest and worked for 3.5 years as both a researcher and a research administrator of Veteran Studies. Situated within a Veteran center, I built a framework at a top-tier Midwest, land-grant university for doing "research *with, not on*, Veterans." I drew from my own experiences of what it feels like to not be included in the research, to not have my military service "count" or be considered a legitimate Veteran (by not only formal institutions such as the VA, but by peers and colleagues as well), and, most importantly, to not qualify for much-needed benefits or resources because my military story doesn't align with the dominant narrative. All this experiential knowledge served me well as a liaison between university researchers and community organizations where Veterans of all military experiences inhabit. Transforming what was originally the dissertation project that I completed in 2018 into this book has felt like another form of creating unity between my disparate selves. *It has brought me full circle and continues to help me heal.* When I finished my dissertation in 2018, I was starting a new life chapter employed at a Veteran center in a Midwestern university. Now, in finishing this book, I have concluded my time employed with this Midwestern university and I am on to creating new forms of understanding and healing with military/ Veteran communities in an entrepreneurial way.

In my last month working in the Veteran center at this Midwest university, I attended a faculty talk for a prospective new hire of assistant professor. This scholar, Rachel Hoopsick, was presenting a talk on her research that focused on never-deployed National Guard and Reservist Service Members. Rachel was part of "Operation Safety," which is a longitudinal research study examining the health and wellbeing of U.S. Army Reserve/National Guard soldiers and their partners out of the Department of Community Health and Health Behavior at the University of Buffalo. Her interview faculty talk at my university happened over zoom, so I watched it from the comfort of my own home.

As I was getting ready to sit down and watch her talk, I felt a familiar suspicion arising around what I might hear during her talk. *I didn't want to hear another researcher who wasn't a Veteran tell me my military service experience didn't count or wasn't included.* Through my time at the University of Denver (DU) and in the Midwestern university, I had grown to understand that not all scholars who worked with (or tried to work with) Veteran communities were well intended. Even for those who were, if they didn't understand the intricacies of military/Veteran culture and if they didn't approach the research with a "research *with, not on,* Veterans" mentality, then the impact often didn't match the intent. I knew from my own lived experience that *research that is not culturally attune could actually hurt Veterans through further reproducing inaccurate assumptions and narratives about our service.* As Rachel's talk began, I gently reminded myself to remain open and curious.

After her introduction and background, she began by prefacing the data she was sharing in her presentation within a larger narrative, "A general assumption that deployment is the primary catalyst for psychological and social difficulties may contribute to underrecognition and undertreatment of problems among never-deployed service members" (Hoopsick et al. "Deployment Status" 1). *What?! I couldn't believe what I was hearing. This was a good sign! I could feel my emotions starting to stir.* She went on to explain that the research team from Operation Safety had explored if ever-deployed Service Members (having a history of at least one deployment) and never-deployed Service Members (no history of deployment) differed in mental health, substance use, and resiliency factors. They not only found that soldiers did not significantly differ based on deployment experience, but that deployment status was the least salient factor across the measured variables for psychosocial problems. Given these findings, she told us, they went on to develop a scale to measure what they had coined as "non-deployment emotions." *Non-deployment emotions! A tear trickled down my cheek. Her words resonated with me powerfully. My military experience counted! I was included! I felt moved, seen, and finally understood.*

In applying this scale, she went on to explain, they studied never-deployed National Guard and Reservist soldiers and found that more than half of never-deployed soldiers experienced negative emotions. These Service Members "experience negative emotions related to having never been deployed, such as feelings of guilt, decreased value, decreased connectedness, and decreased camaraderie" (Hoopsick et al. "Developing a Measure" 1). *She was talking about me. I had those feelings.* Though more work is needed in applying this scale across different components of the military (i.e., active duty and various branches), **this data suggests that all military personnel, regardless of deployment experience, may experience or be at risk for negative outcomes**, she told us. *I couldn't believe what I was hearing. I felt validated more than I ever had when it came to understanding my own military experiences through research. Someone finally gets it. Someone is finally paying attention. Someone is finally asking the right questions!*

The work of Hoopsick and her colleagues from the Operation Safety project is the closest I have seen to date that grasps the complexities of emotions and dissonance of service members whose narrative does not fit into the dominant narrative of military service, particularly that of deployment experiences. Non-deployed emotions encompass a new line of research that warrants much more attention and future work. With it, however, we must still consider identity. We must examine the impact of serving in a total institution. We must ask *why*. *Why* would service members have negative emotions about not having to fight in a war? *Why* is there not a difference in psychosocial outcomes between those who went to war and those who didn't? I know, through my own narrative of Veteran identity and military service, that it is because regardless of whether we went to war or not, if we graduated Initial Entry Training in the military, our *very being* was *imprinted* and we can never go back. *We are forever changed. We are forever Army Green. We are betwixt and between worlds, permanently, and we don't have tools for how to navigate this space of in-betweenness.* I am thrilled to see the consciousness around experiences of military service beginning to expand. My aim now, however, is to present a new model, definition, and reconceptualization of Veteran identity to foster even greater expansiveness around this lived experience. I begin with a new model of Veteran identity that helps to illuminate and illustrate how current conceptualizations and definitions are harmful.

Model of Veteran Identity Hierarchy

Currently, only certain types of military experiences qualify one for "Veteran" status (and, consequently, facilitate access to specific benefits, resources, and opportunities). As I've illustrated through my own lived experiences and through explicating relevant literature and theoretical constructs, this is inadequate at best and gravely harmful (pun fully intended) at worse. My proposed Model of Veteran Identity Hierarchy argues that an invisible hierarchy of Veteran identity exists among all who have served in the U.S. Military and aims to illustrate how the further one is from the apex of Veteran identity, the more psychosocial difficulties one experiences. Understanding the ideograph of freedom, the military as a total institution, and Army Greens all as interrelated concepts helps to understand this model. First, as previously articulated, the ideograph of freedom is an ideology shared and accepted through story/true events. In the context of the post-9/11 generation (though this model is an application to all eras of Veterans), terrorists attacked American citizens on September 1, 2001. The narrative surrounding this historical event is that terrorists want to take our freedom. Thus, the War on Terrorism began in 2001 to protect our freedom as Americans. Service Members are the *guardians of freedom and the American way of life*. Second, in the total institution of the U.S. Military, *who you are entirely depends on your willingness to surrender who you are*. The ultimate sacrifice of self for country is dying while fighting for freedom. *Give me liberty or give me death.* Anyone who does not die fighting for freedom has fallen short of paying the ultimate sacrifice; they are not the gold star.

Finally, being able to die in combat has not always been accessible to everyone. Through discriminatory policies throughout U.S. history, groups of people have been excluded from participating in the military completely (ban on transgender individuals from serving) or have been limited to only certain types of military activities (Combat Exclusion Policy for women service members). Though certainly the military has come a long way and continues to incrementally work toward complete inclusiveness, the U.S. Armed Forces is still comprised of predominately white, cisgender, able-bodied, heterosexual males. *Army Green does not fit us all the same way.* Because of these interrelated (and very hard to identity) truths, every single person who serves (and survives service) in the military (1) falls short of the ultimate sacrifice and (2) experiences some degree of psychosocial difficulties as a result. The Model of Veteran

Identity Hierarchy posits that because of these interrelated truths, a hierarchy of Veteran identity exists, and this hierarchy dictates not only movement around and embodiment of the Veteran identity, but more importantly, it influences who has access to help, resources, benefits, and even healthcare after separation from military service. Figure 7.1 illustrates this hierarchy and illuminates the interplay between military experiences and individual identity characteristics. Following Fig. 7.1, seven propositions of the model are articulated as well. The purpose of the propositions is to highlight the most relevant facets of the model in a way that can be easily understood. The overarching aim of creating and sharing this model is to highlight how this invisible hierarchy functions to create psychosocial difficulties for everyone who has ever been part of the U.S. military.

This model can be understood through seven propositions:

1. There is an (invisible) apex of Veteran identity, influenced by both military experiences and individual identity characteristics.
2. In the military, who you are, or your status, entirely depends on your willingness to surrender who you are (Junger).

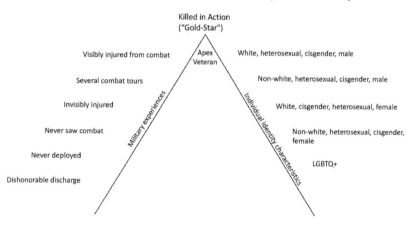

Fig. 7.1 Model of veteran identity hierarchy
The figure shows a triangle and has word descriptions at the peak of the triangle as well as on both sides

3. Loss of life while fighting for freedom is considered the ultimate sacrifice (in the military, in non-military proximal and distal settings, and in media framings) and grants the highest possible status within military/Veteran culture.
4. Due to historical exclusionary policies in the U.S. Military, individuals with specific identity characteristics do not always have access to military experiences that would foster the ultimate sacrifice (loss of life through being killed in combat while fighting for freedom).
5. The hierarchy of military experiences stems from ideologies and ideographs within and about the military and is imprinted into the very being of service members through military initial entry training and through time in service.
6. Everyone who falls short of the ultimate sacrifice of loss of life/Killed in Action (which is every person who survives military service), experiences some form of psychosocial difficulties.
7. The further one is from the apex on this invisible Veteran identity hierarchy, the more psychosocial difficulties one experiences.

As a critical scholar (and just as a human), I believe that simply identifying a problem is not enough. We must also propose solutions. Before I move into my proposition for a new framework and conceptualization of Veteran identity, I want to first make a necessary clarification. It might be easy to assume, given my direct critique of the military institution up to this point in the text, that I indeed did *choose a side*—that I am *against* the military. Allow me to correct you. Despite all I have experienced myself—my own psychological darkness in which I experienced clinical anxiety, depression, disordered eating, addiction, and suicide ideation—I would not change a single thing. *I would do it all again.* I still believe, with every ounce of my militarized *very being*, that the military did indeed redeem me from the adverse life circumstances I was experiencing at the time I joined. It did indeed throw me a metaphorical rope to *get out.* It gave me resources, community, and structure. It taught me resiliency and tools for adaptation in a way nothing else in my life did or could. The military changed my life in a powerful, complicated, chaotic, redemptive way.

Not only is this true for myself, but I know countless others with the same truth—that the military threw them a rope. It doesn't mean the rope didn't come at a cost—for some, like SGT Baker, or for all those brave warriors who have sacrificed their lives fighting for our so-called freedom, the cost was life. For others, it's the loss of a literal part of their body (amputees) or the loss of psychological health (PTSD). And for some, if not most, it's simply the loss of who we were before we joined. Nonetheless, regardless of what it is, regardless of what our military experience was, there is loss, for each one of us. There are psychosocial difficulties in existing *betwixt and between* the perpetual world of liminality between the military and the civilian world. It's the constant inner battle of straddling this line between worlds. I am not against the military—nor am I completely for it—but I am for healing; I am for *union*. I am for alchemizing experiences of pain and loss into opportunities for growth and evolution, as individuals and as a collective. *This* is what I am doing here and now, with this book and with my own professional path as an advocate and researcher working *with, not on*, Veterans. The purpose of this book is to show and tell the truths, as I see and interpret them, about (my) Veteran identity and military service experiences of transition. I have shown and I have told and, next, I want to end my story (up to this point) by planting a seed in all who engage with me through this text. I propose that we reconceptualize and redefine "Veteran" to be holistically inclusive of all who have ever graduated from military IET. Further, I propose that we conceptualize "Veteran" not just as a noun—as a thing that we are or an identity we have—but also as a *verb, as something that we do*.

Reconceptualizing Veteran as a Noun and a Verb

"Veteran" is not just something that I am, but it is also something that I do as I continuously adapt/resist my *very being* between military and non-military structures and systems. "Veteran" comes from the early sixteenth-century Latin word "vetus," which means "old." Tyson Smith and Gala True explain that upon ending military service, Veterans often confront identity questions: such as "How have I changed?" and "Who is my *new* self?" (149). "Old" and "new" are relative terms, meaning, we come to understand each term/concept in relationship to each other. You cannot have something new without there being something old and vice versa. Thus, anyone who has aggregated from IET (sacred liminality) becomes a product, or a "new" *very being* which inherently also includes something "old." If we redefine "Veteran" to include everyone who has graduated from IET, then through this lens, something "old" is *who we were before we joined the military*, rather than who we are during our time in service. As we know, who we are during military service depends entirely on our willingness to surrender who we are (Junger).

Victor Turner taught us that sacred liminality (IET) is both *a grave and a womb*. Once we complete/aggregate from sacred liminality, our *very being* is anew, which means we have an "old" *very being* that has been *imprinted*. Thus, our "old," *imprinted, very being* is the product of this aggregation into something "new." *My very being is the product—the subject—the noun.* Considering the etymology of the word "Veteran," as inherently meaning something "old," then it makes sense to understand that "Veteran" is the *product of imprinting our old, very being* through IET. "Veteran" is not becoming something new once we separate from the military. *What "new" thing do we become once we separate?* We do not become anew at that time. We do not undergo a sacred liminality, marked by intense ceremony and ritual once we separate from the military institution. Further, given that the military institution becomes *impressed in our very being* during IET, *we can never completely wash the Army Green off*, anyway. Rather, we become anew *after our sacred liminal experience of IET*.

However, within our current conceptualizations, we do not consider one to be a "Veteran" after completion of IET. Currently, we name and understand the *product* of military IET as "Service Member" or, more specifically, "soldier, sailor, marine, airman, coast guardsman, national guardsman, or reservist." Using myself as an example, within this framework, we can see that once I aggregated into institutionalized liminality (joined my unit for my time in service), I became someone who did "soldiering." According to Oxford languages, "soldier" is both a noun and a verb. "Soldier" is both a person who serves in an army (noun) and "soldier" means to "serve as a soldier" (verb). The current language and subsequent understandings of "Soldier" versus "Veteran" are helpful in differentiating between who is actively/currently serving in the military and who has completely separated from military service, but it falls short of grasping the full picture. It does not capture both something "new" and something "old," which, likely, is the point, given the totality of the military institution. *Who you are in the military entirely depends on your ability to surrender who you are.* Once you are part of the military institution as a service member/soldier who has aggregated from military IET, there is no room for what was "old." Herein lies the problem and the solution.

The problem with this conceptualization and understanding of military service is that it assumes all who are part of the institution are passive subjects who assimilate. Yet, as we learn from De La Garza and Ono, *we do not assimilate—we adapt/resist* assimilation. We *are active subjects. Army*

Green does not fit the right way. All who survive military service fail to reach the apex of Veteran. Is it this truth, which becomes deeply buried within our subjective selves during the sacred liminal experience of IET, that shows us "Veteran" is not only a subject/noun? I am a Veteran "whose form was impressed upon [me] by [the military]" (Turner 105), but I am also a subject who *adapts to and/or resists* this "impression upon me." In IET, if you do not adapt, you risk discharge for a literal "failure to adapt." This discharge can only occur during one's first 180 days of military service—which is during IET. However, after we graduate from IET and enter the institutionalized liminality that encompasses our time in service, we *actively adapt/resist*. In my case, I adapted every time I got ready for the weekend drill with my NG unit. Everyone who is currently serving in the military is always actively adapting/resisting. Regardless of whether it's adapting/resisting to go to weekend drill, to go to annual training, to report for duty during the day as an active-duty Service Member, to go to war, to come home from war, or to separate from military service completely, it is an action—it is something that we do—because we are active subjects. To "Veteran" is "to adapt and/or resist."

Again, I propose that we reconceptualize and redefine "Veteran" to include all who have ever graduated from military IET because it is during IET that we create something "old" through adapting to become anew. Further, as we are active subjects who adapt/resist assimilation, I propose that we reconceptualize "Veteran" also as a *verb*. Specifically, I propose that military **"Veteran" is a social identity product and process of differentially adapting and/or resisting transition between distal and proximal factors of the U.S. Military structure and an outside system**.

First, "Veteran" is a **social identity** because it's subjective, social, and about *identity*. Within this framework, *everyone's experience of military service is included*. With this new ideation, I intentionally aim to disrupt and shift conceptualizations of all military experiences to center social identity, account for differences in lived experiences, and highlight the liminality of these experiences. I draw from both the Model for Analyzing Human Adaptation to Transition (Schlossberg) and the theory of differential adaptation (De La Garza and Ono) to create the definition/new concept.

Next, "Veteran" is both a **product and a process of differentially adapting and/or resisting**. Sacred liminality has finality, which creates an outcome, or a "product," yet institutionalized liminality does not, which means it is an ongoing process of "doing." Again, we do not experience another form of sacred liminality once we separate from military service;

there is no rite of passage that marks us as *anew* once we separate from the military institution. There cannot be because the military is a total institution. *We cannot ever completely wash Army Green off.* Beyond IET, not adapting is not akin to a *failure to adapt*, as perhaps we are finding ways to resist instead. Maybe we are changing the host culture. *Maybe we report the MST. Maybe we decide to keep the nose ring in when going to that interview for the job at the Veteran center.*

This conceptualization of "Veteran" as a verb recognizes that we are active agents that do not "assimilate," but rather, we adapt/resist assimilation that is *impressed upon us.* To be a military Veteran is to be a product of sacred liminality and to understand "Veteran" as a verb is to both see and recognize how Veterans adapt and/or resist institutionalized liminality. During time in service, it is much more difficult to resist assimilation because in the military *who you are entirely depends on your willingness to surrender who you are.* It is once you completely separate from military service that resistance as an active subject becomes more accessible—becomes a thing we do more easily without consequence of tangible repercussions from the military institution. However, because *we can never completely wash the Army Green off,* resistance after separation (whether that looks like growing a beard, piercing your nose, naming and reporting your experiences of service-connected disabilities, or writing a book critiquing the military institution) is still a difficult thing to do. But nonetheless it is an act of doing—a verb—of either adapting or resisting during transitionary military experiences.

We adapt/resist military assimilation in moments marked by **transition**. A transition is an event or non-event that results in a change in assumptions about oneself and the world and thus requires a corresponding change in one's behaviors and relationships (Schlossberg). When we join the military, ship to Basic Training, graduate IET, deploy for war, attend weekend drills, come home from war, come home from weeks of training in the field, or separate from military service, we experience a military transition. We go through a process and we—our *very being*—is the product of going through that process of transition. This new definition and concept account for all experiences of military transitions and makes any need for the term or concept of "reintegration" moot and irrelevant. It acknowledges that *we do not go back.*

Instead, we differentially adapt and/or resist transition **between the distal** (organizational and institutional) **and proximal** (peer, leader, environmental) **factors of the U.S. Military structure** (a total and persistent physical and psychological structure) **and an outside system** (drawing from ecological framework and family systems theory). The military is a total institution (distal), which means it encompasses every area and component of our lives. Yet, the military as an institution is comprised of individual people (proximal)—we come to know ourselves through our relationships with others. This is why the aforementioned Model of Veteran Identity Hierarchy is so relevant. When I separated from the military, I did not consider myself a Veteran and I didn't think my military service mattered at all, to anyone. This is because my experience of military service did not fit the dominant narrative. I knew others who had military service experiences that included deployments to war, combat experience, being raped or sexually assaulted during service, losing a limb during service, or contending with PTSD. I understand my own military service experience within and through relation to that of my peers, leaders, and the environment in which I was situated.

I realize that proposing a new definition and concept of "Veteran," as I have done so here, is disruptive. I also realize that disruption is exactly what is needed. Understanding things such as Veteran suicides, reintegration, and most importantly, identity, as is, is not working. I would even go so far as to say it is harmful. Too many Veterans are dying by suicide; too many Veterans experience psychosocial difficulties after separating from the military; too many Veterans do not have language to be able to name and articulate what they are going through. My story of military service is unique—it is my own. Yet, the psychosocial difficulties I experienced once I separated from the military are not unique. Not only could I not name or articulate what I was going through when I separated from military service, but worse, I couldn't get any help. I did not—I still do not—qualify for most (healthcare) services from the nation's largest organization serving Veterans, the VA. In fact, according to the VA's definition of "Veteran," I am not one. This is unacceptable.

Within the new definition and conceptualization of "Veteran" that I have proposed here, *there is room for my and others' differential experiences of military service*; it is inclusive of all forms of military transitioning. It doesn't associate our realities of adapting to being solely about active duty, war, and/or combat experiences; it highlights the proximal and distal factors that influence our adaptation. *It sees and identifies power.* It recognizes our experiences of adapting and resisting transition are *differential* because we all have intersecting identities (Crenshaw). It gives us space to resist without positioning us as *broken, wounded,* or *failures* for doing so. It knows the U.S. Military is a total institution made up of a persistent societal structure that is unique from outside systems. It recognizes we are all products through the processes we experience in the total military institution. It recognizes that institutional liminality is perpetual and ongoing, which means our experience of it is ongoing. "Veteran" is not just an identity we have; it's an identity we actively adapt and/or resist. It is both something that we are and something that we do. This new conceptualization creates space for naming, which creates space for healing. If we understand this identity as something we have power over through adaptation/resistance, then we have awareness of our own agency, our own subjective reality, our own differences. With knowledge comes power. As I continue to *drive on* through my own institutionalized experience of both being and doing "Veteran," I continue to uncover new forms of redemption. I continue to name my own experiences of military service—the good, the bad, and the ugly—and in doing so, continue my own work of unifying my "old" and "new" selves.

Let me be clear, my work is not done. I will never be able to completely wash *Army Green* off. Since the psychological darkness in the form of an identity crisis I experienced my first year out of the NG, I have gathered an abundance of tools to heal, to reclaim, to form union within and between my disparate selves. But this work is ongoing. There are still days I have panic attacks, there are still days I feel depression creeping in, there are still days I crave the numbness of smoking too much cannabis, there are still days I struggle with food. I have come a long way, but I realize there will never be a finality to this limbo. Further, it's important for me to acknowledge that these challenges of psychosocial difficulties cannot be and are not sole correlations of my time in (or experiences of) the military. As many others do, I joined the service as an escape. This means I joined the military with trauma already part of my being. I believe my experiences of IET, TIS, and separation from service compounded and exacerbated trauma I already had and layered more on top of it. My identities and experiences cannot be separated; they are all interrelated. The military both *saved me and constrained me.* Now, outside of the military, it is up to me as an active and engaged subject to find and create moments of union within myself.

Unifying Ambivalence: Moving Toward Indigenous Perspectives

Gloria Anzaldúa imparts *la mestiza* as the product of living between borderlands. "Cradled in one culture, sandwiched between two cultures, straddling all three cultures and their value systems, la mestiza undergoes a struggle of flesh, a struggle of borders, and inner war" (100). *La mestiza* is pressured to assimilate, yet she experiences *differential adaptation and/or resistance to transition*. One culture is already imprinted into her—she must find a way to *integrate* and unify the old with the new. The work of la mestiza is to create a new consciousness. Anzaldúa imparts the wisdom of her own mestiza consciousness when she eloquently articulates this *continual creative motion* of *soul work*:

> She has discovered that she can't hold concepts or ideas in rigid boundaries. The borders and walls that are supposed to keep the undesirable ideas out are entrenched habits and patterns of behavior; these habits and patterns are the enemy within. Rigidity means death. Only by remaining flexible is the mestiza able to stretch the psyche horizontally and vertically. La mestiza constantly has to shift out of habitual formations; from convergent thinking, analytical reasoning that tends to use rationality to move toward a single goal (a Western mode), to divergent thinking, characterized by movement away from set patterns and goals and towards a more whole perspective, one that includes rather than excludes. The new mestiza copes by developing a tolerance for contradictions, a tolerance for ambiguity.... She learns to juggle cultures. She has a plural personality, she operates in a pluralistic mode—nothing is thrust out, the good the bad and the ugly, nothing rejected, nothing abandoned. Not only does she sustain contradictions, she turns the ambivalence into something else. She can be jarred out of ambivalence by an intense, and often painful, emotional event which inverts or resolves the ambivalence. I'm not sure exactly how. The work takes place underground—subconsciously. It is work that the soul performs. That focal point or fulcrum, that juncture where the mestiza stands, is where phenomena tend to collide. It is where the possibility of uniting all that is separate occurs. This assembly is not one where severed or separated pieces merely come together. Nor is it a balancing or opposing powers. In attempting to work out a synthesis, the self has added a third element which is greater than the sum of its severed parts. That third element is a new consciousness—a mestiza consciousness—and though it is a source of intense pain, its energy comes from continual creative motion that keeps breaking down the unitary aspect of each new paradigm. En unas pocas centurias, the future will belong to the

mestiza. Because the future depends on the breaking down of paradigms, it depends on the straddling of two or more cultures. By creating a new mythos—that is, a change in the way we perceive reality, the way we see ourselves, and the ways we behave—la mestiza creates a new consciousness. The work of mestiza consciousness is to break down the subject-object duality that keeps her a prisoner and to show in the flesh and through the images in her work how duality is transcended. The answer to the problem between the white race and the colored, between males and females, lies in healing the split that originates in the very foundation of our lives, our culture, our languages, our thoughts. A massive uprooting of dualistic thinking in the individual and collective consciousness is the beginning of a long struggle, but one that could in our best hopes, bring us to the end of rape, of violence, of war. (Gloria Anzaldúa 101–102)

In the work that I do, I think a lot about war. When I'm deep in the throes of trying to find a way to reconceptualize reintegration, to redefine Veteran identity, or to find some grand solution to the Veteran suicide phenomenon, I always come back to the same thought: *if we could only end war*. I feel so silly when I think that, like I should be standing on a stage wearing a long gown and tiara, spouting about "world peace." But it's true. *I do want world peace*. Don't we all?

Unfortunately, I don't know how to end war and accomplish world peace...yet (*Drive on, Soldier, drive on!*). But I do know that Veteran transitionary experiences and suicides are not about war; they are about belonging to an institution that exists to *construct and conquer* in the form of war. I know that like la mestiza, *the work of a Veteran is to create a new consciousness*. We must look in the mirror and ask ourselves "How have I changed?" and "Who is my new self?" (Smith and True 149). We must have language that accounts for our disruption to and process of identity related to our military entrance, service, and exit. We need a way to identify and understand the *imprinting into our very being* that occurred through IET and TIS. Especially because outside of these contexts, *these habits and patterns are the enemy within. Rigidity means death*. We need outlets for understanding and articulating how belonging to the military institution imprints habits and patterns within us that can become *the enemy within* outside of that system. We must shift to divergent thinking, where we consider the whole perspective of social identity and include rather than exclude. We should not focus solely on deployment and combat experiences when talking about military/Veteran transitionary experiences. As Veterans, we must cope by developing a *tolerance for ambiguity*.

200 J. R. HUNNIECUTT

Uncle Sam taught us to *adapt and overcome*. We must learn to *juggle the binary cultures* we live among and operate in a *pluralistic* mode where we take the good, the bad, *and the ugly*. And then, we must turn that ambivalence into something else—something *unified*. This is work only the *soul* can perform. We must *change the ways we perceive reality, the way we see ourselves, and the ways we behave*. We must disrupt paradigms and *show through our flesh and the images of our work* how our *duality is transcended*.

Critical Reflection

Exactly how, though, do we do that? For me, this book—the stories I've told, the literature I've analyzed, the conceptualizations I've shifted—is work *my soul performed*. It is work that asked me to be vulnerable, share deep, raw parts of myself, and invite you to sit in my psychological darkness with me. Sandra Faulkner and Shelia Squillante, as well as Anne Harris and Stacy Holman Jones, suggest practical strategies for writing about the self performatively. They categorize strategies for purpose, audience, ethics, structure, craft, and evaluation criteria. They first ask, "What are your goals of this writing," and "What do you want your piece to do?" My professional goals for this book are (1) to argue that the current ways we are researching topics such as Veteran suicides, transitions, and identity are exclusive and inhibiting and have led to conceptualizations and understandings of Veteran identity to be *solely* about post-war and, more explicitly, post-combat difficulties; (2) to illustrate the nature of liminality in military IET and TIS and to shift our thinking toward identity; (3) to illuminate social struggles and challenges of [the] Veteran identity during [my] reintegration experiences; (4) to highlight how Veteran identity dissonance is rooted in the conditioning that happens during military Initial Entry Training (IET) and experiences during Time in Service (TIS;) and (5) to propose and advocate a new term and subsequent conceptualization for military transitions and Veteran identity that is comprehensive and inclusive and centers the social manifestations this experience.

My personal goal for this book was to take some space to heal—to write through my own experiences of IET, TIS, and transition out of the military so that I can more fully understand how my struggles are connected. This work is my *new consciousness*, my new *redemption*. I write to speak my truth, and though I realize that all our truths are different, I both expect and hope that my stories also shine some truth into the realities of all my brothers and sisters in arms—because all of you are part of me, this story is both for and about you too. As I chose to employ tools in this project that call for critical reflection, I must consider "how does my story speak in relationship to larger stories of cultural Others like myself? Where do the 'I' and the 'we' separate? Do they?" (Calafell 9). I wrote about experiences of struggling with *my* Veteran identity to shine light on dominant discourses of *the* Veteran identity. I identified the inherent assumption that exists in current conceptualizations of reintegration and Veteran identity to be predominantly about deployment and combat experience. I illustrated how the diversity of individual experiences is being excluded; I showed how the "'I' and 'we' separate." I wrote to heal, and now after this process, I have more clarity around my experiences of military IET, TIS, and Veteran identity. I better understand how my psychosocial difficulties are connected. I also recognize my work is not done—that is, will never reach a point of finality, because I know my Veteran identity is both a product *and* an ongoing, perpetual process. My aim for this new understanding of Veteran identity is to influence transdisciplinary research on military/Veteran suicides, transitionary experiences, and identity in a way that leads to more comprehensive, inclusive, and effective program and policy development. If they are going to prepare us to go to war, I want them to prepare us *to know how to heal from being prepared to go to war.*

I want Veterans to be positively impacted by this work. Considering audience, Faulkner and Squillante, as well as Harris and Holman Jones, propose, "Whom do you want to reach?" and "What do you want the audience to do, feel, and believe after experiencing your work?" I wrote this work for myself, Veterans, and scholars doing military/Veteran research. For myself, I wanted to claim space to voice my experiences, make sense of them, and learn and heal through the process. I want Veterans who experience this work to be inspired to tell their own stories, question their own experiences of military service and how it changed them, and move toward their own form of a mestiza consciousness. And for scholars, my hope is that this work influences your discourses and conceptualizations around Veteran identity and experiences of military service in ways that lead to more inclusive, comprehensive, and holistic research inquiries. I urge you: *research with, not on, Veterans.*

For ethics, Faulkner and Squillante ask, "Are you able to write this piece now," and "Who is implicated in the writing?" I first wrote this piece four years ago. I rewrote it again now. If I wrote it again in four more years from now, I suspect there would still be more to tell. This is because the Veteran identity is not fixed; it is an identity of perpetual in-betweenness;

there will always be more to tell. It has taken a lot of time and a lot of *soul work* to try to wipe the Army Green off my lenses, only to realize a tint of green will always remain. Even now, when I think of who is implicated in this writing, I think of my brothers and sisters in arms and about what some of them will think and say after they read this work—after they read the things I wrote about our military, our Uncle Sam. I worry about how *I* am implicated through the stories I have told about myself.

Faulkner and Squillante urge me to reflect on structure and craft in my writing and ask: "What structure will work and how can you include research in your writing to achieve your purpose and establish veracity," and "Have you paid attention to the line, the music in the piece, form, aesthetics, voice, narrative truth?" (4). I chose to employ autoethnography, which combines subjective experiences, power and culture, and theory and writing, to achieve my purpose of disrupting and shifting conceptualizations of reintegration and Veteran identity. I drew on auto-archeology (Fox), a form of autoethnography that relies on institutional artifacts as anchors to elicit stories to achieve veracity and narrative truth in my work. The institutional artifacts I presented throughout this project represent accurate truths throughout my experiences of military IET, TIS, and separation. Finally, considering criteria, they propose, "How should your piece be evaluated," and "How will you know if you have achieved your goal(s) for the piece?" (4).

This piece is not intended to be evaluated using measures of evaluation pertinent to objectively scientific or clinical research. This is not an empirical, quantitative, objective research project. Rather, it is intentionally designed to be a decolonizing, demilitarizing, critical, qualitative, subjective research project. In the broad landscape of military/Veteran social science research as I know it, this piece perhaps will be cast into the realm of "complementary" or "alternative." "The borders and walls that are supposed to keep the undesirable ideas out are entrenched habits and patterns of behavior; these habits and patterns are the enemy within. Rigidity means death" (Anzaldúa 101). This piece is intended to disrupt and evolve paradigms. For a lot of people, that can be uncomfortable. "Only by remaining flexible is the mestiza able to stretch the psyche horizontally and vertically" (Anzaldúa 101). Thus, my own work remains to *differentially adapt.*

I now have a better understanding of "How have I changed" and "Who is my new self?" (Smith and True). I realize that I am privileged in that I have access to higher education where I can learn and gather tools to critically reflect on these questions. I realize the military gave me access to this privilege. I still find myself moving between a binary way of thinking about the military and my time in it—good or bad, right or wrong, gain or loss. *How I have changed* is that I realize it's not either/or, it's both/and. I focused on military structure and community throughout my stories, as I believe these two things encompass the proximal and distal, primary and secondary military group cohesion, reflect the ecological framework for reintegration, and emphasize the interconnectedness of relational and familial systems. I see the assimilated structure and community that I differentially adapted to throughout all my forms of military transitions as *both* good *and* bad, gain *and* loss.

In terms of structure, the military gave me access to higher education and provided me with resources to move up and out of what I was born into. It gave me a mission—a greater sense of purpose and social responsibility. It taught me discipline, responsibility, maturity, and new skills. It gave me new, unique experiences. *And* the structure of the military system also took away my individual freedom over self. It forced me to adapt to assimilation. It branded me with an Army Green uniform that *never quite fit just right*. Instead of changing the uniform to fit me better, it forced me to adapt myself to fit the uniform. It told me the uniform *fits us all the same way*—that our differences did not matter because the uniform represented a shared meaning, a shared purpose, a shared identity. And sometimes, that shared identity is powerful and beautiful and fosters an untouchable connection between strangers. I will always have Battle Buddies. *I will never leave a fallen comrade* and they will *never leave me*. *And*, despite our shared identity, purpose, and connection, we still need room for our differences. Our intersecting identities matter. We need language, concepts, and tools that account for both/and rather than either/or.

Suggestions for Future Research

This is where I believe contributions from the field of Communication Studies would be most useful. This project is primarily rooted within intercultural communication, as it is a study on identity that employs a critical identity framework of liminality. Likewise, the theory of differential adaptation is housed within intercultural communication. Much of the literature on Veteran suicides, reintegration, and identity, however, emerges primarily from mental and behavioral health disciplines. Yes, *some*

Veterans' experiences can be medicalized—but what about social identity implications that aren't diagnosable? The main theme of this project is that these topics are *about identity;* and as identity is communicative in nature, research in these domains at large needs to expand to, include communicative modes of inquiry. For instance, the sub-disciplinary area of organizational communication would be helpful in directing research that explores military organizational assimilation, organizational exit, group cohesion and dismantling, and organizational and institutional identity. Further, family communication researchers can contribute much by exploring how military units and groups function as family systems and what a loss of such system then entails. Likewise, it would be useful to understand the role of familial relationships within the new concept of Veteran identity I proposed in this book. We know that Veteran suicides are a pressing issue. We know that adaptive transitionary struggles exist. What we need to understand is *why*. Critical, qualitative, communicative research inquiries can help explain the *why*.

Finally, once we have a better understanding of the *why*, we need to move toward *how* to help. When Anzaldúa writes about the new mestiza consciousness, she explains that *la mestiza* operates in a "pluralistic mode" and thrusts nothing out. *La mestiza* knows how to sit with and sustain the "good, the bad and the ugly" (101). Anzaldúa tells us that *la mestiza* takes the ambivalence of sitting with these contradictions and turns it into "something else." This happens when she is "jarred out of ambivalence by an intense, and often painful, emotional event which inverts or resolves the ambivalence" (101). Anzaldúa tells us she doesn't know how this happens or what prompts the jarring. All she knows is that "the work takes place underground—subconsciously. It is work that the soul performs…it is where the possibility of uniting all that is separate occurs" (101). Anzaldúa is writing about the *unification of mind, body, and soul.* La mestiza consciousness is the product of such unification.

As I inch closer toward my own new consciousness of Veteran identity and reflect on "how I have changed" and "who is my new self," yoga comes to mind. As I shared throughout my story, it was the practice of meditation and yoga that centered me most through my own storm of psychological darkness. I traveled to India, and I learned the word "yoga" means "union." The job of the Veteran is to create a new consciousness— to *unify* the conflicting structures of *all that are separate*. To be able to unify, we need tools and outlets for doing so. Warren Price writes about how the leisure activity of fly fishing gave him tools he needed to cope with combat-related PTSD after returning home from war: "Once my friend got me to the river, something changed. Knee-deep in the water and surrounded by nature's grandeur, the symptoms plaguing me began to dissolve, and for the first time in years, I finally felt at peace" (Price et al. 197). The way Price writes about his experience ("something changed...I finally felt at peace") mirrors what Anzaldúa wrote about reaching union after being "jarred out of ambivalence by an intense, and often painful, emotional event which inverts or resolves the ambivalence" (101). We need research that helps us to understand how people become *jarred out of ambivalence*, turn inward, and *feel the peace of a unified self*.

Complementary and Alternative Medicine (CAM) or integrative/comprehensive health modalities offer an abundance of tools and strategies that teach one skills necessary to reach physical and psychological states of union. Helané Wahbeh and colleagues conducted a systemic review of CAM studies for PTSD and found scientific evidence of benefit for repetitive transcranial magnetic stimulation and acupuncture, hypnotherapy, meditation, and visualization. However, evidence was unclear or conflicting for biofeedback, relaxation, Emotional Freedom and Thought Field therapies, yoga, and natural products. As I learned when I dove into research on yoga and meditation practices with military/Veteran populations, this work is also very rigid, empirical, objective, and quantitative. To clarify, I am not saying more quantitative work is not needed; it is. I invite quantitative inquiries measuring the variables I presented in the Model of Veteran Identity Hierarchy. More quantitative research will give us more information about *what* is happening among and between the Veteran identity and our experiences of adapting/resisting. Yet, we need to take it further. Not only do we need to understand more of the *why*, but we need more *solutions*. We need new programs, policies, services, and treatments that help us create a unified self. Baldwin and colleagues surveyed 508 Veterans and 252 (49.6%) reported CAM use. *We want ways to unify ourselves*. Our adaptation to transition is *differential*—we need tools that account for this. We need room for our difference *and* our collective militarized selves. If we change the way we frame and talk about Veteran suicides, transitionary experiences, and identity, it will change the way we think about solutions. We must *adapt and overcome* to establish a new consciousness of Veteran identity.

206   J. R. HUNNIECUTT

WORKS CITED

Anzaldúa, Gloria. *Borderlands: The New Mestiza/La Frontera* (4th ed.). Aunt Lute, 2012.

Baldwin, Carol M., et al. "A profile of military veterans in the southwestern United States who use complementary and alternative medicine: implications for integrated care." *Archives of Internal Medicine*, vol. 162, no 15, 2002, pp. 1697–1704.

Bavelas, Janet Beavin, and Lynn Segal. "Family systems theory: Background and implications." *Journal of Communication*, vol. 32, no. 3, 1982, pp. 99–107.

Baxter, Leslie A., and Dawn Braithwaite. "Relational dialectics theory: Crafting meaning from competing discourses." *Engaging Theories in Interpersonal Communication*, 2008, pp. 349–362. Thousand Oaks, CA: Sage.

Bronfenbrenner, U., & Morris, P. A. "The bioecological model of human development." In R. M. Lerner & W. R. Damon (Eds.), *Handbook of child psychology: Vol. 1: Theoretical models of human development* (6th ed.), 2006, pp. 793–828. Hoboken, NJ: Wiley.

Calafell, Bernadette Marie. "(I)dentities: Considering Accountability, Reflexivity, and Intersectionality in the I and the We." *Liminalities: A Journal of Performance Studies*, vol. 9, no. 2, 2013, pp. 6–13.

Collinge, William, Janet Kahn, and Robert Soltysik. "Promoting reintegration of National Guard veterans and their partners using a self-directed program of integrative therapies: a pilot study." *Military medicine*, vol. 177, no. 12, 2012, pp. 1477.

De La Garza, Antonio Tomas, and Kent A. Ono. "Retheorizing adaptation: Differential adaptation and critical intercultural communication." *Journal of International and Intercultural Communication*, vol. 8, no. 4, 2015, pp. 269–289.

Demers, Anne. "When Veterans Return: The Role of Community in Reintegration." *Journal of Loss and Trauma*, vol. 16, no. 2, 2011, pp. 160–179.

Di Leone, Brooke AL, et al. "Women's veteran identity and utilization of VA health services." *Psychological Services*, vol. 13, no. 1, 2016, pp. 60.

Elnitsky, Christine A., Michael P. Fisher, and Cara L. Blevins. "Military Service Member and Veteran Reintegration: A Conceptual Analysis, Unified Definition, and Key Domains." *Frontiers in Psychology*, vol. 8, 2017.

Faulkner, Sandra L. and Shelia Squillante. "Writing the Personal: Getting Your Stories on the Page." *Sense Publishers*, 2015.

Fox, Ragan. "Tales of a fighting bobcat: An "auto-archaeology" of gay identity formation and maintenance." *Text and Performance Quarterly*, vol. 30, no. 2, 2010, pp. 122–142.

Gil-Rivas, Virginia, Ryan P. Kilmer, Jacqueline C. Larson, and Laura Marie Armstrong. "Facilitating successful reintegration: Attending to the needs of military families." *American Journal of Orthopsychiatry*, vol. 87, no. 2, 2017, pp. 176.

Hall, Lynn K. "The Importance of Understanding Military Culture." *Social Work in Health Care*, vol. 50, no. 1, 2011, pp. 4–18.

Harris, Anne and Stacy Holman Jones. Writing For Performance. *Sense Publishers*, 2016.

Hinojosa, Ramon, and Melanie Sberna Hinojosa. "Using military friendships to optimize postdeployment reintegration for male Operation Iraqi Freedom/ Operation Enduring Freedom veterans." *Journal of Rehabilitation Res Dev*, vol. 48, no. 10, 2011, pp. 1145–1158.

Hoopsick, Rachel A., et al. "Is deployment status the critical determinant of psychosocial problems among reserve/guard soldiers?." *Psychological services*, vol. 17, no. 4, 2020, pp. 461.

Hoopsick, Rachel A., et al. "Developing a measure to assess emotions associated with never being deployed." *Military medicine*, vol. 183, no. 9–10, 2018, pp. e509-e517.

Junger, Sebastian. Tribe: On homecoming and belonging. *Hachette*, UK, 2016.

Kirchner, Michael J. "Supporting Student Veteran Transition to College and Academic Success." *Adult Learning*, vol. 26, no. 3, 2015, pp. 116–123.

Knobloch, Leanne K., et al. "Generalized anxiety and relational uncertainty as predictors of topic avoidance during reintegration following military deployment." *Communication Monographs*, vol. 80, no. 4, 2013, pp. 452–477.

Mascarenhas, Mridula. "Uniform to Pulp: Performance of Transformation, Critique, and Community-Building for Veteran Soldiers." *Western Journal of Communication*, vol. 78, no. 1, 2014, pp. 78–96.

McGee, Michael Calvin. "The "ideograph": A link between rhetoric and ideology." *Quarterly Journal of Speech*, vol. 66, no. 1, 1980, pp. 1–16.

Pfeiffer, Paul N., Adrian J. Blow, Erin Miller, Jane Forman, Gregory M. Dalack, and Marcia Valenstein. "Peers and Peer-Based Interventions in Supporting Reintegration and Mental Health Among National Guard Soldiers: A Qualitative Study." *Military Medicine*, vol. 177, no. 12, 2012, p. 1471.

Price, Warren D. "I Tie Flies in My Sleep: An Autoethnographic Examination of Recreation and Reintegration for a Veteran with Posttraumatic Stress Disorder." *Journal of Leisure Research*, vol. 47, no. 2, 2013, pp. 185–201.

"Recommendations from the Independent Review Commission on Sexual Assault in the Military." *Center for Homeland Defense and Security*. July 2021. https://www.hsdl.org/c/recommendations-from-the-independent-review-commission-on-sexual-assault-in-the-military/#:~:text=In%20February%20 2021%2C%20a%2090,sexual%20assault%20and%20sexual%20harassment. &text=Recommendations%20to%20Prevent%20Sexual%20Harassment, Recommendations%20for%20Climate%20%26%20Culture

Reger, Mark A. et al. "Risk of Suicide Among US Military Service Members Following Operation Enduring Freedom or Operation Iraqi Freedom Deployment and Separation From the US Military." *JAMA Psychiatry*, vol. 72, no. 66, 2015, pp. 561–569.

Schlossberg, Nancy K. "A model for analyzing human adaptation to transition." *The Counseling Psychologist*, vol. 9, no. 2, 1981, pp. 2–18.

Siebold, Guy L. "The essence of military group cohesion." *Armed Forces & Society*, vol. 33, no. 2, 2007, pp. 286–295.

Smith, R. Tyson, and Gala True. "Warring Identities: Identity Conflict and the Mental Distress of American Veterans of the Wars in Iraq and Afghanistan." *Society and Mental Health*, vol. 4, no. 2, 2014, pp. 147–161.

Theiss, Jennifer A., and Leanne K. Knobloch. "A relational turbulence model of military service members' relational communication during reintegration." *Journal of Communication*, vol. 63, no. 6, 2013, pp. 1109–1129.

Turner, Victor. The Ritual Process: Structure and Anti-Structure. *Aldine de Gruyter*, 1969.

Wahbeh, Helané, Angela Senders, Rachel Neuendorf, and Julien Cayton. "Complementary and alternative medicine for posttraumatic stress disorder symptoms: a systematic review." *Journal of evidence-based complementary & alternative medicine*, vol. 19, no. 3, 2014, pp. 161–175.

Wilson, Laura C. "The prevalence of military sexual trauma: A meta-analysis." *Trauma, Violence, & Abuse*, vol. 19, no. 5, 2018, pp. 584–597.

Zogas, Anna. "Costs of War: US Military Veterans' Difficult Transitions Back to Civilian Life and the VA's Response." *Watson Institute International & Public Affairs*, Brown University, 2017, pp. 1–14.

Index[1]

A

Adapt and overcome, 169–205
Advanced Individual Training (AIT), 18, 19, 63, 78–81, 159, 171
Aggregation, 76–78, 81–84, 159, 171, 178, 185, 193
Anzaldúa, Gloria, 83, 84, 165, 198, 199
Appalachia, 4–7, 16, 103, 107, 141, 163, 169, 177
Army Combat Uniform, 39, 139, 160
Army Green, 17, 19, 63, 80, 85, 91, 111, 137, 138, 140, 141, 147, 150, 151, 153, 154, 158, 163–165, 171–174, 177–179, 181, 183, 184, 188, 189, 193–195, 197, 202, 203
Artifacts, 76, 87, 91–92, 95, 132, 133, 137, 138, 141, 150, 161, 164, 165, 172, 202
Autoarcheology, 76, 91–92, 95, 133, 137, 202
Autoethnography, 1, 3, 38, 76, 87–92, 175, 202

B

Baker, Travis, 4, 5, 23, 24, 54, 169, 191
Basic Combat Training (BCT), 3, 63, 78, 140, 171
Battle, 15, 16, 24, 43, 54, 112, 118, 123, 192
buddies, 15, 44, 48, 80, 81, 91, 106, 107, 111, 118, 138, 140, 141, 147, 150, 164, 165, 183, 203
Betwixt and between, 76, 110, 132, 156, 188, 192
Borderlands, 83, 84, 87, 165, 198
Brothers and sisters in arms, vii, 1, 129, 183, 200, 202

C

Cannabis, 9, 12, 29, 30, 34, 42, 43, 53, 197
Cheerleader, 9, 10, 14, 39, 63, 162, 163, 173

---

[1] Note: Page numbers followed by 'n' refer to notes.

© The Author(s), under exclusive license to Springer Nature Switzerland AG 2022
J. R. Hunniecutt, *Rethinking Reintegration and Veteran Identity*, https://doi.org/10.1007/978-3-030-93754-6

209

210 INDEX

Civilian, 4, 16, 18, 19, 26, 37, 39, 59, 63, 65, 68–70, 78, 79, 85, 88, 90, 91, 98, 106, 110, 125, 127, 132, 137, 148, 150, 152, 155–158, 160–163, 171, 173, 174, 177–182, 192
civilian-soldier, 18, 158, 162
Colonialism
colonizing, 105, 111, 147, 148
settler, 104, 105, 107, 147, 164
Communitas, 76–82
Complementary and Alternative Medicine (CAM), 125, 205
Consciousness, 3, 17, 90, 106, 144, 159, 174, 186–201, 204, 205
Critical
narrative inquiry, 75
reflection, 3, 89, 90, 200–203

D
Dakota Access Pipeline, 124
Deep South, 6, 15, 17, 40, 85, 104
Department of Veterans Affairs, 44, 45, 54, 69, 177
Disordered eating, 43, 44, 47, 177, 191
Don't Ask, Don't Tell, 14, 17, 142
Drill, 3, 4, 11, 18, 19, 21, 23, 24, 28, 29, 31–33, 39, 43, 45, 126, 127, 151, 152, 158, 160, 161, 184, 194, 195
sergeants, 13–16, 79–81, 138, 139, 150, 152
Drive on, soldier, drive on, 24, 27, 127, 175, 186, 199

E
East Tennessee State University (ETSU), 21, 27, 38
Ecological framework, 176, 182–186, 196, 203

Embodied, 78, 90, 104, 122, 133
End of Time in Service (ETS), 27, 32, 33, 158

F
Family systems, 6, 38, 39, 97, 176, 182–186, 196, 204
Freedom, vii, 26–34, 105, 111, 113, 126, 131, 133, 138–166, 171–174, 176, 177, 182, 186, 189, 191, 203, 205

H
Hoopsick, Rachel A., 187, 188

I
Identity, 2, 15, 17, 18, 75, 76, 80, 83–92, 95, 96, 101, 102, 104, 110, 125, 128, 133, 137–139, 141–143, 146, 149–153, 155, 156, 158, 160, 161, 163–166, 169–173, 175, 178, 181, 183, 186, 188–192, 194, 196, 197, 199–201, 203–205
crisis, 37–70, 101, 102, 128, 155, 161, 165, 169, 197
Ideograph, 138, 144–149, 164, 165, 172–174, 189, 191
Ideology, 17, 80, 105, 111, 138, 144, 145, 147, 154, 164, 165, 173, 185, 189, 191
India, 113, 117–123, 132, 204
Indigenous, 103–106, 108, 111–113, 118–120, 125, 132, 143, 147, 164, 198–205
Initial Entry Training (IET)
Advanced Individual Training (AIT), 18, 19, 63, 78–81, 159, 171

INDEX   211

Basic Combat Training (BCT);
   Basic, 14, 63, 78, 80, 81, 140,
   157, 171, 195; Boot
   Camp, 13, 63
Ivory Tower, 2, 40

L
Liminality
   institutionalized, 75, 77, 82–86, 96,
      105, 110, 113, 137, 138, 141,
      149, 150, 155–159, 165, 171,
      178, 182, 185, 186, 193–195
   sacred, 75, 77–84, 106, 113, 137,
      139, 141, 147–150, 154, 159,
      165, 171, 172, 174, 178,
      182–186, 192–195
Lynch, Jessica, 139, 140

M
Meditation, 49, 113, 117, 119–122,
   141, 177, 204, 205
Mestiza, 83, 84, 166, 198, 199, 201,
   202, 204
Military
   assimilation, 2, 37, 61–65, 137,
      170, 181, 182, 195, 204
   civilian divide, 2, 37, 66–70, 86,
      171, 182
   culture, 2, 13, 37, 62, 65–68, 88,
      91, 105, 106, 111, 113, 121,
      126, 146–148, 181, 187, 191
   family, 5, 48, 65, 68, 84, 97, 105,
      107, 111, 112, 125, 148, 182,
      183, 204
   militarism, 67, 105, 107, 147, 182
Military Occupational Specialty
   (MOS), 14, 23, 66, 78
Military Sexual Trauma (MST), 45,
   51, 180, 195
The Mission Continues, 96, 101, 123

Model for Analyzing Human
   Adaptation to Transition,
   176–179, 194
Model of Veteran Identity Hierarchy,
   3, 189–192, 196, 205
Myth, 144, 145, 148, 173

N
National Guard (NG), 2, 3, 8, 10, 11,
   13, 18–20, 23, 28, 37, 39, 44,
   45, 52, 54, 57, 85, 90, 98, 102,
   110, 121, 124–126, 129, 130,
   141, 155–158, 161, 162, 169,
   187, 188, 194, 197
Non-commissioned officer
   (NCO), 4, 23
Non-deployment emotions, 187

O
Operation Safety, 187, 188

P
Panic attack, 42, 47, 197
Performative writing,
   87–89, 92
Photo voice, 104, 108, 110
Post-Traumatic Stress Disorder
   (PTSD), 28, 30, 45, 51, 58, 68,
   86, 122, 143, 145, 180, 192,
   196, 205

R
Recruit, 5, 13–15, 63, 64, 66, 78–83,
   85, 102, 119, 130, 140, 148,
   151, 152, 170, 171
Redemption, 39, 123–126, 133, 144,
   147, 149, 157, 161–164, 175,
   197, 200

212 INDEX

Reintegration
    post deployment to war, 184
    post separation from service, 170
Rite of passage, 76–79, 81, 83, 85,
    173, 174, 178, 195
Ritual, 22, 64, 65, 76–78, 81, 89, 97,
    111, 140, 151, 193

S
Separation
    from the military, 2, 3, 39, 45, 49,
        51, 56, 57, 59, 61, 66, 67, 85,
        86, 95, 96, 141, 149, 158,
        161, 165, 178, 183, 186, 193,
        195, 196
    from service, 56, 58, 67, 70, 75,
        132, 159, 161, 163, 165, 166,
        169–171, 173, 178, 182, 185,
        186, 197
Service, vii, 1–34, 37, 39, 40, 42, 44,
    45, 49–60, 62, 66–70, 75, 85–87,
    89–92, 95–99, 101, 102, 111,
    124, 126, 128, 130, 132, 133,
    137, 138, 141, 149, 150, 155,
    157, 159, 161, 163–166,
    169–171, 173, 174, 178–182,
    184–197, 199, 201, 205
    member(SMs), vii, 49, 55, 57, 60,
        63, 64, 66, 67, 76, 78, 83,
        89, 104, 112, 120, 122, 124,
        125, 127, 130, 132, 150,
        154–156, 158, 159, 161,
        172, 175, 177, 178,
        186–189, 191, 193, 194
Soldier's Creed, 39, 137–141, 144,
    148–150, 154, 161, 164, 165
Story, vii, 1–3, 5, 7, 37, 38, 45, 70,
    75, 86–92, 95, 96, 104, 108,
    110–112, 118, 128, 133,
    137–140, 144, 145, 151, 152,

    169, 172, 173, 175, 186, 189,
    192, 196, 200–204
Student Veterans of America (SVA),
    49, 102, 113, 120, 121, 123, 126
Sturm Specialty in Military Psychology
    (SSMP), 99, 101, 103, 120, 121,
    125, 126, 128
Suicide, 1, 2, 24, 37–70, 86–88, 96,
    101, 102, 113, 123, 125, 143,
    164, 166, 169, 170, 172, 183,
    184, 186, 191, 196,
    199–201, 203–205
Symbols, 68, 76–78, 91–92, 99

T
Theory of Differential Adaptation,
    176, 179–182, 194, 203
Time in Service (TIS), 18–26, 31, 44,
    56, 87, 113, 133, 137, 138, 140,
    141, 149–152, 156, 158, 159,
    163–166, 171, 172, 174, 181,
    182, 186, 191–195,
    197, 199–202
Total institution, 65, 82–86, 90, 98,
    165, 173, 178, 182, 183, 185,
    188, 189, 195–197
Transition, 2, 16, 18, 45, 56, 58, 66,
    68, 76, 78, 82–84, 92, 106, 133,
    138, 150, 155, 156, 160, 161,
    165, 170–172, 174, 176–179,
    181–183, 185, 186, 192,
    194–196, 198, 200, 203, 205
Trauma, 6–10, 12, 21, 34, 38, 44, 59,
    69, 161, 170, 197
Traumatic Brain Injury (TBI),
    45, 51, 68
Turner, Victor, 64, 65, 70, 75–79,
    81–83, 85, 107, 132, 139, 155,
    156, 159, 165, 171, 173,
    184–186, 193, 194

U

Uncle Sam, vii, 12, 21, 23–25, 31, 32, 105, 107, 118, 126, 133, 143, 147, 148, 157–161, 172, 182, 183, 200, 202

Union, 119, 166, 175, 192, 197, 204, 205

Unite the Right rally, 129

University of Denver (DU), 30, 31, 50, 52, 68, 98–100, 102, 113, 120, 123, 125, 126, 187

V

Very being, 78, 85, 105, 113, 120, 132, 139, 141, 147, 159, 160, 166, 172, 173, 184, 185, 188, 191–193, 195, 199

Veteran
identity, 1–3, 37–70, 75, 76, 85–90, 92, 95, 96, 101, 102, 104, 112, 128, 131–133, 138, 149, 150, 164, 165, 170, 172, 174–176, 178, 179, 181, 185–197, 199–202, 204, 205

reintegration, 2, 56–70, 85, 89, 100–102, 113, 137, 164, 170, 172, 174, 182, 183

suicides, 1, 2, 37, 54–56, 59–62, 68–70, 86–88, 96, 123, 125, 164, 166, 169, 170, 172, 184, 186, 196, 199–201, 203–205

Veteran Service Organization (VSOs), 53, 96, 101, 123

W

Warrior, 63, 66, 80, 85, 139, 148, 171, 173, 191
ethos, 140, 141

White supremacy, 8, 15, 17, 84, 113, 130, 143, 153, 154

Y

Yoga, 46, 49, 113, 117–123, 125, 141, 177, 204, 205

Young Men's Christian Association (YMCA), 8, 10

Printed in the United States
by Baker & Taylor Publisher Services